Simulating
Organizations

Simulating Organizations

Computational Models of Institutions and Groups

Foreword by Michael D. Cohen

Edited by Michael J. Prietula,
Kathleen M. Carley, and Les Gasser

AAAI PRESS / THE MIT PRESS
Menlo Park, California, Cambridge, Massachusetts, London, England

Copyright © 1998, American Association for Artificial Intelligence
445 Burgess Drive
Menlo Park, CA 94025

Copublished and distributed by The MIT Press, Massachusetts Institute of Technology, Cambridge, Massachusetts and London, England.

Library of Congress Cataloging-in-Publication Data
Simulating organizations : computational models of institutions and groups /
  edited by Michael Prietula, Kathleen Carley, and Les Gasser ; foreword by
  Michael D. Cohen.
      p. cm.
    Includes bibliographical references and index.
    ISBN 0-262-66108-x (paperback : alk. paper)
    1. Organization. 2. Organizational sociology—Mathematical models.
  3. Artificial intelligence. I. Prietula, Michael J. II. Carley, Kathleen M.
  III. Gasser, Leslie George, 1949– .
  HD31.S565 1998
  302.3'5'011—dc21   97-51313
                                                                            CIP

Printed on acid-free paper in the United States of America.

*To those who have intellectually
inspired this new field
through their research and their spirit of
interdisciplinary conversation:*

*Richard Cyert, James March,
Allen Newell, and Herb Simon.*

Contents

Foreword

Michael D. Cohen

This volume adds forceful new evidence that computational modeling of organization is experiencing a sudden burst of new vitality and maturation. There has been an immense gain in the sophistication of the computational tools employed, and—more importantly—in the integration of those tools with fundamental concepts derived from social science studies of human organizations.

The sporadic growth history of this area is actually rather puzzling. Organizational issues were among the first to be attacked when computational modeling developed in the 1950s around the work of Herbert Simon and his colleagues at what was then Carnegie Tech. By 1963 we had "a behavioral theory of the firm," with half a dozen interesting organizational models created by Cyert and March and their numerous colleagues and students. From that point on, however, the rate of advance was rather slow. While there have been, of course, some notable additions to the repertoire of interesting organizational models, nothing has occurred that is comparable to the explosion of computational modeling of cognition.

There are a number of candidate explanations of the slow growth of organizational modeling relative to cognitive modeling. Among them are (1) high costs of acquiring organizational data to which models can be compared (relative to laboratory cognitive data); (2) lower formalization of established theories in the organizations field; (3) low exposure to computing among practicing organization theorists; (4) poor intuitive match of process control structures in traditional computing languages to naturally occurring organizational processes.

All of these factors may be improving now. For example, increasing computerization of the workplace is making data on organizational activities far more available to would-be simulators than at earlier times. But it is recent changes with respect to the fourth item on the list that seem to me to deserve special notice.

One major development on this front has been the wide diffusion of object-orientation in the software community. Instead of controlling processes in organizational models using iterative loops and conditional branching, it is now natural to represent processes as activation of object methods modulated by message passing. Objects provide a highly natural way of implementing model agents who have specialized capabilities and subtle, implicit, networks of interaction. This is a far more congenial framework within which to express intuitions about organizational processes.

The "organization-friendly" character of object-orientation is hardly an accident, of course. Alan Kay's early writing about Smalltalk, for example, made explicit use of analogies to organizational phenomena characterizing the design of the new language (1977).

A second development is the growing interest in organizational questions shown by researchers in the field of distributed artificial intelligence, who have recognized that distributed computers an programs must deal with many issues that are profoundly similar to those facing human organizations. (Here one should acknowledge early work by Carl Hewitt [1977], Victor Lesser [Durfee, Lesser and Corkill 1987], and the Hayes-Roths [1978].) Again the result has been a series of new ways of thinking about processes that are highly congenial to expressing intuitions about human organizations.

Both of these developments trace out an intriguing, round-about, path in which ideas about human organizations serve as analogies that inspire developments in computer science which in turn become tools useful for building computational models of organizations.

The influence of these developments can be seen clearly in the contents of this volume. Object-oriented methodology now underlies many of the systems being developed, and ideas from the field of distributed artificial intelligence are directly in evidence in many of the chapters.

The results are at last beginning to look highly promising. The increased interest in formal tools for organization theorists I clearly signaled by the emergence of a new journal on the topic: *Computational and Mathematical Organization Theory*. While there is still a great deal of hard work to be done, we can begin to imagine a day when theorists of organizations will routinely state theories and derive their implications using computational tools that are easily comprehended and widely shared - though sharing the tools will only happen if the field commits itself to the special efforts it requires.

The three editors of the volume have played a central role as catalysts of these developments. All of us interested in making computation a viable intellectual tool of organization theory are in their debt.

Ann Arbor, Michigan

Acknowledgements

The direct seeds of this book reside unequivocally in the AAAI Workshop on Artificial Intelligence and Theories of Groups and Organizations, put together by Kathleen Carley, Les Gasser, David King, and Mike Prietula. The presentations, discussions, e-mails, and collaborations emerging from that workshop and from the annual Computational and Mathematical Organization Theory Workshop associated with the INFORMS meetings have helped to energize a direction of theory and research reflected in this volume. The ultimate value of this book stems from the contributions of the authors. Significantly, the expertise reflected in these chapters is spread across a broad spectrum of disciplines: computer sciences, organization theory, sociology, operations research, management science, psychology, information systems, and beyond. It is not easy to get a group as diverse as this to speak to, and not by, each other. We believe such a conversation is well under way. Out of such activity emerges fascinating discussions. Out of such discussions science progresses. We thank them.

We also thank the American Association of Artificial Intelligence for taking a risk on this workshop, and the AAAI Press for taking a risk on this volume. Specifically, we thank Kenneth Ford of NASA and the University of West Florida (our AAAI Press editor) and Mike Hamilton of AAAI Press.

We also thank our colleagues for their insightful comments and our families for their support. Finally, we thank Kathy Murphy at the Fisher School of Accounting of the University of Florida for helping shepherd the process of accumulating chapters and other desiderata from us all. This one is done....

A Computational Approach to Organizations and Organizing

Michael J. Prietula, Kathleen M. Carley, and Les Gasser

O rganizations and groups permeate our lives, and their influence is growing. Indeed, each of us is so familiar with being in or being affected by organizations that we may tend to think we know how they work—-as Giddens has pointed out, people must be in some sense fairly good social theorists just to get along in daily life (Giddens 1984). However, naive theories about organizations are often wrong, and it can be dangerous to rely upon them. Organizations are large complex highly volatile systems whose behavior affects and is affected by the environment in which they operate. Individuals can, but do not always, affect how organizations operate. The character of information technology that is available can affect organizational processes, and so on. For effective guidance in organization design, management, and operation, stronger principles, and the methods for generating and deriving them are needed.

Clearly, organizational behavior is affected by a large number of interacting factors. Organizational theory can be characterized as the study of how this multiplicity of factors combine to influence the behavior of organizations and the people and technologies comprising them. Some would even argue that across such factors there are general principles of organizing that are true for all groups and organizations regardless of whether the actors within the organizations are human or artificial. As such, organizational theory can also be characterized as the search for these general principles.

Computational organization theory (COT) is the study of organizations as computational entities. COT researchers view organizations as inherently computational because they are complex information processing systems. An organization as a computational system is composed of multiple distributed "agents" that exhibit organizational properties (such as the need to act collectively and struggles for power), are assigned tasks, technology, and resources, and across which knowledge, skills, and communicative capabilities are distributed. Computational organization theory focuses on understanding the general factors and nonlinear dynamics that affect individual and organizational behavior with a special attention on decision making, learning, and adaptation (Carley 1995). In computational organization models, information, personnel, decision responsibility, tasks, resources, and opportunity are distributed geographically, temporally, or structurally within, and sometimes between, organizations.

Computational organization theories are meso-level theories of organizations. An idealized characterization of organizational studies partitions research into two types. A macro perspective, (conventional organization theory) treats the complexities of individual behavior as largely irrelevant, or simplifies variety across individuals into an ideal individual type. A micro (i.e., organizational behavior) perspective focuses on the individual and often minimizes the constraints on action afforded by tasks and social-situations, and institutions. Computational organization theories are typically meso-level in the sense that they seek to explain and predict macro-level behavior, such as overall organizational performance, from micro-level actions, such as the interaction among agents, each of which are "cognitively" limited.

Computational analysis can help us to grasp some fundamentals of human information processing behavior (Simon 1973). Thus, computational modeling can be valuable for the study of organizations as collections of intelligent agents. Further, compared with experiments using human subjects, computational models are generally less noisy, easier to control, more flexible, more objective, and can be used to examine a larger variety of factors within less time. Computational analysis also makes it possible to determine whether or not important nonlinearities in behavior emerge as scope conditions are extended. For example, computational models may be larger (e.g., more agents) or may cover a longer period (more tasks) than can be covered in a human laboratory experiment. Ostrom (1988) argues that computer simulation offers a third symbol system in studying social science (with natural language and mathematics being the first two symbol systems) and notes that "computer simulation offers a substantial advantage to social psychologists attempting to develop theories of complex and interdependent social phenomena." This same advantage is true for organizational theorists, perhaps even more so given the nature of organizations.

Organizations are complex, dynamic, nonlinear adaptive and evolving systems. Organizational behavior results from interactions among a variety of adaptive agents (both human and artificial), emergent structuration in response to non-linear processes, and detailed interactions among a large number of other factors. As such, organizations, or at least many aspects of them, are poor candidates for analytical models. Thus, computational analysis becomes an invaluable tool for theory building as it enables the researcher to generate a set of theoretical propositions from basic principles even when there are complex interactions among the relevant factors. The computational model can be thought of as a hypothesis generator that generates a set of propositions that can be more easily assured precise and internally consistent. In addition, computational models allow researchers to demonstrate proof of concept; i.e., to demonstrate whether or not a set of factors that are completely modelable are capable by themselves of generating certain phenomena. Used in this way, computational models can be used to show the potential legitimacy of various theoretical claims in organization science. Finally, using computational models it is often possible to determine the logical consistency of a set of propositions and the extent to which theoretical conclusions actually follow from the underlying assumptions. In some areas, formal logic plays this role. However, currently, multi-agent logics are not sufficiently developed to play this role.

Computational techniques for theorizing about organizations and organizing are invaluable tools for both the researcher and the manager. Most of the work in this book focuses on the scientific rather than the administrative side of this enterprise. Nevertheless, some hints (Chapters 1, 7, 8 and 10) are given as to how these tools might ultimately be of use to managers. Essentially, these computational models, once appropriately validated, can be used as decision aids to help the manager think through the impacts of new information technologies, organizational redesigns, or the reengineering of tasks. Clearly the models are not quite there yet, but that is one of the ultimate objectives.

Given such a computational model, three general evaluation criteria can be brought to bear: sufficiency testing, process testing, and component analysis. Sufficiency testing is the weakest form of validation and focuses entirely on the outcome of the behavior. In essence, it states that a computational model should at least be able to produce the behavior it purports to explain and is similar to the achievement criterion in cognitive modeling (Simon and Baylor 1966). Chapters 1, 2, 3, 4, 5, 6, 9 and 10 meet this criteria. Process testing makes a stronger statement, and is similar to the process criterion in cognitive modeling (Simon and Baylor 1966). This test goes beyond showing that an unspecified set of mechanisms produces a certain result by demonstrating that particular mechanisms (or knowledge) can produce the behavior. In this test, comparisons are made at some level of abstraction between the model and a referent (a proposed gold standard). Chapters 1, 2, 3, 4 and 9 are movements in this direction. Component analysis examines specific contributions of the mechanisms or knowledge represented in the reasoning events. The relative impact of different components are contrasted. Chapters 1, 3, 4 and 9 have this characteristic. Computational theorists can build theories of organizations and organizing by hypothesizing about the behavior of their models, testing these hypotheses through a series of virtual experiments, generating a new consistent set of hypotheses derived from these computational results, and then testing these hypotheses with "real" data. The chapters that move farthest in this direction are Chapters 4 and 9.

Hypothesizing about the behavior of computational models may seem trivial and obvious, as the program components are well defined; however, the complexities of today's simulation systems inhibit accurate a priori specifications of their behavior. Even with simple models, such as Team-Soar (Chapter 3), the model of cooperation (Chapter 5), and the original garbage can model (Cohen, March, and Olsen 1972), new findings emerged that were not hypothesized given the program components and new insights were gained into organizational performance. Though predictions may be made concerning the behavior of such models, tests of actual program performance must be made to verify them. To this end, researchers often use these models to run virtual experiments, collecting data that is then analyzed graphically and statistically.

Within the field of computational organization theory, computational analysis is used to develop a better understanding of the fundamental principles of organizing multiple information processing agents and the nature of organizations as computational entities. Research in this area has two main foci. The first foci is has to do with building new concepts, theories, and knowledge about organizing and organization. Most of the chapters have this foci. The second foci has to do with developing tools and procedures for the validation. Chapters 7, 8 and 11 have this foci.

This book is divided into four sections. Each of these sections corresponds to a major area in which there is on-going research. Section One is titled "Organizations as Multi-Agent Systems." Human (or human-derivative) organizations, like games, are "artificial" in the sense that they are crafted by humans (Simon 1981). Organizational behavior emerges both from the artificial construct that constrains individual interactions and the natural limits on human (or agent) behavior. This type of emergent behavior is seen in the results presented in Section One. All three chapters in this section draw heavily on work in artificial intelligence. Unlike most games, however, organizations are highly volatile with no specifiable (or perhaps predictable) equilibria. Indeed, within organizations it is the norm that the rules change, the players change, and the situations change. This volatility is due in large part to the agents which comprise them and the way in which the agents interact. Hence, within organizations, the form of the rules and procedures depends on the agents and their personal history as they respond to the changing environment. The first chapter (Chapter 1, "Web-Bots, Trust, and Organizational Science"), by Carley and Prietula, describes an experiment in which a strong model of artificial intelligence called Soar (Laird, Newell, and Rosenbloom 1987) is used to explore the significant issue of trust between intelligent agents. Not only is this a unique direction of inquiry, but the study produces quantifiable data on deliberation and communication derived directly from the theoretical stance articulated in code. In the second chapter of this section (Chapter 2, "Team-Soar: A Model for Team Decision Making"), Kang, Waisel, and Wallace also incorporate a Soar approach. In this chapter, the authors model a naval command and control team tasked with making critical decisions regarding the hostility of an incoming aircraft. Events such as those occurring with the U.S.S. Stark and the U.S.S. Vincennes have been traced to dysfunctional team behaviors. Their approach is to simulate and analyze possible sources of team dysfunctionality to improve team decision making behaviors. In the third chapter in Section One (Chapter 3, "Designing Organizations for Computational Agents"), So and Durfee describe a framework for understanding organizational design design for computational agents, use that framework for analyzing the expected performance of a class of organizations, and describe how the analyses can be applied to predict performance for a distributed information gathering task. An interesting component of this chapter is the concept of organizations re-designing themselves, addressing an emerging critical problem in network administration.

Section Two ("Organizations and External Conditions") explores the relationship between organizational action, agent behavior, and environmental volatility. Part of the volatility within organizations comes from the advent of new technologies. Further, organizations often try to employ technologies to curb the impact of other forms of organizational volatility. Lin (Chapter 4, "The Choice between Accuracy and Errors: A Contingency Analysis of External Conditions and Organizational Decision Making Performance") uses a version of the radar task described in Chapter 2, but focuses on exploring the relationship between organizational performance, organizational designs, and environmental properties. It appears that the reliability of an organization resides in the fit between the design and the task the choice of design becomes a strategic decision between what type of errors the organization is willing to accept or minimize. Huberman and Glance (Chapter 5, "Fluctuating Efforts and Sustainable Cooperation") show that when individuals confronted with a social dilemma contribute to the common good with an effort that fluctuates in time, they can generate an average utility to the group that decreases in time. This paradoxical behavior takes place in spite of the fact that typically individuals are found to be contributing at any one time. This phenomenon is the result of an intermittency effect, whereby unlikely bursts of defection determine the average behavior of the group. Thus, typical behavior of individuals comprising a group, can be inconsistent with a groups average properties. In the final chapter in this section (Chapter 6, "Task Environment Centered Simulation"), Decker describes the TÆMS framework (Task Analysis, Environment Modeling, and Simulation) to model and simulate complex, computationally intensive task environments as multiple levels of abstraction, and from multiple viewpoints. TÆMS is a tool for building and testing computation theories of coordination. This framework permits researchers to mathematically analyze (when possible) and quantitative simulate (when necessary) the behavior of multi-agent systems with respect to interesting characteristics of their task environment. As such, it is a testbed for exploring centralized, parallel, or distributed control algorithms, negotiation strategies, and organizational designs. To illustrate TÆMS, Decker investigates a simple question: Is there a difference between performance due to either the choice of organizational structure or the decomposibility of the technology?

The chapters in Section Three ("Organizations and Information Technology") address issues of technology, but within the realm of information technology and information systems. Most computational models of organizations do not consider the role of information technology, Thus, the chapters in Section Three represent initial forays into the how to think formally about the role of information technology in organizations. Fox, Barbuceanu and Lin (Chapter 7, "An Organizational Ontology for Enterprise Modeling") begin to address the next generation of Enterprise Model. Specifically, they propose that the next generation be a common sense enterprise model, which possess the capability to deduce answers to queries requiring relatively shallow knowledge of the domain. Thus, a key component of future information systems is an enterprise model that goes well-beyond the capabilities of current database or enterprise systems. Key to the articulation of such a model are the fundamental ontologies upon which the model is defined. The authors present a discussion of their approach to defining ontologies and ontological competence in their pursuit of the next generation enterprise model. In Chapter 8 ("Modeling, Simulating, and Enacting Complex Organizational Processes: A Life Cycle Approach"), Scacchi describes the approach and mechanisms to support the engineering of organizational processes throughout their life cycle. Organizations are, in part, defined by their processes. As events change (e.g., technology, tasks, environment) an organization may have to review and redefine its processes and process streams. Scacchi describes a knowledge-based computing environment, the articulator, that supports the defining and simulation of complex organizational processes. Kaplan and Carley (Chapter 9, "An Approach to Modeling Communication and Information Technology in Organizations") describe the communicating and information technology (COMIT) computational framework used to investigate information processing impacts of changing either the information technology or the communication structure on organizational performance. COMIT generates aggregate and detailed statistics on the number and duration of actions (e.g., communication, information lookup) and task completion quality. To illustrate, the authors describe a study in which levels of technology (high, low) are crossed with levels of experience and work structure (solo, collaborative). Their results suggest that technology, training, and organizational design can interact in complex ways to influence performance, and that computational approaches as COMIT can help reveal those complexities and their effects. In the final chapter of this section (Chapter 10, "Organizational Mnemonics: Exploring the Role of Information Technology in Collective Remembering and Forgetting"), Sandoe presents a conceptual model of organizational remembering and forgetting, and describes a simulation derived from the conceptual model. Sandoe argues that organizational remembering (and forgetting) occurs in three ways: an organization can remember (1) structurally, through the establishment of rules, roles, policies; (2) mutually, through advisory relationships among its members, and (3) technologically, through the creation of physical or symbolic artifacts. Sandoe then conducts a study where three organizational forms (hierarchy, network, hub) are simulated and tested with respect to environmental turbulence, turnover, and cost.

In the concluding essay ("Validating and Docking: An Overview, Summary and Challenge"), Burton addresses the chapter contributions in three contexts. First, Burton discusses the chapters with respect to the important issue of validity in the context of a framework which summarizes a computational model along three dimensions: its purpose, its process, and the analysis of its results (Burton and Obel 1996). Second, Burton categorizes the chapters according to a scheme developed by Carley (1995) which situates a computational simulation with respect to its explanatory role, of which four are proposed: organizational design, organizational learning, organizations and information technology, and organizational evolution and change. Finally, Burton speculates on the contribution of the collective in the context of "docking" or aligning simulation models for comparative purposes (Axtell, Axelrod, Epstein and Cohen 1996).

Computational organizational theorists are trying to use computational techniques to develop a firm scientific base for the study of organizations. As noted, organizations are often complex, nonlinear, adaptive systems. The natural complexity of organizations is reflected in the fact that many of the existing models and theories of organization are vague, intuitive, and under-specified. The more explicit and well-defined these theories, the greater our ability to make scientific progress. Computational theorizing about organizations helps to achieve this. The chapters in this book contribute to this endeavor. These chapters are the outgrowth of the tremendous outpouring of work in this area in the second half of the twentieth century since Cyert and March's *A Behavioral Theory of the Firm* in 1963. Recent work in this area combines traditional organizational concerns with performance, design, and adaptation with technique and approaches informed by work in the area of distributed artificial intelligence (Bond and Gasser 1988, Gasser and Huhns 1989). However, the computational organization theories of today, unlike much of the early work in distributed artificial intelligence work, are often grounded in existing cognitive, knowledge-based, information-processing theories of individual behavior and information processing, institutional, population ecology, or other models of organizations. Computational organization theorists extend the work on individual behavior to the organizational level (e.g., Simon 1947). This combination and extension gives precision to the notion of bounded rationality by specifying the nature of the boundaries and the role of social and historical information in defining organizational action (Carley and Newell 1994, Carley and Prietula 1994). This book contributes to our understanding of both organizations and organizing and provides illustrations for how to conduct research in this area.

Simulating
Organizations

Organizations as Multi-Agent Systems

I

WebBots, Trust, and Organizational Science

Kathleen Carley and Michael Prietula

WebBots are artificial creatures. Now, by "artificial" we do not mean that they do not exist, for they do. In fact, we built some. Yet, Web-Bots are neither biological nor mechanical creatures. WebBots are computer programs, but they are computer programs of a very special type. WebBots are programs that help their human counterpart(s) to achieve goals and solve problems. What is unique about WebBots is that they do much of their work on their own over webs of interconnected networks.

One of the major applications we see for WebBots is to be "intelligent explorers" on networks (including the Internet) for their human (i.e., corporate) counterparts. Thus an organization might have dozens, hundreds, or even thousands of corporate WebBots actively searching, communicating, traveling, and even reproducing over networks around the world for a wide variety of purposes. Simpler types of such creatures are being researched or even employed by firms such as AT&T, IBM, Apple Computer, Xerox, Microsoft, Hertz, Ford, and even the White House (Houlder 1994; Keller 1994). Although the specifics of any vibrant and emerging technology is extremely difficult to predict with certainty, the current trends in information technologies all point to a single, inescapable prediction: *the WebBots are coming!*

WebBots (or whatever you wish to call them) can take on a wide variety of forms. In this chapter, we will briefly mention some of these, but we are going to describe a different kind of WebBot. The WebBots we describe have very unique properties. To get these unique properties, we propose a very unique architecture for WebBots. The interesting elements of the proposed architecture are that it provides a fundamental framework for general WebBot intelligence and permits a unique set of mechanisms for defining, measuring, and sharing corporate learning, memory, and knowledge.

In this chapter, we first offer a brief look at WebBotlike programs. This is not a new concept; rather, we are building our approach on a long stream of incre-

mental research from several different perspectives. We then present an architecture that can realize a specific type of intelligent WebBot agent, an agent that
can reason and communicate with other WebBots. Since a central point of this
chapter is exploring the social aspects of WebBots, we next describe a computational experiment in which we simulate an organization of WebBots. In this experiment, we assign tasks to a small group of WebBots, adjusting and experi-
menting with a particularly important aspect of WebBot interaction—trust and
forgiveness in information exchange. We conclude with a speculative discussion
on the implications of applying an organizational science perspective to an organization of WebBots. Should we begin to define an organizational science of
WebBots? Is it possible? We argue that this is not only possible (though certainly not easy), but essential, in order to successfully assimilate such technology (or
technologies) into the corporate environment. We propose that the foundations
for studying WebBot organizational science have already been formed.

About WebBots

In one sense, this chapter is quite speculative. The WebBot creatures of the type
we are addressing are not quite ready for prime time—but close. They are in
the digital Catskills of information technology: corporate and university laboratories. The WebBots in our world are related to digital creatures that go by
many names, depending on their particular capabilities, or even on the particular laboratory or organization where they are being created. There is no commonly accepted definition for the term WebBot; however, the concept of a Web-
Bot has emerged at various times over the past decades in both formal and
informal settings.

We have witnessed lively discussions at our research conferences over who
invented or used what term first, who actually constructed the first (fill in your
term here), and what stream of research was actually most responsible for the
current perspective(s). It is perhaps easiest to think of WebBots as belonging to a
large family of computational architectures that differ on various dimensions of
form or function but possess a general family resemblance. Recall the wide variety of droids depicted in the *Star Wars* trilogy? Similarly, we can imagine a wide
variety of WebBotlike "digital analogs."

The research lineage of approaches such as ours can be traced to several
sources, with perhaps the general theme mostly related to Negroponte (1970),
though the concept of an "intelligent agent" has been around in thought, if not
in form, since at least the 1960s. Several fascinating perspectives abound in the
field, such as knowbots (Kahn and Cerf 1988), softbots (Etzioni, Lesh, and Segal
1994), varieties of software agents (Genesereth and Ketchpel 1994; Greif 1994,
Guha and Lenat 1994; Keller 1994), apprentices (Dent et al. 1992), intelligent

agents (King 1995; Roesler and Hawkins 1994), distributed intelligent agents (Hayes—Roth 1990; Rosenschein 1992), and a host of similar creatures in the distributed artificial intelligence literature (e.g., Gasser and Huhns 1989; Sycara et al. in press). Furthermore, there is an important convergence of several aspects of these themes that are opportunistically being applied to the Internet (e.g., Cheong 1996).

Additionally, this work draws from the work in computational organization theory (Carley and Prietula 1994; Carley 1995) and addresses the issue of organizational design. Like the work on intelligent agents, rigorous research using computational methods to explore issues of organizational design dates back to the 1960s (Cyert and March 1963). This work uses computational techniques to examine how organizations of intelligent, and often adaptive, agents should be coordinated (Masuch and LaPotin 1989; Levitt et al. 1994; Prietula and Carley 1994; Lin and Carley in press).

The options for organizations currently range from purchasing available application—specific software (e.g., generally for information retrieval, data mining, web mining, or news filtering) to building their own agents within a particular technology using a form of scripting language, such as General Magiclike Telescripts (White 1994), crafting their own proprietary systems for specific purposes, or hiring a firm to build or apply agent technology (e.g., Comshare or Andersen Consulting's Enterprise Intelligent Systems group). Additionally, research projects are underway to provide general agent design languages and open architectures (e.g., Cohen et al. 1994; Shoham 1993). However, one must be careful to understand the "granularity and form" of the architectures and languages. For example, there are large differences between building agents from enhanced components of a programming facility, like a predefined object package within C++, and building agents from a much higher architectural level, such as those often afforded by the distributed artificial intelligence approaches (Bond and Gasser 1988). One goal of this chapter is to add an approach to this last list of efforts that brings a quite different perspective on agent design.

Our collective role in this chapter is not one of historian; consequently, we are permitted to exploit the available degrees of freedom afforded by this claim to offer our own interpretation and work from there. Our first interpretation is as follows:

A *WebBot* is a computer program that operates autonomously to accomplish a task or set of tasks as an intellectual advisor and assistant to a human counterpart.

WebBots of the sort we are describing, then, are presented with goals (explicit or implicit) and turned loose within a system or a network (or within many networks) to accomplish some electronic type tasks. We might tell a *WebBot* (let us ignore issues of natural language communication) to perform the following tasks:

- Monitor intranet work events across a set of terminals and provide a report on Monday of the list of people who … (an intranet monitoring WebBot).

- Engage a search every day for new additions to telecommunications home pages that … (a watcher WebBot] and then add them to a resource list … [a fetch WebBot).

- Keep an up-to-date list on the references of recent hearings on the cable industry where … (a fetch WebBot) and then go get the text, graphics, or audio-feeds if they are available on-line … (a fetch WebBot).

- Watch the corporate knowledge bases for any new additions regarding audit and technology issues in the health care industry … (a corporate watcher WebBot) … and send them e-mail requesting a copy of their knowledge report where … (a corporate communicator WebBot).

- Go out and scan employees' disks checking for viruses and report back the results … (a virus checking intranet WebBot).

- Go out and scan the Web to detect what sites are pointing to your site, then send and collect an information survey over the Web to those sites … (a tracer WebBot).

In the first example, a network administrator might want to check logins, idle time, and workloads for the corporate intranet. For the second, a WebBot will access Internet search resources (e.g., search agents programming other search agents) every day to determine if new home pages (i.e., World Wide Web sites) have been added for a particular topic. The third example addresses what might have been called "library research," where the electronic card catalogs are periodically monitored and text resources are obtained when appropriate. The fourth example depicts a corporation that has set up a type of knowledge base containing experiences (e.g., problems, solutions, and explanations) of client engagements or internal projects. The next example illustrates a WebBot that has virus-monitoring responsibility for software on employees' disks on their company's intranet. In the final example, a WebBot explores to see what links are pointing to a corporate web resource and then engages an automated web-based survey sequence.

The set of WebBots available to their human counterparts are defined in terms of the business processes they are to accomplish at one end with the embedded procedural knowledge of how to accomplish them at the other. The embedded procedural knowledge, as one may surmise, must include aspects of the digital image of the relevant corporate resources that enable it to perform the tasks at hand. WebBots must know about (or have the capacity to figure out) the corporate environment within which they reside.

Four general observations can be made on the requirements of the WebBots we are describing that differentiate them from their fellow agents. First, if an organization (we will assume that organizations may be some of the major investors in such creatures) engages a set of WebBots as assistants for their employees, and employees in organizations often require interaction with other employees, then an obvious observation can be made:

Some WebBots' tasks will necessitate interacting with other WebBots.

Second, business processes themselves can be rather complex and, in fact, constructed (defined in terms) of simpler business processes. That is, business processes will be specified in terms of other business processes. Therefore, a second observation can be made:

Some of the WebBots' tasks will consist of sequences of, or even hierarchically defined levels of, business processes.

Third, the WebBots must be able to engage a sufficient amount of deliberation to reasonably deal with the vague, ambiguous, and uncertain environment encountered in the attempted execution of the business processes within a dynamic corporate setting. That is,

WebBots should have the capacity to reason about and learn from their actions.

Finally, there is a direct implication of two types of potential communication in this simple structure: human–WebBot, WebBot–WebBot. Human–WebBot communication is, essentially, a fundamental question of human-computer interface development. This is a critical element in systems design, since from the perspective of the user, the interface *is* the system. Good systems design teams understand and address this issue. Tell the WebBot what to do (e.g., by means of some scripting language, mouse clicks, voice commands), and have the WebBot report back to the user in the most appropriate (or desired) manner available.

What is interesting are the implications of the WebBot-to-WebBot communications. What might they say to each other? How should they say it? In part, these are also system design questions whose answers depend on the nature of the problems to be addressed and by the particular agent technology. One could imagine that this would involve communication for requesting and providing information for task-related purposes, including coordination. Yet we are envisioning communication also occurring on a fundamentally different level. Because of the particular architecture out of which our WebBots are constructed, they are quite capable of direct knowledge exchange (Zhu, Prietula, and Hsu in press).

The fundamental structures that compose their knowledge can be shared among WebBot agents. Agents do not need to be actually built solely of this particular architecture; rather, they simply have to include this architecture as a subcomponent of their architecture. Thus, the inclusion of a direct knowledge exchange (DKE) capability renders an agent that is DKE-enabled. DKE-enabled WebBots have a remarkable capability:

WebBots can directly share the knowledge they accumulate in the performance of their tasks.

We are describing WebBots that have a fundamental intelligence and that are able to reason about their task and their environment, which includes the behavior of other WebBots. Furthermore, each WebBot is capable of educating any other WebBot by directly communicating its knowledge. There could be, of course, much simpler and specialized forms of WebBots, but in this chapter we are addressing a more ambitious species—a species capable of rudimentary problem solving and learning (thus changing its behavior) in the service of a goal.

Thus we can offer a modestly improved definition:

A *WebBot* is a computer program that operates autonomously and intelligently to accomplish a task or set of tasks as an intellectual advisor and assistant to a human counterpart and other WebBots.

A Computational Study of WebBots

While we are also envisioning many WebBots interacting with each other, we are also describing an embedded electronic population of WebBots interacting within an explicit (or implicit) WebBot organizational structure. On one level, as defined, there is a distinct set of business processes that are defined in terms of the WebBots that instantiate them. On another level, there is a new and different organization of agents interacting in a world influenced by, but not populated with, humans. Our primary interest in WebBots is not in what they might be able to achieve, but rather in the implications of WebBot social interactions with each other in this electronic organizational subculture.

What can we begin to say about an organizational substructure of intelligent WebBot agents? We conducted a computational exploration of a simple organizational situation based on the type of WebBot we have described. We asked the following question: to what extent does WebBot honesty affect individual and collective organizational behavior?

Organizations are composed of individual agents whose collective activity defines the "behavior" of an organization. Similarly, the individual decisions of WebBots affect the behavior of the entire WebBot collective and, consequently, the organization's general behavior. From this perspective, certain types of WebBots' social behaviors (i.e., interacting with each other within the organization in the execution of their tasks) and their effects on organizational performance (individual and collective properties of their behavior) are explored. The WebBot's social behavior is defined by a set of behavioral predispositions they have reflecting specific "rules of social engagement" defining a rudimentary social cognition component of WebBot deliberation. The rules we are investigating are concerned with honesty and benevolence judgments within the context of a socially situated task.

The simulation described in this chapter is unique. It reflects a "theory on a theory" as the fundamental WebBot architecture is itself a theory of individual intelligence, called *Soar*. With this theory of individual WebBot architecture forming the basis for creating WebBots, an assemblage of WebBots are linked together, interacting in a social environment in their performance of a task. Two types of knowledge are encoded in each WebBot: task-specific knowledge, enabling the task to be accomplished, as well as social-interaction knowledge, reflecting the social cognition rules of social engagement for the properties investigated (honesty, benevolence). By situating these WebBots in an organizational task permitting social interaction, a small organizational unit is defined. How each WebBot behaves is based on the nature of the goals, the knowledge to work on those goals, and how the task unfolds in the context of other WebBots.

In cognitive science terms, each WebBot defines its own problem space reflecting critically perceived aspects of the task environment (Newell and Simon 1972). Each WebBot's problem space also contains models of other encountered WebBots and their behaviors, for these other WebBots are also components of the task environment. It is from models of each other's behaviors that decisions are made regarding interactions, and it is the nature of these social interactions (i.e., interaction decisions) that define collective organizational behavior. Yet, each WebBot constructs its task-specific social reality and performs its problem-solving behaviors in the same manner and with the same underlying architecture. It is entirely knowledge-based, with a single set of mechanisms operating under a unified approach to defining all aspects of deliberate problem solving—Soar.

The Soar Architecture

Soar is a symbol-oriented computational architecture for general intelligence (Laird, Newell, and Rosenbloom 1987; Newell 1990). In the Soar architecture, tasks are represented as search, through the application of operators to monitor and manipulate symbol structures in working memory, within problem spaces to achieve goals (existence of a particular symbol structure). Knowledge in Soar is represented as *if* <antecedent> *then* <consequent> productions of the following general form:

if   <a structure is found in working memory>
then <propose a change in working memory structures>

Changes in working memory are proposed until sufficient evidence has accumulated to support a specific change in memory structure. This is accomplished through a preference system embedded in the architecture itself. Details can be found in Laird et al. (1990).

If Soar cannot directly and unambiguously achieve a goal with its current knowledge base, the architecture automatically generates an impasse, causing a new goal, called a subgoal, to be created and addressed—the resolution of the impasse. This, in turn, may cause further impasses.

Essentially using a depth-first, look-ahead search, the subgoaling process proposes envisioned subproblem spaces that correspond to each of the available actions. Soar traces the decision trees that would unfold if each possible subproblem space was in fact chosen, and then evaluates the outcomes of each alternative action in terms of the current goal. Since both the production memory and the working memory are always accessible and the same problem solving mechanisms apply in any subproblem space, the full problem solving power of Soar is available to be brought to bear for each subproblem.

Once Soar resolves a subgoal, an analysis of the working memory elements (symbol structures) leading to the resolution of the subgoal is made, linking them to the eventual working memory elements of the resolution. From this, new long-term productions are created, called *chunks*, which represent accumulated knowledge to directly resolve the state causing the impasse if it is again encountered, thus avoiding subgoal deliberations. Soar has learned.

All decisions in Soar are made in a two-phase decision cycle. During the first phase, called the *elaboration* phase, any and all productions whose antecedent conditions have been satisfied fire, proposing their consequent contributions to working memory. As working memory structures change, different productions may become able to fire, while others may lose support. This process continues until no more productions can fire. Thus, all productions effectively fire in parallel. The decision cycle in Soar represents the fundamental metric for deliberation: the more decision cycles, the more cognitive effort.

Soar-based WebBots

With much of the fundamental effort of intelligent deliberation a component of the architecture, WebBots can be created from Soar by adding task-specific knowledge. The task for the study consisted of a basic simulation of Soar agents making judgments over a network regarding tasks. The network task is interpreted as follows: Soar agents are WebBots that search out electronic information resources over the network. A WebBot receives a net resource target to find (e.g., a Web site that contains some desirable information resources), then proceeds to search for the Web site containing the target. An option available to the WebBot is to send out an electronic message to other WebBots to see if they have encountered this requested resource and can tell where it might be located.

In modeling the access to the various resources, we imposed a sequence of processes required to access them. For example, one might imagine logging in to a mailbox to get an assignment, sending out the e-mail, getting a response, evaluating the response, logging in, and accessing/searching through a variety of interim Web pages or pointers to finally access the resource, which may or may not be at a particular Web site.

The WebBots themselves were provided with the following rudimentary characteristics:

• *Communication*—ability to ask other WebBots if they have seen a resource on the net, and answer other WebBots questions regarding the same issue.

- *Location memory*—ability to recall what resources it has seen when it has visited a net site
- *Social memory*—ability to recall its interactions with other WebBots regarding requests for net site information (i.e., was it correct or not)
- *Rules of social engagement*—when asked for information, consistent truth (trustworthy WebBots), or consistent misleading (untrustworthy WebBots)
- *Social judgment*—a scoring scheme for judging whether a WebBot was trustworthy based on social memory of past communications and engagements.

For this study, five different organizational sizes were examined (one through five WebBots), and each organization was homogeneous with respect to one of two conditions. In the first condition, the WebBots were all honest—they attempted to respond accurately to questions of possible Web resource locations from either their memory or their current perspective (i.e., directly observing it from their location). In the second condition, all WebBot organizational agents attempted to deceive other WebBots when they received requests for Web locations.

In both conditions, all WebBots engaged in social judgments. Consisting of ratings of trustworthiness based on the veracity (or lack thereof) of each of the other WebBots' past communications. WebBots incorporate three levels of trustworthiness of an information source: trustworthy (location of a Web site was correct), possibly untrustworthy (location of last requested Web site was incorrect), and untrustworthy (location of last two requested Web sites were incorrect). Thus, if at some time in the past WebBot X told WebBot Z that net resource A was at net site x, and in acting on this information, WebBot Z finds that net resource A is indeed at net site ξ, then WebBot Z's "opinion" of WebBot X would support a social judgment of trustworthiness. If WebBot Z's prior opinion of WebBot X was "possibly untrustworthy," then that opinion would be upgraded to trustworthy.

On the other hand, if WebBot Z fails to find net resource A at net site ξ, then WebBot Z would downgrade its opinion of WebBot X. If WebBot X was previously considered "trustworthy" (the initial judgment values of all WebBots), then it would be downgraded to "possibly untrustworthy." Two consecutive incorrect messages from a given WebBot results in a judgment of "untrustworthy." Once some WebBot Z deems another WebBot X untrustworthy, WebBot Z automatically presumes that all further communication from WebBot X will also be incorrect. These WebBots are not forgiving.

The characterizations of WebBots are highly stylized but represent the facets of a broad range of behaviors found in functional and dysfunctional human agents (or human-created agents, like computer viruses and cracker codes). As WebBots can be programmed to perform in any particular manner, and as organizational members may compete, in part, in terms of the behaviors of their personal or corporate WebBots, this represents a legitimate investigation of extreme, though possible, (non)cooperative behaviors. The primary point in this chapter is to illustrate a methodology, present a small example of a computational study, and report the results.

The net environment was depicted as having fifteen single net resource orders for each WebBot and twenty possible net locations with three potentially relevant resources at each location. The twenty locations are ordered hierarchically, such that each location has a link to two other locations, specifically a single parent and single child. We can think of linked locations as being adjacent. Agents, when they begin searching this web, always begin at location one.

There are no duplicates in either the task orders or the available resources; therefore, there are forty-five additional extraneous resources distributed throughout the net locations (accounting for occasional additional local search effort). Each WebBot would request one net task order at a time, locate the resource in the net environment, then request another net task. The simulations were run until the order queue was completed. The simulations were conducted on networked workstations, each running a single copy of a Soar WebBot agent.

The Results

Several dependent measures were used to examine the behavior of the individual and collective WebBots. "Cognitive effort" is a general metric based on decision cycles. *Average cognitive effort* is the total cognitive effort (in terms of decision cycles) divided by the number of WebBots in the organization. Figure 1 presents the data for all five organizations, and for both organizational types. As can be seen in figure 1, the more WebBots in the organization, the less each WebBot has to do. Yet, except after the first precipitous drop (from one to two WebBots), the additional reduction in load does not seem that remarkable.

Maximum cognitive effort reflects the most cognitive effort put forth by a WebBot in an organization. By making a simplifying assumption that all decision cycle efforts are equivalent in duration, this is also a measure of the total time required to complete the task. From the figure it is clear that some events are affecting the two organizations differently. The organization composed of untrustworthy agents first declines in terms of total time taken to complete the task (with organizations consisting of one, two, and three WebBots), then begins to increase (with organizations of four and five WebBots). The organization with trustworthy agents has a similar profile, but its periodicity is smaller, where the decline–increase cycle occurs twice, with local minima at two WebBots and four WebBots, respectively.

This graph begs three questions: What is happening to trustworthy organizations with three WebBots? What is driving the curves up as the size of the organi-

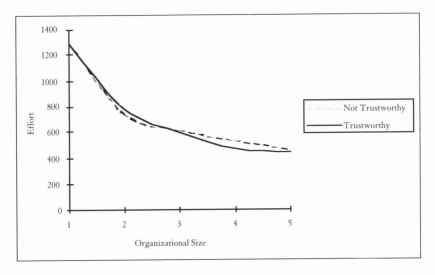

Figure 1. Average effort per WebBot to complete the task.

zation increases? What is causing the interaction between trustworthiness and organizational size (i.e., untrustworthy WebBots dominate at lower organizational sizes, trustworthy WebBots dominate at large organizational sizes)?

Regarding the first question, the answer is found in the distribution of effort among the WebBots. Essentially, in this organization there was a significant, but anomalous, maldistribution of effort centered around one WebBot that accounted for over 53 percent of the search effort, which was highly unusual (e.g., the distribution for the three untrustworthy WebBots was 34 percent, 34 percent, and 31 percent).

The second question concerns the curves themselves as they eventually rise (i.e., the time to complete the task increases) as the number of WebBots increases beyond four or five because of several interacting events. Contributing to this is a general increase in wait time as the WebBots begin (slightly) to interfere with each other as they try to access resources. *Wait cycles* indicate the amount of time the WebBot spends simply in queues to access a net resource. This usually represents a wait when multiple WebBots are trying to access a net location, which, in this model, locks out all but one WebBot at a time. In figure 3, the rate of increase of wait cycles is apparent with the graph of average wait cycles per WebBot.

Also influencing the general rise in task time is the contribution made by the ability to communicate. Communication, in this model, takes time and effort for a WebBot. Therefore, asking and answering questions represents a general contribution to task time, as shown in figures 4 and 5, respectively. An examination of figure 4 reveals a general increase in communication ef-

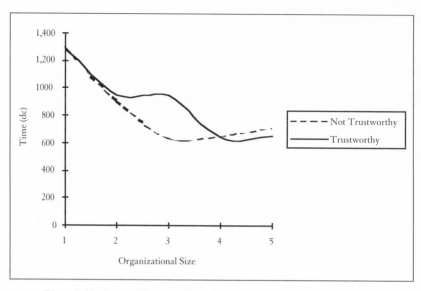

Figure 2. Maximum effort as total time (in decision cycles) to complete the task.

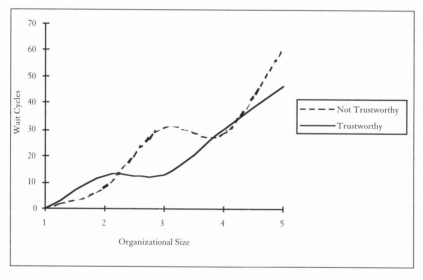

Figure 3. Average number of wait cycles (in decision cycles) for each organization.

fort as the size of the organization increases. This is expected, as more agents are attempting to communicate. Similarly, in figure 5, more answers are being generated in response to the questions.

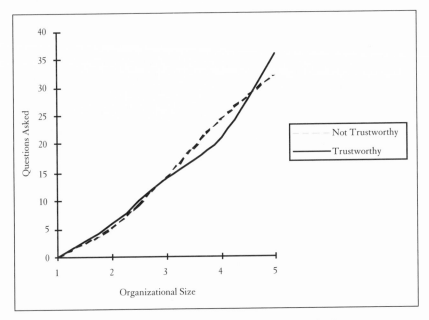

Figure 4. Total number of questions asked in the organization.

Thus, both wait time and communication time drive up the overall time to complete the task. But what about the third question? That is, why the interaction between task time and WebBot trustworthiness? In part, this has already been addressed. The differential contributions of both wait cycles (figure 3) and questions answered (figure 5) account for this interaction.

It is important to make a distinction between the total time it takes an organization to complete the task, and the total effort (in terms of aggregate WebBot decision cycles) it takes to complete the task. From figure 1, it is clear that the average WebBot effort is decreasing, and from figure 2 it is clear that the total time is decreasing (then increasing slightly). Figure 6 shows the cumulative organizational effort it takes to complete the task. The total cognitive effort to complete the task steadily increases as more WebBots are brought onboard. Total cognitive effort is measured as the total number of decision cycles that all WebBots in an organization require to complete a task. Note again the slight interaction between organizational size and WebBot trustworthiness.

Finally, there seems to be another recurring periodicity occurring in Figure 6 for both types of organizations across sizes, though the "phases" are off. Of interest, then, is the attenuation of the graph for the untrustworthy WebBots and the increase of the graph for the trustworthy WebBots at the larger organizational sizes.

The answer to both questions can be found in an investigation of question

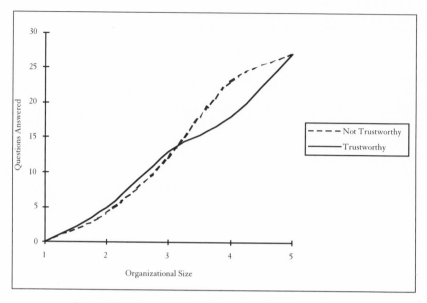

Figure 5. Total number of questions answered in the organization.

and answer events. Figures 7 and 8 show the average number of questions asked (figure 7) and answered (figure 8) for the organization sizes.

As the number of WebBot agents increases, trustworthy agents ask and answer more and more questions. The reason is that more information is being discovered as the WebBot agents search the net. The more they search, the more they learn. The more they learn, the more they can communicate useful information. On the other hand, untrustworthy WebBots are actually decreasing the number of questions they are asking and answering.

As the number of WebBot agents are able to encounter and communicate wrong or unreliable information, specific decisions are made not to ask specific agents. Remember that WebBot agents give wrong information about a net resource only if they have encountered that resource. As the organization learns about its environment, it learns not to trust more and more of its WebBots. The penalty incurred (at first) for trusting untrustworthy agents is that a WebBot accesses specific locations (based on information from other WebBots), only to find the desired resource not there (see figure 9). In this figure, trustworthy WebBot agents never intentionally mislead (i.e., all of the values are zero for this graph), and untrustworthy WebBot agents begin to incur effort costs as the size of the organization grows.

But we must be careful. Our little study examined the extremes of a task—all trustworthy, all untrustworthy. There is, no doubt, a strong task × agent proper-

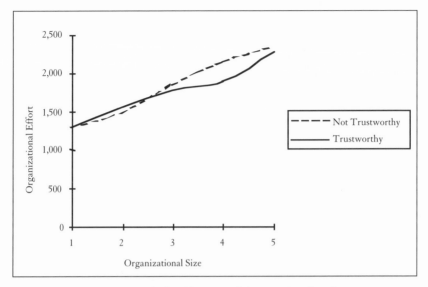

Figure 6. Total effort (decision cycles) to complete the task.

ty interaction. Agent properties work well (or behave in a certain manner) in one type of task environment, but may perform quite differently in another. For the task at hand, there is a relatively small number of agents interacting with a sparse task. There is little agent interference (i.e., changing the state of the world as a trustworthy agent knows it) in this task. It would be interesting to investigate how agent trustworthiness (i.e., variations on the social rules of engagement), organizational trustworthiness (i.e., the number agents of a certain type in a group), and task properties (i.e., the number of different resources, the number of mirror sites replications) interact to produce error rates, intentional or unintentional.

Conclusion: About Organizational Science

Human agents base their behaviors on the vast quantities of knowledge garnered through years of experience and the remarkable capacity of the human brain. However, many types of organizational tasks and roles impose a variety of constraints that effectively inhibit much of the reasoning capabilities of the employee. Consequently, it could be the case that interesting variance in performance in organizational settings may be accounted for by a relatively small set of recurring response behaviors (perhaps expressed as rules) to individual goals under the particular organizational constraints. Thus, by selecting a small set of

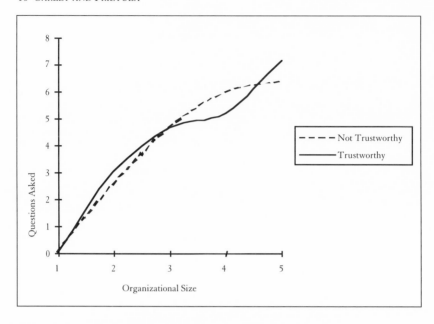

Figure 7. Average number of questions asked per WebBot.

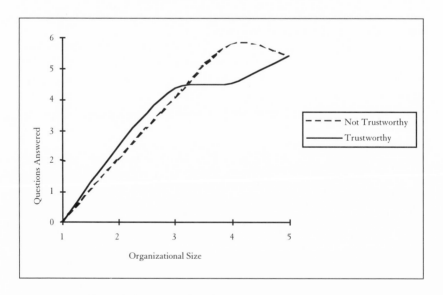

Figure 8. Average number of questions answered per WebBot.

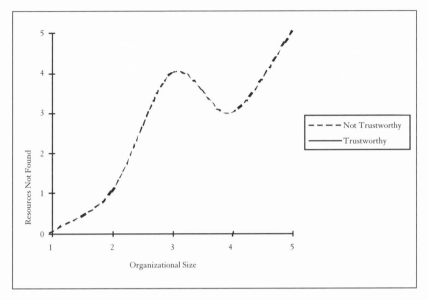

*Figure 9. Number of resources failed to be found at communicated location.
(Note: Value for trustworthy WebBots is zero.)*

response behaviors (in this case, rules of social engagement) occurring in a task situation that is highly constrained (the task is both simple and restricted in execution), we can model the behavior of organization agents.

By systematically manipulating the social rules of engagement and the knowledge (and thus social behavior) of individual agents, we can systematically observe the emergent organizational behavior, for organizational behavior is derivative from the nature of the individual agents and the context within which they interact. As such, this chapter is an incremental step in exploring the cognitive as well as social aspects of organizational theory (human or machine) through computational modeling (Carley and Prietula 1994b). Consider two particular features of the proposed model—the role of trustworthiness and the role of DKE.

The fundamental issues underlying trust in an organizational setting is an important and emerging topic in organizational science (e.g., Kramer and Tyler 1996) and information systems (Lerch, Prietula, and Kulik in press). It may seem strange in this initial exploration of WebBots to look at the issue of trustworthiness. After all, one might expect that WebBots, as artificial agents, will not intend to lie. However, what we have termed a lack of trustworthiness in these artificial agents can arise in a number of ways. First, the basic concept of trust is already embedded in the concepts underlying today's distributed computational environment. This form of trust is actually an administrative and communication link between systems, which includes privilege granting for access to resources (Microsoft 1994).

Second, WebBot agents may simply be based on an erroneous algorithm. For example, it is unreasonable to expect a WebBot to "know" the location of a resource if a sufficient amount of time has elapsed since the validity of the URL was assessed. The web world is changing faster than the WebBot's image of it. Its knowledge is dated, as is its value—and time matters (Keen 1986).

Third, problems in portability and interactions with other software or tasks may lead these agents to act in an increasingly suboptimal fashion. In this case, over time, WebBots may degrade from trustworthy to untrustworthy in effect, though not in intent, for example, the evolution of organizational routines interpreted as a procedural memory implies, if we carry the metaphor, automated application and resistance to change, and difficulty to assess (e.g., Cohen and Bacdayan 1994).

Finally, the agents might indeed be crafted to lie. This is a simple extension of the recurring events of computer fraud, intentional denial of service, cracking, and so forth that, unfortunately, are elements of risk associated with doing business with, and connecting to, machines (e.g., Neumann 1995). Perhaps WebBot certification is required. Or is this actually a component of business? Is it ethical to craft a WebBot to mislead under certain circumstances? Is it simply a version of the "business is war" philosophy? There might be broader issues of industrial espionage, ethics, and business conduct by computers (Schwartau 1994).

We note that not only are the WebBots coming but they represent and will possibly control a great deal of wealth. Raj Reddy of Carnegie Mellon University predicts that soon you will be able to buy these intelligent agents, such as WebBots, (as you would) templates for spreadsheets (Anthes 1995, February 1995). Not only are they coming, but they represent a major financial investment. For example, it is estimated that by the year 2000, intelligent agent revenues in the United States and Europe could reach $4 billion (Fletcher 1994). This is not counting the funds affected by such WebBots acting as personal intelligent financial assistants. Microsoft is reportedly building the successor to (the unfortunate) Microsoft Bob, called Peedy, an anthropomorphic 3-D rendered parrot to serve as an intelligent assistant (Rupley 1995). It is a small step from such a general assistant to one fine-tuned to aid in financial planning, investment, and the dispersion of funds, to WebBot agents that autonomously negotiate and broker over the net and perform other dynamic multiagent interactive tasks (Sycara et al. in press; Sycara and Zeng 1996).

Consequently, it may be financially advantageous (although potentially illegal) to give such agents the capability of lying. Since the appearance of a lack of trustworthiness can occur in a number of ways, it is important to understand how organizations of WebBots might react in such situations. This preliminary study suggests that the effects of a lack of trustworthiness will be most felt when large numbers of WebBots must act in a coordinated fashion to perform some task.

An important capability of our WebBots is that they can search out skills (as knowledge) on networks. The DKE capability of these types of intelligent agents is critical in evolving the nature of the intelligent agent to a form that is capable of both accumulating and sharing in knowledge for the performance of organizational tasks. These agents are not simply intelligent explorers, they are intelligent knowledge explorers. As such, our WebBots bear a striking resemblance to various artificial agents currently in existence on the World Wide Web.

Indeed, there are already a variety of agents (a.k.a. webcrawlers, robots, spiders) that are used to search, index, and retrieve information on the World Wide Web, even one that simply (and usefully) measures the growth of the Web (Indermaur 1995). As we saw, the DKE capabilities of our WebBots makes it possible for them to take advantage of others' knowledge and so reduces the amount of effort that any one agent needs to expend on a coordinated task. Such DKE capabilities at the individual level also lead to the emergence of important organizational behaviors, such as determining the shape of the communication network in and between organizations. There are emerging proposals for a variety of general guidelines for knowledge exchanges (e.g., Genesereth and Fikes 1992; Gruber 1993) and experiments using specific intelligent architectures for knowledge exchange (e.g., Zhu, Prietula, and Hsu in press). On a broader note, Sun's Java language provides a generic coding platform for object-based agents. Of interest is Netscape's object signing capability (and other X.509-compliant certificate authorities), which helps provide, in their words, "shrink-wrapped trust for downloaded software."

We conclude this chapter with speculations about the future of a form of organizational science. That is based on conducting computer-based simulations of computer-realized organizations made up of artificially intelligent and adaptive agents. Why can we feel confident in the prediction that such computational models will play an important part in the future of organizations? Why might we argue for the organizational science of WebBots? The answer lies in the very nature of the emerging information technologies, the organizations embracing these technologies, and the business environments where the organizations use these technologies.

First, a wave of technological change is assaulting corporations and laying the groundwork for the opportunity and need for organizational WebBots. For example, the software crafted for Internet applications is directly applicable for a firm Intranet structure. The ubiquity and rapidity with which these changes are occurring creates a need for managers, technologists, and scientists to understand the potential organizational impact of these emergent technologies without necessarily investing in them and under novel conditions. Computational techniques are particularly useful in providing insight under these conditions.

Second, researchers who examine organizations theorize and study both organizations and organizing (Burton and Obel 1996). We are actually faced with an interesting phenomenon. To the extent that both the structure and components of an organization exist as intelligent agents on a network, a simulation of that organization *is* the organization. How will WebBot (or other types of intelligent agent) organizational structures work? What will the underlying economics look like? What will the fundamental principles be?

Will there be any fundamental principles? At issue is whether there are underlying principles that govern the behavior of organizations of humans, organizations of artificial agents, and organizations of both humans and artificial agents. A variant of this issue is not whether there are principles, but whether they are knowable. A computational organization theory is necessary if we are either to demonstrate that such principles do not exist or to discover and examine such principles if in fact they do exist.

These issues are probably less of a philosophical puzzle and more of a quandary of computational complexity. We have seen this in other disciplines. For example, biology, physics, and astronomy all have important branches that rely on computational modeling as a strategy for discovering or confirming the underlying regularities of interest. As organizations, society, and economies move toward computational realizations of decisions, representations, coordination, communications, interactions, and markets, they move away from human involvement.

The implications bring us around to our opening sentence: WebBots are artificial creatures. We add to that a closing comment: WebBots are artificial creatures operating in the context of an organization—an artificial structure. What nature of organizational science can deal with these types of social artifacts? The general implications of this have been foretold over twenty-five years ago by the Nobel prize-winning organizational theorist (economist, computer scientist, and psychologist) Herbert Simon in his book *The Sciences of the Artificial* (1969). But that is another chapter ... .

Acknowledgments

The authors would like to thank our colleagues for their helpful comments, the Soar group at Carnegie Mellon University for the use of the Soar machines, and David Park for running the original experiments. This work was supported in part by the National Science Foundation under grant IRI9633.

2

Team Soar

A Model for Team Decision Making

MinCheol Kang, Laurie B. Waisel, and William A. Wallace

Teaming, the use of groups with shared leadership, both individual and collective responsibility and accountability, and a special goal to be achieved, is considered by some practitioners to be "the primary unit of performance in high-performance organizations" (Katzenbach and Smith 1993). Some of the highest-performing organizations in terms of dealing with rapidly unfolding events with high uncertainty and potential for catastrophic impacts are in the military. In these organizations, events like those that involved the U.S.S. *Stark* and the U.S.S. *Vincennes* have demonstrated the need for greater understanding of the dynamics of teams. As described in a series of reports on incidents of team dysfunctional behaviors (Hollenbeck et al. forthcoming), the U.S.S. *Stark* incident involved an air patrol team of the U.S.S. *Stark* itself, an AWAC's reconnaissance plane, a land-based radar unit, and an Aegis Cruiser. The team misjudged the intention of an Iraqi jet, resulting in an attack that left thirty-seven U.S. service personnel dead. In the case of the U.S.S. *Vincennes*, a team consisting of the captain, supervisors, and radar operators misinterpreted an aircraft identification signal and the flight path of the civilian aircraft, resulting in the death of 290 people from 6 nations. A less dramatic but equally important example of a lack of understanding of teaming is the pervasive belief by management that all one has to do to achieve high performance from the workforce is to ask employees to work in groups. Creating a group doesn't, in and of itself, result in a team. Although there exist guidelines for team management based upon cases and anecdotal evidence (such as Katzenbach and Smith 1993), rigorous research complementing these efforts is needed in order to provide a foundation for prescribing the formation, operation, and performance of teams in organizational settings. The objective of the work described in this chapter is to contribute to this research.

What Is a Team?

If we define a group as two or more people who share something in common, then teams are a special class of groups. A team is a group whose members share a common goal and a common task (Ilgen et al. 1995; Orasanu and Salas 1993). The most critical distinction between teams and groups is the degree of differentiation of roles or expertise relevant to the task and the degree of member interdependence. Teams consist of highly differentiated and interdependent members while groups consist of homogeneous and interchangeable members with little or no interdependency. Team members bring to their teams different knowledge and skills that apply to the team's tasks (Ilgen et al. 1995). Furthermore, teams consist of interdependent and mutually accountable members who interact over time (Katzenbach and Smith 1993). In short, teams are sets of two or more experts who interact interdependently and adaptively toward a common goal.

The Team as Problem Solver and Decision Maker

Newell and Simon (1972) view problem solving as a fundamental human activity. Problem-solving activities and other symbolic, goal-oriented behaviors have been characterized as a search in problem space (Masuch 1992; Newell 1980). Humans solve a problem by finding a sequence of actions that transforms the initial problem state into the desired goal state. The domain of these actions is called the *problem space*. Solving a problem usually involves transformations through one or more intermediate states (Newell and Simon 1972). This decomposition of the problem into a series of subgoals often is crucial to success. When solving problems, humans act as knowledge systems (Newell 1990), using available knowledge to search for and choose a course of action that is appropriate to achieve the goal.

After examining more than fifty different teams in thirty companies, Katzenbach and Smith (1993) found that teams must be able to identify the problems and opportunities they face, evaluate the options they have for moving forward, and then make necessary trade-offs and decisions about how to proceed. This statement implies that a team should be a problem solver (Newell and Simon, 1972). In fact, a team is a collection of problem solvers, which, in turn, can be viewed as a collective problem solving system.

Although teams act as problem solvers, they work differently than individual humans when solving problems. One notable distinction between team and individual problem solving is that in team problem solving, the searches for alternatives are carried out by multiple intelligences. Teams solve problems in distributed fashion. Often, a team decomposes its team problem into a set of subproblems; then, different team members, who are problem solvers themselves, work on the different subproblems simultaneously. When all the subproblems have been solved, the results are integrated into a team-level solution to the team problem.

The problem solving process of a team can be divided into three phases: problem formulation, alternative generation, and choice (Massey and Wallace forthcoming). In the problem formulation phase, the team gains an understanding of the problem with a formal conceptualization. This phase consists of constructing and/or recognizing the team goal, the team problem space, and the initial team state. During alternative generation, the team generates and evaluates alternatives, which are the means used to transform the initial state into the goal state. The alternatives are sometimes referred to as operators, since the act of selecting and implementing an alternative transforms the state of the problem within the problem space. During the choice phase, the team selects what it believes to be the best alternative (or operator). Note that the problem-solving process is recursive, since each task may be decomposed into multiple subtasks.

Teams are rational systems of human interaction, where "rational" means performing the search based on relevant available information in order to find solutions (Masuch and LaPotin 1989). Although teams are more rational than individuals, teams still are subject to bounded rationality (Masuch 1992; Lucas and Jaffee 1969); that is, they are neither completely rational nor completely thorough in their use of knowledge and in their search for alternatives when solving problems. Lucas and Jaffee (1969) discovered that decision-making teams often, perhaps typically, do not use new information in a particularly rational manner.

Mental models are abstract constructs used by humans to represent their knowledge about problems and to guide problem-solving behavior (Newell 1990). When each team member engages in a task, she or he develops a mental model, a unique mental representation that reflects his or her perspective, expertise, experience, role, and so on, of the task and its domain. As team members interact with one another while carrying out the task, a shared mental model evolves. If they are successful, this shared representation will encompass common understanding, common goals, and shared viewpoints among the team members. The shared mental model is believed to affect team performance. Research by Katzenbach and Smith (1993) reveals that failed teams rarely develop relevant shared mental models, while high performance teams do.

Characteristics of Team Decision Making

The literature on group dynamics suggests that teams make better decisions than individuals, especially for complex tasks. A team has more information, knowledge, and reasoning capacities than an individual. Teams are expected to cope with the problems of complexity by increasing information processing capacities. Complex problems can be decomposed and assigned to individual members based upon their expertise or roles. The additional information resources available to a team can aid in reducing complexity and uncertainty by identifying constraints and therefore identifying regions of infeasibility (Zannetos 1987). As a result, the team can carry out tasks, particularly in turbulent environments, that are beyond the capabilities of an individual member.

What distinguishes team decision making from individual decision making are the existence of sources, varied expertise, and multiple perspectives, all of which must be integrated to reach a decision (Orasanu and Salas 1993, Stasser 1988). This integration often results in conflicts among team members. The resolution of these conflicts by a team requires more processing time than would be needed by an individual to reach a decision on the same problem. Therefore, for timely, simple decision making tasks, individuals may outperform teams.

The performance of a team depends on the task environment and the characteristics of the individual members as well as on the design of the team (McGrath 1984). Although each of these factors has an impact on team performance, most previous researchers manipulated only one or a few variables in any one of these domains (Duffy 1993). But, according to contingency theorists, organization performance is a function of the fit among variables across the three domains (Robbins 1990, Lupton 1976). Furthermore, team performance can be viewed as group behavior that has emerged from the interaction of the factors in the three domains (of task environment, characteristics of the members, and design of the team) (Prietula and Carley 1994). These views suggest the need for comprehensive research on teams that consider the three domain variables together.

Computational Modeling as a Research Method

Computational modeling with distributed AI as the paradigm will be used as the research methodology to study team behavior. A model that describes a class of systems in terms of a set of operations on entities, where the operations can be described in computational terms, will be considered a computational model (Yost and Newell 1993). Such a model can describe a system's structure and behavior and how the behavior is determined by its structure (Newell et al. 1993). For example, the Plural-Soar model, which models a warehouse where multiple workers fill orders by retrieving items stored in stacks located in different places, permitted researchers to examine how different combinations of cognitive constraints (such as communication and memory capabilities) combined with varying organizational structures (for example, different sizes) result in different organizational behaviors (Carley et al., 1992).

A computational model can be used as an instrument in a laboratory setting. Simulation experiments with a computational model can be performed at lower cost and with less time and effort than laboratory experiments with the real system (Stasser 1988). Questions can be addressed in a systematic fashion and repli-cated as necessary. A computational model is also useful for cases in which data is insufficient or unattainable, such as when the cost of experimentation is pro-hibitive, or where the problem domain is too risky in terms of safety and securi-ty for real-life experiments (Doran 1989, Masuch and LaPotin 1989).

Another valuable aspect of computational modeling is the ability to construct a theory by generating propositions to be tested by experimentation with the ac-tual system (Stasser 1988). Computational modeling has the capacity to integrate separate theoretical propositions into a single model, with the possibility of at-taining unanticipated, novel results (Abelson 1968). Such results can add new insights and may form the bases for further research.

These characteristics of computational models make the methodology useful in modeling human systems, particularly when cognition is involved. Cognition or human information processing can be viewed as computations using symbol-ic representations (Newell 1990, Pylyshyn 1989, Hunt 1989). Humans are sym-bol systems that achieve their intelligence by symbolizing external and internal situations and manipulating those symbols (Simon and Kaplan 1989). As sym-bol systems that process information, humans receive symbol structures for in-puts and produce symbol structures as output (Masuch 1992, Cohen and Feigenbaum 1981). Computers also process information by manipulating sym-bols. A computer can be thought of as a knowledge system that has a body of knowledge and a set of goals; it can take action to attain its goals according to what its knowledge indicates is appropriate (Newell et al. 1993). A computer can exhibit intelligent behavior while pursuing goals, that is, when it knows that a particular action will lead to a preferred situation, it will, when possible, select that action (Newell et al. 1993).

A demonstration that a particular system can support the wide range of rep-resentations that human cognition must use would be a powerful argument for that system as the appropriate model of human cognition. This is called the *suf-ficiency argument* (Hunt 1989). At the most abstract level, computers are the only known mechanisms that are sufficiently plastic in their behavior to match the plasticity of human cognition. They are also the only known mechanisms capa-ble of producing behavior that can be described as knowledge dependent. Therefore, computational models are an appropriate representation system for human cognitive activity in general, and for the process of decision making in particular (Hunt 1989, Pylyshyn 1989).

Computational modeling is an especially appropriate methodology for studying teamwork. It forces researchers to be specific about relationships among the enti-ties, which in this study means how the individual team members work together. Concepts from cases and anecdotal evidence must be formalized into operators on entities. This design process forces one to be systematic in describing the behavior of the team members as individuals and as a collective unit (Carley and Prietula 1994, Jin and Levitt 1993).

Distributed AI as a Paradigm for Computational Modeling of Teams

Distributed AI (DAI) is a subfield of AI that focuses on how a collection of artificially intelligent agents in a problem-solving situation can interact to achieve a common set of global goals (Chaib-Draa et al. 1992, Bond and Gasser 1988). DAI studies distributed problem solving by using groups of artificial agents, whereas team decision making can be considered as distributed problem solving by a group of humans. Therefore, DAI has potential as a framework for modeling the behavior of teams.

There are analogies between human groups and DAI systems. Both human groups and DAI systems are arrangements of parallel distributed intelligence for multiagent problem solving (Masuch 1992, Gasser and Hill 1990). Like a DAI system, a group can be thought of as a network that consists of agents as nodes and communication channels as connections between nodes. Furthermore, properties of both human groups and DAI systems are not derivable or representable solely on the basic properties of their component members or agents (Chaib-Draa et al. 1992). They both display social behavior (Carley and Newell 1990). They even face the same problem of allocating tasks, resources, and information to sets of intelligence (Fox 1981). These analogies and others support the argument that DAI systems could serve as models of human groups for supporting theoretical work (Masuch 1992, Huberman 1992, Gasser and Hill 1990, Doran 1989). In this sense, DAI is the experimental branch of organizational science (Crowston 1992).

Decision making is cognitive behavior, and all intelligent behavior can be conceived of as problem solving behavior. Thus, decision making can be viewed as a problem-solving activity, and a decision task can be considered a problem to be solved (Mackenzie 1978). Furthermore, team decision making can be thought of as a distributed problem-solving activity. Therefore, a DAI system can be used to model the distributed problem-solving process of a team just as an AI system can be used to model the problem-solving process of an individual human (Griffiths and Purohit 1991). DAI computational models provide symbolic-level frameworks that can capture the distribution of processing or computation embedded in team decision making (Chandrasekaran 1981).

Team decision making is a macrolevel phenomenon that emerges from microlevel interactions. DAI modeling is a promising approach for studying the micro-macro link because DAI systems can explore global behavior of a collection of agents based on local knowledge and local procedures of each agent (Huberman 1992). One of the most important features of DAI computational models is that each independent computational unit has its own local knowledge and controls its own execution (Sueyoshi and Tokoro 1991). Therefore, DAI systems can model the problem-solving behavior of a team based on local knowledge and the local problem-solving activities of each individual member.

DAI provides a means of studying a multiplicity of factors that influence team decision making. Traditional research on teaming typically employs surveys or other techniques for gathering anecdotal evidence (Katzenbach and Smith 1993) or uses experimental methods in quasi-laboratory settings (Hollenbeck et al. forthcoming). Both approaches have their benefits: surveys can help identify research questions or hypotheses, while experimental methods can provide in-depth understanding of one or two factors in team decision making. However, simulation using artificial agents provides a setting where a multiplicity of theoretical constructs, such as the characteristics of the agents and their interactions, can be incorporated into models and assessed by simulation. In addition, DAI models of team decision making require detailed descriptions of members' cognition, interaction, group design, and task (Carley and Prietula 1994, Jin and Levitt 1993). Hence, DAI models enable researchers to study the complex relations that characterize teams analytically.

Team-Soar: A DAI Computational Model of Team Decision Making

Team-Soar is a DAI computational model of team decision making that consists of a group of interconnected individual AI agents. Soar, an AI computational model of human cognition, is used to model individual group members, and the multiagent Soar technique is used to model the team collectively (Laird et al. 1993). The group of AI agents is called Team-Soar to emphasize that it models a goal-oriented, distributed-expertise group, a naval command and control team consisting of four members who have different areas of expertise and are located apart from one another. The goal of the team is to identify aircraft and make decisions based on the identification. Members of the team cooperate interactively to make the decisions. This problem has been used for academic research because it is a realistic problem having sufficient complexity and requiring distributed problem solving activity (Lin 1993, Papageorgiou and Carley 1993, Hollenbeck et al. 1991). Also, the naval carrier team case is a good vehicle for displaying the relationship between individual capabilities and group achievements because each member has a different role and expertise in a different area.

Design of the Team-Soar Model

The team being modeled by Team-Soar consists of commanding officers (CO) of four units in a naval carrier group. The leader is the CO of the aircraft carrier (CARRIER). The other members are the CO of a coastal air defense (CAD) unit, the CO of an AWACs air reconnaissance plane (AWAC), and the CO of an Aegis cruiser (CRUISER). Figure 1 shows how Team-Soar models the four roles of the naval command and control team and their activities. Lines with arrows

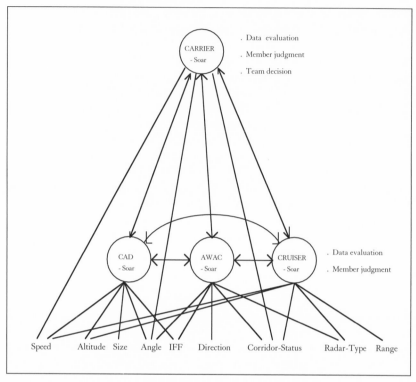

Figure 1. Team-Soar models a naval carrier team of four experts.

represent communication links between team members, while lines without arrows indicate which members can access the raw data for which attributes. The
four AI agents are realized on a SUN machine by using a multiagent Soar technique developed for distributed problem solving (Laird et al. 1993). In Team-
Soar, four individual Soars are interconnected to represent the communication
channels among team members. Each AI agent has specific knowledge in its
long-term memory about the different role, expertise, and experience of the
team member it models.

In the Team-Soar model, aircraft are tracked by radar and evaluated in terms
of the nine attributes shown at the bottom of figure 1. To participate in a team
decision, each member first makes a judgment about the best course of action by
using the information available to it, then recommends this judgment to the
leader, that is, CARRIER. To make a judgment, a member first interprets the raw
data for the attributes and evaluates each attribute on a scale of one to three. It
also may ask other members for their evaluations of certain attributes. When a
member has made the required evaluations, it then makes a judgment about
which of seven possible courses of action to recommend to the leader. The seven

possible courses of action range in degree from ignore, which has a value of zero, to defend, which has a value of six (Hollenbeck et al. 1995). Intermediate actions on this scale are review (1), monitor (2), warn (3), ready (4), and lock-on (5). Upon receiving all other members' judgments, the leader makes a team decision based all members' judgments, including its own (CARRIER's). The correct decision is predetermined by the Team-Soar mechanism.

In Team-Soar, each member is an independent goal-oriented problem solver with its own knowledge about the world. A candidate model for Newell's (1990) unified theories of cognition, Soar models the human cognitive capabilities of knowledge-based problem solving, learning, and interacting with the external environment. Soar also incorporates into its model the view of the human as a general problem solver (Newell and Simon 1972), a symbol system (Newell 1990, Newell and Simon 1976), and a knowledge system (Newell 1990). Finally, Soar implements the idea of the problem space hypothesis (Newell 1993, Newell 1980), arguing that all human symbolic goal-oriented behavior can be conceived of as a search in a problem space.

As modeled by Soar, each member maintains both long-term memory and working memory. All knowledge, including expertise, is stored in each member's long-term memory in the form of a production, that is, an "if-then" rule. Working memory, on the other hand, keeps only the knowledge that is relevant to the current cognitive activity of the member. The content of working memory is decided by a decision mechanism using the preference concept and is selected from the knowledge in long-term memory. The preference concept is part of the Soar architecture. See work by Laird and his colleagues (1993) for a detailed description of Soar's architecture.

According to the problem space paradigm, the Soar model can be described in terms of goals, problem spaces, states, and operators (Laird et al. 1993). The problem space description of Team-Soar is as follows. During the team decision making, each member in Team-Soar develops two problem spaces: a *team problem space* and a *member problem space* (figure 2). In the team problem space, the member tries to achieve the team goal, that is, to make the team decision correctly; in member problem space, the member tries to achieve the member goal, that is, to make a good recommendation to the leader. The team and member goals are achieved by applying appropriate operators to states in the corresponding problem spaces. When a team member first perceives an unidentified target, it develops its own version of a team problem space in its working memory. Each member's team problem space has an initial state and a goal state. The initial state is refined with *group knowledge*, the metalevel knowledge about group factors, other members, and other members' expertise. After constructing and refining its team problem space, each member develops an individual member goal as a subgoal of the team goal in accordance with its position on the team, and then develops its member problem space. The member that first spotted the unidentified target announces the appearance of that target to the other mem-

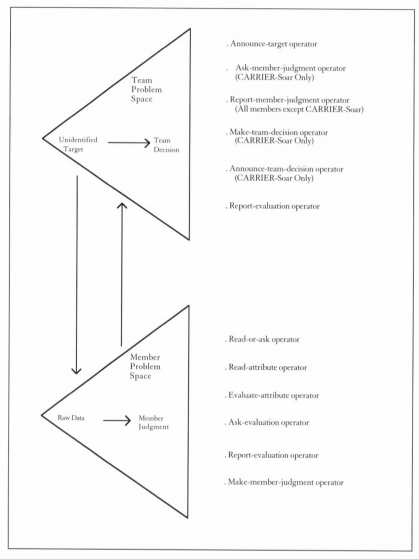

Figure 2. Team and member problem spaces with major operators of Team-Soar.

bers using the announce-target operator. After receiving this announcement, the other members follow the same problem space development process as the first member, except for the announcing activity.

In its member problem space, each member reads the raw values of attribute data (read-attribute operator), evaluates the values (evaluate-attribute operator), or asks other members their evaluations of some attributes (ask-evaluation operator). The member may also voice its evaluations to other members upon request (report-evaluation operator). After collecting all the required information, the member makes its judgment (make-member-judgment operator), and then returns to the team problem space.

When the leader (CARRIER) has returned to the team problem space, it asks the other members for their judgments (ask-member-judgment operator), and the other members report their judgments to the leader (report-member-judgment operator). Upon receiving all others' judgments, the leader makes a team decision by using a team decision scheme (make-team-decision operator), and announces the decision to all other members (announce-team-decision operator). Then all members close their team problem spaces and wait for a new task. (In the above description, some lower-level operators, such as the waiting operator, were not mentioned for the sake of clarity.)

Team-Soar models the naval command and control team in terms of three domains—team-level, member-level, and task/environment—since the performance of a team depends on factors belonging to the three domains. The team-level factors include team size, team structure, resource allocation, communication method, and team decision scheme.

Team-Soar consists of four members who perform the four roles of the naval carrier team; CARRIER, CAD, AWAC, and CRUISER. Team structure refers to the hierarchy of authority. The structure of Team-Soar is a one-level hierarchy, where a leader exists and all other members act as subordinates of the leader. Resource allocation refers to which member can access which and how many attributes of the aircraft. Team-Soar can manipulate resource allocation at three different levels by using the variable of team informity. Team informity and its three levels are explained later in this chapter.

Two communication methods, one-to-one and broadcasting, are used. *One-to-one* communication occurs when one member sends a message to another member of the team. *Broadcasting* occurs when one member sends a message that goes simultaneously to all members of the team. Four different types of information can be communicated: raw data, evaluations, judgments, and decisions. Raw data are the numeric values of the nine attributes from figure 1. Evaluation is an interpretation of raw data. A judgment is a member's recommendation of what decision should be made. The decision is the team's final decision.

To make a team decision, the leader uses a decision rule that contains a mechanism for combining member judgments into a team decision. This decision rule is referred to as the *team decision scheme*. Four different team decision schemes are used in Team-Soar; majority win (tie breaker: leader), majority win (tie breaker: member), average win (fixed weight), and average win (dynamic weight). The team decision schemes will be explained in detail later in this chapter.

The model of a team member includes such factors as expertise, metaknowledge, member judgment scheme, and agent type. A member's expertise is characterized by the attributes the member can access, the member's ability to evaluate raw attribute data, and the knowledge of which attributes were interrelated. The accessibility of attributes is tied to the resource allocation factor in the team model. Each member has the ability to evaluate the attributes it accesses. Knowledge about interrelations between attributes is also considered as expertise. An interrelation between two attributes means that those attributes must be considered together. For example, speed and direction must be considered together. In this interrelation, fast targets headed toward the team are most threatening, while fast targets not headed toward the team are not considered threatening. Each member has one or two pieces of interrelation knowledge.

Possession of metaknowledge can affect team performance. In Team-Soar, metaknowledge refers to the knowledge about other members' expertise, i.e., who has what expertise. This subject will be covered later in this chapter.

A judgment method is used to combine evaluations of attributes into a member judgment. Unlike humans, who have the freedom of using whatever judgment method they choose, members of Team-Soar are limited to one of the two different judgment methods: the proportional method and the uniform method. In both methods, a member's evaluations are combined to produce a score. The member's judgment is based on that score. With the proportional judgment method, members have a scorecard of sorts that tells them which judgment to recommend based on the combined evaluation score. This scorecard reflects all nine attributes, so the member must transform the score ranges for nine attributes into score ranges for whatever number of attributes it actually has access to. The uniform judgment method simply divides the total possible score (for example for seven attributes, each having a maximum value of two, the maximum total score would be fourteen) by the number of possible judgments. So, if a member has access to seven attributes, then the total possible score would be fourteen, and fourteen divided by seven (the total number of possible judgments) equals two. Then, evaluation score totals of zero and one would translate into a judgment recommendation of zero (ignore), evaluation score totals of two and three would map to a judgment recommendation of one (review), and so on.

Members of Team-Soar can have different degrees of cooperativeness and activity. Each member has one of the three different levels of cooperativeness: selfish, cooperative, and neutral. Cooperativeness comes into play for the activities of making judgments and providing information to other members. Selfish members tend to give higher priority to making their own judgments than to providing information to other members, whereas cooperative members are willing to sacrifice their own judgment-making activities in order to help other members. Neutral members assign equal priorities to their own and others' activities. There are two levels of activity: passive and active. Passive members participate in team activities passively, that is, only upon request, whereas active members involve themselves voluntarily.

Modeling of the task and its environmental factors considers target distribution, task complexity, and task uncertainty. The actual threat levels of the targets are uniformly distributed among seven-point levels. Task complexity, which is used to calculate the actual threat levels of the targets, is defined in terms of relational complication among target attributes. The current version of Team-Soar uses two different task complexities. The first type of task complexity can be represented as $2x_1 + x_2x_3 + x_4x_5 + x_6x_7 + x_8x_9$ where x stands for an attribute. The multiplication reflects interrelations between target attribute pairs. The second type of task complexity, which is simpler than the first, is represented as $x_1 + x_2 + x_3 + x_4 + x_5 + x_6 + x_7 + x_8 + x_9$. There is no interrelation among target attributes for the second type of task complexity. Task uncertainty refers to the unpredictability or unknown nature of tasks. Any attribute for which the team has no information is considered as task uncertainty. For example, none of the team members can access the attribute of angle.

So far in this chapter, we have examined the characteristics of team and team decision making and how computational models, especially computational models using DAI, can be used to study team decision making. The Team-Soar model was introduced as an example of a DAI computational model. In the remainder of this chapter, we will show how the Team-Soar model can provide insights about team decision making.

Two Studies Using Team-Soar

Using a DAI computational modeling technique, Team-Soar permits researchers to explore different combinations of modeling factors and allows them to analyze the modeling subject systematically. This is how Team-Soar can provide insights about team decision making. As examples, two group studies done with Team-Soar will be introduced in the following two subsections. The purpose of Study I is to examine the relationship of team decision scheme used and the amount of information available to teams with the measures of team effectiveness. The purpose of Study II is to explore the relationship of *metaknowledge* (knowledge about the knowledge that other team members have) and the amount of communicated information with how long it took the team to reach a decision.

Study I

One benefit of using DAI models for studying team decision making is that they can provide researchers with data on both an individual member's decision behavior and the team's collective behavior. Such models therefore enable researchers to examine processes at the individual level and also in relation to team behavior. Study I will demonstrate the power of DAI models to provide these kinds of data.

Experimental Design

Study I was undertaken to examine the role of team decision scheme on team performance at different levels of available information. In Study I, team performance was measured by two standards of team effectiveness: decision deviation and disaster rate. Decision deviation refers to the deviation of the decision that the team made from the correct decisions. Disaster rate is a function of the frequency of decisions that were off by four or more points from correct decisions (Hollenbeck et al. 1995). Study I used a 4 x 3 design where team decision scheme and *team informity* were manipulated. Team informity is a variable that quantifies the amount of available information. Each of the twelve team models made 10,000 team decisions.

Four team decision schemes were examined in the study: majority win (tie breaker: CARRIER), majority win (tie breaker: CAD), average win (fixed weight), and average win (dynamic weight) schemes. In majority win schemes, the team's decision was determined by the recommendation that was made by the majority of the team members. When there was a tie, the leader (CARRIER) either followed its own judgment (majority win with tie breaker leader) or followed the judgment of the member CAD, who had accessed more information than the leader (majority win with tie breaker CAD). In the average win schemes, a rounded-off average of all the weighted member judgments determined the decision. To compute this average, for both fixed and dynamic versions of the average win scheme, member judgments were converted into quantitative values and weighted appropriately according to the leader's assessment of the quality of each member's judgment. This assessment was based on the member's expertise or past performance. In the fixed weight version of the average win scheme, the leader assigned a fixed and equal weight to each member's judgment; this weight was used for all decision tasks. In the average win scheme with dynamic weights, the leader, for each task, assigned weights to each member's judgment by considering past performance history of the member up to the decision point. Therefore, in the decision scheme, the dynamic weight assigned to a member's judgment was derived from the member's performance rating at that point in time. A member's performance rating consisted of points accrued from the correctness of its judgments on previous decision tasks: each member received seven points whenever its judgment was correct, six points whenever its judgment was off by one from the correct decision, and so forth.

It was assumed that teams with more information would perform better than teams with less information. To vary the team informity in Study I, the number of target attributes whose data were directly accessible for each member was controlled in three levels. In the low informity level, the leader, CARRIER, could access only two of the nine attributes, while the other members could access three attributes each (figure 2). In the medium informity level, the leader could access three attributes, whereas each of the other members could access five. In the high informity level, the leader and other members could access four and seven attributes, respectively.

Hypothesis Tests and Results

To statistically examine the effects of team decision scheme and informity level on team decision deviation, the following three null hypotheses were tested:
1. The four team decision schemes affect team decision deviation equally.
2. The three different levels of team informity affect team decision deviation equally.
3. There are no interaction effects of the decision scheme and the level of team informity on team decision deviation.

Two-way ANOVA was used for the hypothesis tests. All three null hypotheses were rejected at the .0001 level of significance. Thus, the test results strongly support the existence of main and interaction effects of team decision scheme and team informity on team's mean decision deviation. Since interaction effects were significant, Tukey's studentized range test was performed at the 0.05 level of significance in order to determine which combinations of decision scheme and team informity differ significantly. Note that because each team model of the simulation experiment was configured with a combination of the two decision variables, the total number of observations for both the ANOVA procedure and the Tukey test was 120,000 (= 4 X 3 X 10,000). Tukey's test results are shown in table 1. The lower the team decision deviation (shown in column two), the better the team's performance. In the Tukey grouping, teams with the same letter are not significantly different. MAJ/LDR represents the majority win scheme with leader as tie-breaker, MAJ/CAD represents the majority win scheme with CAD as tie-breaker, AVG/FIX represents the average win scheme with fixed weights, and AVG/DYN represents the average win scheme with dynamic weights.

The occurrence of disaster was quite small; team models using majority win with leader as a tie breaker were the only ones that produced a nonzero disaster rate. The majority win schemes produced disaster at low (19 times) and medium (3 times) levels of team informity. When the same hypothesis tests were done with disaster rate as the dependent variable, the main and interaction effects of decision scheme and informity level on mean disaster rate were found to be significant at the 0.0001 level. Furthermore, Tukey's test (see the last column of table 1) revealed that the majority win scheme with leader as tie breaker team model at the low informity level was the only one whose mean disaster rate differed significantly from the mean disaster rates produced by other team models.

Discussion

Figure 3 shows a graph of the mean decision deviations at each combination of

Team Configuration (Informity level and win scheme)	Team Decision Deviation (Tukey Grouping at $\alpha = 0.05$)	Average Member Decision Deviation	Deviation Difference	Mean of CARRIER Deviation (Leader)	Mean of CAD Deviation	Mean of AWAC Deviation	Mean of CRUISER Deviation	Disaster Rate (Tukey Grouping at $\alpha = 0.05$)
Low MAJ/LDR	0.564 (A)	0.693	0.129	0.801	0.628	0.635	0.708	0.0019 (A)
Low MAJ/CAD	0.537 (B)	0.698	0.161	0.804	0.625	0.633	0.731	0 (B)
Low AVG/FIX	0.316 (F,G)	0.694	0.378	0.815	0.624	0.624	0.711	0 (B)
Low AVG/DYN	0.317 (F,G)	0.700	0.383	0.808	0.632	0.638	0.722	0 (B)
Medium MAJ/LDR	0.465 (C)	0.558	0.093	0.717	0.483	0.487	0.544	0.0003 (B)
Medium MAJ/CAD	0.414 (D)	0.553	0.139	0.706	0.479	0.481	0.548	0 (B)
Medium AVG/FIX	0.404 (D)	0.560	0.156	0.724	0.489	0.482	0.546	0 (B)
Medium AVG/DYN	0.368 (E)	0.562	0.194	0.717	0.489	0.488	0.553	0 (B)
High MAJ/LDR	0.367 (E)	0.428	0.061	0.659	0.339	0.330	0.385	0 (B)
High MAJ/CAD	0.313 (F, G)	0.426	0.113	0.650	0.329	0.337	0.387	0 (B)
High AVG/FIX	0.332 (F)	0.422	0.090	0.643	0.326	0.333	0.386	0 (B)
High AVG/DYN	0.296 (G)	0.425	0.129	0.653	0.335	0.332	0.379	0 (B)

Table 1. Results of simulation experiments in Study I.

the decision variables. Throughout all levels of team informity, the scheme of average win with dynamic weight worked quite well in terms of keeping team decision deviation reasonably low. The scheme of average win with fixed weight became especially effective when team informity decreased to low. In general, the average win schemes resulted in lower decision deviations—in other words, better decision accuracies—than the majority win schemes. Note that the scheme of majority win with leader as a tie breaker was the only one that resulted in disastrous team decisions in this experiment. Judging from the experimental results, it appears that the majority win decision scheme may not be the best one for tasks that require a choice from among several possible alternatives.

With high team informity, all decision schemes worked fairly well (figure 3). But the difference in mean team deviations between the team using the decision scheme that gave the best results and the team using the decision scheme that gave the worst results became larger as team informity went down (figure 3). Furthermore, for all the team decision schemes, the difference between expected and actual team decision deviations increased as team informity decreased (see figure 4). In particular, team models using the two average win schemes had actual team decision deviations that were less than half of their average member decision deviations at low-level informity (table 1). The team's expected decision deviation, that is, the average member decision deviation (see the third column of table 1), is the average of all individual members' mean decision

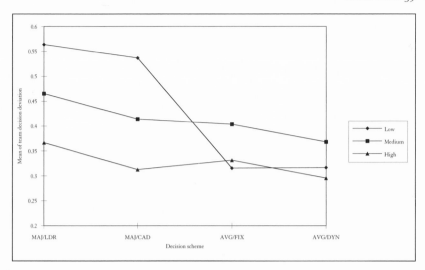

*Figure 3. The impact of team decision scheme on
team decision deviation at different team informaties.*

deviations. One way of interpreting these results is that the choice of team decision scheme becomes more critical when less information is available.

In the majority win schemes, for all levels of team informity, the change of tie
breaker from the leader to CAD resulted in an improvement of team performance despite the fact that average member deviation was almost the same for
both team models in each team informity level (table 1). The improvement in
team deviation turned out to be due to an increase in the ratio of correct tie
breaks. This result suggests that in an equivocal decision making situation, rely-
ing on the member who accesses more information is beneficial, provided the
member uses the information rationally.

Terms like *bonus-assembly effect* (Collins and Guetzkow 1964) and *collective
work-products* (Katzenbach and Smith 1993) have been used to explain the phenomenon that a group (or team) can produce a better outcome than would be expected given the abilities of individual members; that is, a group (or team) is more
than the sum of its member parts. This phenomenon was observed for most team
models used in Study I. Table 1 shows that the team performances of most experimental models are better than the performances of any of the individual members.

According to human group research, team decisions often are not as good
as judgments made by the best team members (Tindale and Davis 1983). In
Study I, team models using the schemes of majority win with leader as tie-
breaker and average win with fixed weights at high informity displayed the
same phenomenon (table 1). In these cases, the deviation of an individual
team member was lower than the deviation for the team; for example, com-

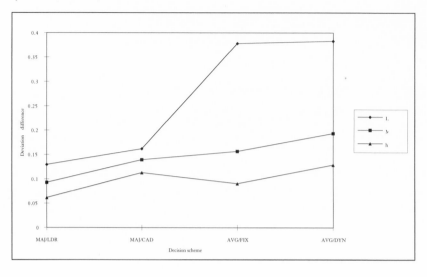

Figure 4. The impact of team decision sceme on the difference between actual and expected team decision deviations at different team informities.

pare CAD's deviation with the team's deviation in the scheme using high informity and majority win with leader as tie-breaker.

Study II

Study I rated team effectiveness by examining external measures of team process: decision deviation and disaster rate. Study II, in contrast, used the internal measures of team wait time and team decision cycles to rate team efficiency. These internal measures shed light on what are normally hidden cognitive processes. Such internal measures can be used because Team-Soar was built from individual cognitive models displaying the power of cognitive computational models. Team wait time and team decision cycles are variables that are related to the amount of time it takes a team to reach a decision. In the Soar model (from which Team-Soar was derived) a decision cycle is a cognitive measure, an elementary deliberation unit that consists of an information processing step and a decision step (Carley 1989). In Team-Soar, the variable team decision cycles is the sum of the number of decision cycles that each member goes through to complete a task. The other variable, team wait time, is simply the sum of the idle times of all the members; idle time is counted in terms of decision cycles. An example of idle time is the time a member spends doing nothing while waiting to receive a reply to a request.

Experimental Design

Study II used a 2 x 3 design to examine the impact of metaknowledge on team performance for different amounts of communicated information. To explore the impact of metaknowledge, six teams performed 10,000 decision tasks each. Since the metaknowledge examined in Study II refers to knowledge about which members can access what attribute data, it is reasonable to examine the impact of metaknowledge in conjunction with team informity. As stated in Study I, team informity was manipulated by changing the number of attributes that each member could access directly. In Study II, the three information levels introduced in Study I were used to control team informity. Another reason for manipulating team informity in Study II is that metaknowledge is related to how members communicate with one another. A member with metaknowledge can communicate directly with the member who has the needed information (one-to-one communication), whereas a member without metaknowledge must broadcast its message to all other members (broadcast communication). Further, the amount of information to be communicated is proportional to team informity; that is, the more information members have, the more information is likely to be transferred among them. In sum, we expect to find an interaction effect between metaknowledge and team informity on the efficiency of communication, since metaknowledge has an impact on the communication method, whereas team informity constrains the amount of communication.

Hypothesis Tests and Results

The following three null hypotheses were tested in order to study the effects of metaknowledge and team informity on team decision cycle:
1. There is no difference in how presence or absence of metaknowledge affects team decision cycles.
2. There is no difference in how the three levels of team informity affect team decision cycles.
3. There are no interaction effects of the metaknowledge and the level of team informity on team decision cycles.

As in Study I, two-way ANOVA was used to test the above hypotheses. The results of the statistical analysis showed that all three null hypotheses were rejected at the 0.0001 level of significance. In order to discover what combinations of varying levels of the decision variables (metaknowledge and team informity) differ significantly in their effects, Tukey's studentized range test was done at the 0.05 level of significance. In Study II, there were 10 observations of average team decision cycle per team model, where each average team decision cycle was acquired from every 1,000 decision tasks. Therefore, the total number of observations used for the statistical tests is 60 (2 x 3 x 10).

Team Configuration (Informity level and status of meta-knowledge)	Mean of Team Decision Cycles (Tukey Grouping at α = 0.05)	Mean of Team Wait Time (Tukey Grouping at a = 0.05)
High / ABSENT	264.6 (A)	33.5 (B)
High / PRESENT	254.6 (B)	41.3 (A)
Medium / ABSENT	215.2 (C)	30.5 (C)
Medium / PRESENT	212.7 (D)	33.8 (B)
Low / ABSENT	166.3 (E)	21.1 (D)
Low / PRESENT	166.2 (E)	21.1 (D)

Table 2. Results of simulation experiments in study II.

To examine the effects of metaknowledge and team informity on team wait, the hypothesis tests were repeated, substituting team wait time for team decision cycles. The main and interaction effects of the metaknowledge and the informity level on mean team wait time were found to be significant at the 0.0001 level. Tukey's test performed at the 0.05 level of significance showed that the effect of metaknowledge became insignificant as team informity decreased to low.

Discussion

Table 2 shows the results of Study II. For the tests on team decision cycles, each team made ten observations. For the tests on team wait time, each team made 10,000 observations. In the Tukey grouping (N = 60 for team decision cycles; N = 60,000 for team wait time), the teams with the same letter are not significantly different. "Present" and "absent" refer to the presence or absence of meta-knowledge. Low, medium, and high refer to levels of team informity. We see that team wait is not always positively correlated with team decision cycle. At medium and high informity levels, team models without metaknowledge had less team wait time than team models with metaknowledge, whereas the former team models used more team decision cycles than the latter. How can this phenomenon be explained? In the teams whose members do not have knowledge about each other's expertise, one way of getting information is to ask all other members by broadcasting a general request whenever one member needs information. Members of teams with metaknowledge, however, directly query a randomly selected member among those who are experts in the required area. Teams without metaknowledge are likely to have less team wait time, since any available experts can respond to the asker, while in teams with metaknowledge, only the selected member can respond, and then only when it has time to do so. On the other hand, teams without metaknowledge are likely to require more team decision cycles because, often, more than one member expends time to respond the same question. At low informity, there were no significant differences between the team models with and without metaknowledge with respect to both measures of team efficiency. This is because the degree of overlapping of expertise was quite low at low informity level. The low informity level was designed so that there was only one member able to answer the other member's request. The limit on the number of possible responders caused there to be no difference between broadcasting and one-to-one communications, which, in turn, caused there to be no difference between the team models with and without metaknowledge with respect to both efficiency measures. We therefore conclude that the degree of expertise redundancy can affect team efficiency by constraining the number of possible responders.

Figure 5 and figure 6 indicate that average amounts of wait time and average numbers of decision cycles increase as the amount of information to be communicated increases. Another result that is evident from figures 5 and 6 is that the size of the advantage or disadvantage of having metaknowledge depends on the level of team informity. As is evident in figure 5, the mean difference of team decision cycles between the team models with and without metaknowledge became larger as team informity increased. The same is true with the team wait time (see figure 6). These results imply that the impact of having or not having metaknowledge on the team efficiencies become stronger as greater amounts of information are communicated.

Conclusion

The use of computational modeling and distributed AI provided both tools and a conceptual framework for studying team behavior. A computational model based on the Soar paradigm, Team-Soar, was constructed to test the value of the DAI approach. Two illustrative virtual experiments were run to assess the Soar paradigm and demonstrate the value of Team-Soar in studying team behavior. We found first, that simulation is valuable as a research tool for studying teams and second, that some of the results of studies I and II can be matched with existing research results.

Even though only a few design factors were considered, the two studies provided a number of predictions about what happens when people work in teams. For example, one such prediction is that majority win schemes do not seem to be good team decision strategies for this type of command and control task. These results illustrate the power of computational models in providing a large number of nontrivial insights (Carley and Wallace 1995). The predictions from these studies can be tested with human subjects or with empirical data. Computational simulations are useful precursors to experiments with human subjects,

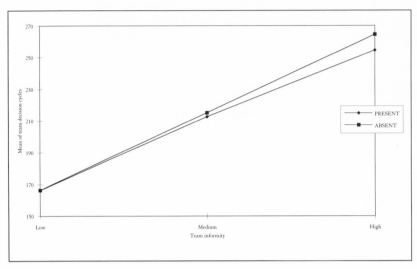

*Figure 5. The impact of team informity on
team decision cycles at different levels of metaknowledge.*

especially when the latter require a lot of time and money. The complexity of
real subjects and the limits of human cognitive capability prevent researchers
from doing systematic and thorough studies of real decision making teams.
Computational models can help researchers in situations like this. Often, computational simulations generate unanticipated results, which may provide new
insights that are not readily perceived by direct observation of the research subjects (Carley and Wallace 1995). In Study II, one such unexpected result was
that the possession of metaknowledge affected team wait time and team decision cycles in opposite directions at medium and high informity levels. The simulation provided an opportunity for the researchers to analyze systematically
the effects of metaknowledge on the team efficiencies.

Matching computational models with the behavior of real modeling subjects
can provide some degree of validation of the models (Burton and Obel 1995).
With Team-Soar, this means matching the simulation results with the behavior
of human teams. Some results of the Team-Soar experiments correspond with
the findings from previous research on human subjects. It has been observed,
for example, that decisions made with less information often result in better
performance than decisions made with more information, even when the information has been processed correctly (Glazer et al. 1992). When the average win
schemes were used in Study I, there were some cases where team models that
had less information performed better than team models that had more information. Also, researchers have recognized that the use of different group decision schemes may lead to the making of different decisions and therefore result

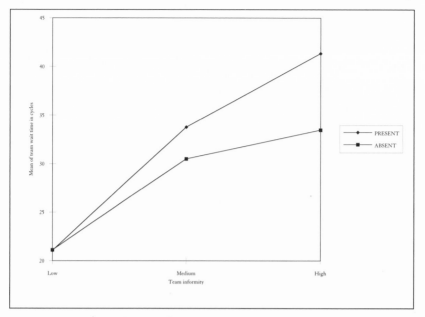

*Figure 6. The impact of team informity on
team wait time at different levels of metaknowledge.*

in different performance levels (Miller 1989). The results of Study I confirmed this result. Furthermore, the results of Study I display such phenomena as bonus-assembly effects (Collins and Guetzkow 1964) and Tindale and Davis's finding (1983), phenomena that has been observed in human teams. In Study I, the team performances of some models were better than the performances of any of the individual members, whereas team performances of other models were not as good as the performances of the best team member. The phenomena observed in Study I help explain the relationships between individual members' performances and team performance. This comparison of observed human team phenomena with the simulation results demonstrates the usefulness of DAI computational models for understanding teaming.

We argue that the study of teams can be advanced by adopting technologies and ideas from the areas of computational modeling and distributed AI. While much work remains to be done, we believe the Team-Soar experiments illustrate how DAI computational models provide deep insights about team decision making by permitting researchers to explore different combinations of modeling factors easily and by allowing them to analyze modeling subjects systematically. Topics that were not covered in this chapter, such as validation of Team-Soar and its flexibility in accommodating different types of team decision variables, will be presented in future publications.

3

Designing Organizations for Computational Agents

Young-pa So and Edmund H. Durfee

Organizing is important in computational systems, just as it is important in human systems. Organizational knowledge allows a computational system to recognize its role, and the roles of others, in accomplishing collective goals. However, as circumstances change, organizational structures must often change also. It is therefore important to understand how different organizations can be designed for different populations of agents, performing different tasks in changing environments, to meet various performance goals. Our work has been directed toward understanding this design space and characterizing the effectiveness of different organizations. In this chapter, we describe a framework for understanding organizational design for computational agents, use this framework for analyzing the expected performance of a class of organizations, and describe how our analyses can be applied to predict performance for a distributed information gathering task. Our ongoing work includes making organizational design an inherent part of a multiagent system, rather than something done by an external designer.

A human or computer agent acting in a world populated by other agents should typically coordinate his, her, or its actions with the actions of others. This action often requires models of what the other agents have done, are doing, and/or will do. In many cases, these models are mutually held. In fact, in multi-agent systems that act in environments that reward cooperation, the agents might actively seek to establish a shared set of models. A shared organizational structure, for example, provides agents with descriptions about their roles and responsibilities in the multiagent context and thus represents guidelines for intelligent cooperation and communication among the agents.

An organization can be thought of as a long-term commitment made by the agents to a particular way of jointly handling the cooperative tasks. In the situation for which the organization was devised, the agents should cooperate effectively and reliably. However, many interesting real-world organizations are situated in complex, often uncertain, and changing worlds. If the collection of agents is to be effective in such circumstances, it must adapt to such changes in at least one of a number of ways. One way is for the agents to actively change their environment so that it once again matches their organizational structure. A second way is for the agents to adopt, at the outset, an organizational structure that provides sufficient flexibility to the agents allowing them to dynamically adapt to new circumstances within the same organizational structure. Finally, a third way is for the agents to reorganize themselves into an organizational structure that they have designed specifically for the expected situation.

Clearly, any system of agents that will survive for an extended time should be capable of adapting in all of these ways. It should be able to perform *task-environment (re)design* in cases when no organizational structure could possibly succeed or where the advantages of the current organization can continue to be realized. The task could be simplified, for example by relaxing some goals. Or the agents could maintain their environment in some way; a fascinating example is the process of sociogenesis, whereby individuals in a population differentiate to form an emergent organized colony with its own internal environment which buffers the individual members from changes in the outside world (Novak 1982). However, organizations can be even more robust if the differentiated individuals have retained some degree of flexibility, such that they can adapt as a whole to changing circumstances while still remaining within the same organizational framework. In such organizations, individual sophistication becomes a more prized asset, since individuals must use local information to decide, within organizational guidelines, on specific actions that further the goals of the entire organization. Pushed to the extreme, of course, even large degrees of latitude of action might not salvage an obsolete organizational structure, and the agents within it must be capable of, at a minimum, reallocating roles within an organization, and more generally of full-scale organization self-design.

This chapter is thus about organizations of communicating, autonomous, computational agents: how the organizations should be designed, and how agents can, among themselves, design, join, maintain, and dissolve organizations in order to jointly perform a set of tasks in an efficient, flexible, and reliable manner. While issues of task-environment (re)design are important, in this chapter we concentrate on the other two approaches to using organizations to provide agents with models of others. We begin with a framework for describing the organizational design problem, and explore some initial strategies for forming organizational designs depending on possible performance measures, task-environment parameters, and agent capabilities. We then turn to the broader considerations of how agents that are part of an ongoing organization might engage in the organizational design process so as to maintain, or even overhaul, their organizational structure. Finally, we summarize our results and indicate our ongoing research directions.

Models of Organizations

In this section, we will discuss the framework for describing the organizational design problem, and explore some initial strategies for forming organizational designs depending on possible performance measures, task-environment parameters, and agent capabilities

Organization-Theoretic Perspective

Human organizations are the subject of study for organizational theory, and many models of various types of organizations have been generated (Scott 1992). The variety of emphases within organizational theory attests to the complexity of the phenomena in human organizations. Since the subject of study is about *human* organizations, various human factors and relations are a primary concern for organizational theory. However, we agree with other researchers within both computer science and organizational theory that many concepts and ideas can be shared between the two disciplines to better understand human organizations and to design more efficient and flexible distributed systems (Cohen 1986, Fox 1981).

Of the various models of organizations in organizational theory, we find two models particularly relevant and useful to our research on organizational self-design. The first is *contingency theory*. Lawrence and Lorsch (1967) who coined the label "contingency theory," stressed the importance of organization-environment match in determining organizational performance.

The main theses of contingency theory are as follows (Scott 1992). First, there is no one best way to organize. There are no general principles applicable to organizations in all times and places. Second, all ways of organizing are not equally effective. Organizational structure is not irrelevant to organizational performance. Finally, the best way to organize depends on the nature of the environment to which the organization relates. Organizational design decisions depend—are contingent—on environmental conditions.

We are indebted to contingency theory for developing our model of organizational performance in which we classify the various factors that affect the performance of the organization into two broad classes: task-environmental factors and organizational factors.

The second school of thought in organizational theory relevant to our research is the *sociotechnical systems perspective* (Trist 1981). Influenced by human relations research, this theory proposed that the distinguishing feature of organizations is that they are both social and technical systems, and insisted that the two systems follow different "laws" and that their relationship represents a "coupling of dissimilars" (Emery 1959). Also, this perspective proposed designing systems that emphasized discretionary behavior, internalized regulations, and work-group autonomy rather than top-down, manager controlled, technical bureaucracies (Scott 1992).

Our model of intelligent cooperation through organizational self-design has a very similar spirit with the sociotechnical systems approach since both are interested in endowing the agents themselves (whether human or machine) with the capability to determine the way they could work together more effectively in various task environments, and to understand exactly under which task environments organizations consisting of members with such capabilities are "good." Also, because our research stems from the distributed artificial intelligence perspective, we are aware of the many rich theories of machine intelligence (such as learning, reasoning, and planning) that are different from the theories of computation and communication in distributed systems. So, in a sense, we are also attempting a coupling of dissimilars by investigating ways to design more intelligent distributed systems.

Distributed Artificial Intelligence Perspective

As the availability of processing systems—and specifically networked processing systems—increased, it became clear that there was power to harness in distributed computing systems if only the various systems could be coordinated to work together. Naturally, notions of organizing the systems came to the fore. Initially, the ideas were simply to decompose large tasks into component pieces that could be carried out in parallel, with little or no interaction among them. More tightly-coupled systems were also considered, with the idea that the interactions *between* the systems could be programmed much like the instructions within the individual systems. These approaches, along with others, have powered distributed computing into increasingly significant applications.

However, another feature of the intuitive notion of an organization, as understood (and populated) by people, was not well captured in these approaches. Human organizations are populated with amazingly versatile and sophisticated agents, at least compared to the computer programs that (still) generally populate distributed computer systems. Organizations, in human terms, do not dictate action at the "instruction" level, by and large; rather, they define roles and responsibilities for organizational participants, who are then expected to elaborate those into action depending on the current task and environmental demands.

This alternative perspective was introduced to computational systems within the field of distributed artificial intelligence, which has typically considered distributed systems in which each individual in such systems possesses, in some degree, what might be labeled as intelligence.[1] With such capabilities, the individual agents in an organization have the capacity to make reasonable local decisions about what they should do, given what they know about their tasks and the environment, as well as what they know about what others are likely to be doing. It is precisely this last bit of knowledge—about what others are likely to be doing—that is available when one knows the organizational structure. That is, if a participant knows the roles and responsibilities of others, he or she can make more informed decisions about what to do locally and how to interact with them. Of course, this in turn means that the agents should abide by their designated roles, so each agent must be able to focus its local decisions toward fulfilling its responsibilities.

Corkill and Lesser (1983; Corkill, 1982), for example, developed computational representations for organizations in terms of interest areas for agents. An agent's interest areas would indicate what kinds of data-processing tasks it was willing and able to tackle, and to what degree. Faced with a variety of possible actions to take, therefore, an agent would be influenced (to a degree that could be modified by an experimenter) by how well those actions fit within its most preferred areas of interest. Moreover, because each agent knew the interest areas of the others, each could identify processing tasks, or information, that would be potentially of interest to them, focusing communication among them to eventually converge to a state where all the most important tasks were accomplished in a coherent, distributed manner.

Of course, the careful design of the interest areas was of primary importance to the success of this approach. Interest areas that were too narrow could mean that processing tasks became unevenly distributed among the agents, leading to longer delays until overall task completion. Moreover, if a subset of the agents failed to participate (they crashed or the network that connected them failed), then some tasks would be left unaccomplished and the overall task would fail to be completed. On the other hand, if interest areas were broadly defined so as to increase reliability and the chances that every agent would have something useful to do, then the situation could quickly deteriorate. Agents would then be duplicating effort and working at cross purposes. In addition, if every agent were made more of a "generalist," communication among agents would explode because every agent would be potentially interested in everything!

In the work of Corkill and Lesser (1983), and in subsequent work (Durfee, Lesser, and Corkill 1987), a variety of organizational structures were evaluated. Techniques were developed whereby agents working within some general organizational structure could also communicate about their more immediate plans, thus avoiding redundant activity and improve differentiation of effort. Performance of these systems was evaluated not only in terms of how quickly the organized agents would complete the overall task, but also in terms of the use of the agents, the overhead of communication and coordination among the agents, the tolerance of the organization to faulty communication channels, and the reliability of the organization to agent failures.

Qualitatively, the conclusions from all of this work closely resembled many of the theses of contingency theory—specifically, that different organizations are more or less effective under different task and environmental conditions. While the agreement with contingency theory is heartening, it is disappointing that the computational realization of organizations provides only domain-specific quantitative prescriptions about organizations to adopt under various conditions. Among the reasons for this difficulty is that the studies were embedded in complex task environments, with agents whose abilities and behaviors were difficult to clearly characterize, and with performance measures that were not clearly articulated.

Our Model

We adopt the main assumptions of contingency theory in our model, but go further in the direction of making the concept of "best match" between organization and environment more precise. At the same time, we avoid tackling too many features of organizations, tasks, environments, and performance measures at once, in an effort to characterize the space of effective organizations within well-defined bounds. In our model, the organizational performance is jointly determined by the features of the organization and the features of the task environment. That is, we pursue a closed-form formula for each of the performance metrics for the organization. The formula, however, need not be expressible in algebraic form. It can be any algorithm that can compute the values of performance metrics given the organizational and task-environmental factors as input.

Our model of organization design (OD) is directly related to our model of organization and the relevant ontologies surrounding it. In order to design an organization, we must first know what is to be designed, that is, know what are the components and features of the organization we can select and combine. These are called *organizational factors*. Second, we need to know what is a good design or a bad design; that is, we need some criteria for evaluation. These are called the *performance metrics*. Third, we need to know how an organization works in order to link the structure of elements and their features to the evaluation criteria. This is called the *organizational performance model*. If we see an organization as a closed system, these three things may suffice. However, many interesting organizations are open systems (Katz and Kahn 1966) and interact with nonorganizational external elements and processes. These are called *task-environmental factors*. Moreover, in many cases, task-environmental factors affect the performance of the organization. Thus we must know about any task-environmental factors in addition to the organizational factors for organizational design. Figure 1 is a diagram showing our model of organizational performance. The arrows indicate the dependency relationships.

The organizational and task-environmental factors define an organizational design space (ODS). A designed organization is a point in ODS. The performance measure is a function over ODS onto the performance metric space. Then, we can define the OD process as a search through ODS for an organization with acceptable performance. In other words, our design process model for

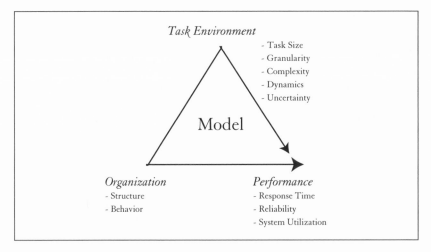

Figure 1. Model of organizational performance.

OD is a generate-and-test or search process model, typically seeking a satisfying (rather than optimal) solution. We note that our model requires the designer to have predictive knowledge concerning exactly how the various factors determine the performance of the organization. This knowledge is then embodied in the performance evaluation function to be used in the design process, thus allowing automation of computational organization design.

In the following sections, we elaborate on the components of our model. The model consists of three components: the organization model, the task-environment model, and the performance model. In its general form, it is still informal and verbal at this stage of research, and thus not amenable to precise computational implementations. However, for specific cases, as we show later in this chapter, it can be realized computationally. Our goal is to formalize the components more generally so that we can embody them as organizational knowledge into autonomous agents capable of intelligent cooperation, enabling them to use it in the process of OSD.

Organizational Model. We initially focus our attention on work organizations, that is, organizations that are designed for some definite work to be done. In particular, we deal primarily with computational organizations in which the type of work done by the organization is the computation (or execution) of a complex function that can be functionally decomposed into subfunctions, and the elements of the organization are agents capable of decomposing and distributing a set of tasks, transferring and routing the (sub)tasks and (sub)results, and executing a set of primitive functions.

We think that the model of organization is tightly related to the model of the task the organization is used for. More concretely, we think that a specification of a work organization should at least include the following elements:

1. The set of tasks and subtasks to be done.

2. The set of agents participating in the organization.

3. An assignment of the tasks and subtasks to the participating agents.

4. A work flow structure which dictates how the tasks and subtasks are to be distributed among agents and how the results and partial results are to be synthesized.

5. Optionally, a set of resources aside from the agents and a set of constraints on the usage of those resources.

Task-Environment Model. By a *task environment,* we mean task and environmental characteristics that affect the performance of the organization. For example, type, size, rate of change, and structure of the task and the world are common important characteristics affecting the performance of many organizations.

In our research, we seek to be able to come up with a more comprehensive model of tasks and environments so that we can explicitly represent and reason about different kinds of task characteristics and also incorporate task and environmental uncertainties, complexities, and dynamics into the task environment model. We believe that many terms such as task complexity, task dynamics, task uncertainty, environmental complexity, environmental uncertainty, and environmental dynamics must be precisely defined.

Performance Model. The following are the potential performance measures we will initially consider:

1. *Response time* is the total time taken to accomplish a task. It is also called the turnaround time.

2. *Throughput* is the number of tasks accomplished per unit time. Without a definition of a unit task this measure is ill-defined.

3. *System utilization* is the fraction of the total system capacity being used at any given time. For a given resource, it is the fraction of time the resource is busy.

4. *Communication cost* is the cost of transmitting a number of bits across the channel. If time is used as the cost, it may include the connection time plus the time to transmit a number of messages across the channel. Alternatively, the number of bits or message packets transmitted across the communication channel may be used as a measure for communication cost.

5. *Reliability* refers to the probability that the system or a component under consideration will not experience any failures in a given time interval. It is typically used to describe systems that cannot be repaired (as in space-based computers), or whose operation is so critical that no downtime for repair can be tolerated. When a system is composed of multiple subsystems and/or compo-

nents, the reliability of each component can be used to evaluate the reliability of the total system. By using redundant components, the system reliability can be improved.[2]

6. *Availability* refers to the probability that the system is operational according to its specification at a given point in time. Availability can be used as some measure of "goodness" for those systems that can be repaired and which can be out of service for short periods of time during repair.

7. *Solution quality* refers to some objective measure of the quality of task results defined for the particular task domain.

A Multiagent Computational Task Using Tree Organizations

As we have mentioned previously, an impediment in studying computational organizations has been that the study of these organizations often involves making sense of a multiplicity of task-environment factors, organizational parameters, and performance metrics. Using our model of the ODS, we have been studying organizations by restricting these various features of task environments, organizations, and performance models, and then incrementally extending our investigations.

For example, our initial studies (So and Durfee 1993, 1994) considered a simple computational task environment (exemplified by a distributed addition task) characterized by its size and by its granularity, defined as the ratio between unit task execution time and the unit message transmission time. The organizations are tree-structured, and comprise homogeneous agents that simply perform their tasks. The performance is measured in terms of the response time of the organizations to accomplish their tasks. Our initial studies focused on how different tree organizations (branching factors and number of levels) performed on different task environments (sizes and granularities). Four specific points can be drawn from our results.

First, cooperative distributed problem solving using tree-organizations is better than centralized problem solving as long as the task is big enough (thus exploiting the benefits of parallelism) and communication is fast enough relative to computation.

Second, tall-thin hierarchies outperform short-fat hierarchies when problem size is sufficiently large (i.e., above some bound).

Third, for certain intermediate problem sizes, short-fat hierarchies may outperform tall-thin ones if the granularity of the task environment is neither too large nor too small.

Fourth, for k-ary trees, there exists a branching factor k' which is larger than 2 but smaller than the branching factor for a single-level tree such that the k'-ary tree generally outperforms both the binary tree and the single-level tree.

Our ongoing work includes applying these analytical models to real problems (see, for example, our later discussion on distributed network monitoring), and extending the scope of our explorations to incorporate other aspects of our model. Specifically, we have been considering also the environmental factor of node failure, the performance measure of reliability, and the ODS extensions that permit redundant task assignments and sophisticated coordination behavior among agents in the organization (So and Durfee 1995).

Organizational Self-Design

Within the distributed AI literature, Corkill (1982) was the first to specifically consider coordination among agents as arising from an organizational structure that is (re)designed and (re)implemented from within, by the agents that populate it. Not surprisingly, this has proven to be an elusive goal involving a chicken-and-egg problem: the objective of the agents is to impose upon themselves an organization, but the means by which they can identify and agree upon such an organization itself requires that they be organized, at least to some extent.

For the time being, however, let us say that the population of agents is already organized in some form. For this organization to be capable of OSD, it should be able to perform at least the following four tasks.

1. Monitor the organizational structure's effectiveness in directing organizational activities. A set of observable parameters that affect the performance of the organization, as well as the formula for computing the performance itself, must be defined. Also, the conditions under which reorganization will be considered must be defined, which will typically involve a performance threshold.

2. Design new organizational structures appropriate to a new situation. For the design task, a way to generate alternative organizational structures for the current situation or for a projected future situation must be available. For systematic generation of organizational structures, an organizational structure should be able to be specified parametrically. Some important parameters include those that specify how the overall task is decomposed into a set of subtasks, how the subtasks are allocated to available agents (determining roles and communication structures among agents), how many agents are involved, and which resources are to be used and how they are to be shared by the agents.

3. Evaluate possible organizations and select the best one. This involves evaluating each alternative organization (including the current one) using a performance measure and selecting the one which is estimated to give the best overall performance.

4. Implement (and execute) the new structure over the network while preserving the network's problem-solving activities. Instantiating the selected structure requires the transfer of each (sub)task to the assigned agent.

An essential problem of OSD is to provide a general enough model of task, environment, organization, and performance. Thus, given a task and an environment, we would like to be able to generate the possible organizations to solve the problem, and evaluate each organization with the performance model. Since there may be different types of tasks and environments and since the possible organizational types as well as the performance of the organization will depend on the type of task and the environment, we would like to classify the different organizational structures in terms of the types of tasks and environments each is well suited for. Once we have such a predictive model of task-environment-organization-performance, the rest of the OSD tasks will be much easier. In sum, we see OSD as essentially involving a generate-and-test process.

Strategies for OSD

From the process just outlined, it is clear that OSD is itself a task (often called a "metalevel" task to differentiate it from the primary task(s) of the organization). As a task to be carried out in the distributed collection of agents, OSD requires that the agents adopt some strategy for its accomplishment, which could well mean that they adhere to a metalevel organization (Durfee and Lesser 1991) that remains unchanged as the organization for accomplishing the primary task(s) is redesigned and reimplemented.

Roles, responsibilities, and authorities could be distributed among agents in a variety of ways in a metalevel organization. At one extreme, a single agent (or a few agents) could be in complete charge of OSD. The agent would supervise the performance of the current organization, design and select a new organization when needed, and impose it on the other agents in an authoritarian manner. For example, in many of the experiments within the distributed vehicle monitoring testbed (Durfee, Lesser, and Corkill 1987), the human experimenter played this role. Corkill's proposed strategy for OSD within his system was not quite as centralized, however. While organization monitoring, design, and selection might be accomplished through shared data structures, it is possible for each of the agents to contribute observations and suggestions into the organization that is cooperatively constructed. Actually realizing such mechanisms computationally, however, is a difficult task. Thus, Corkill's results predominantly focused on computational means for accomplishing the fourth task (implementation) in the list we provided in the previous section.

At the other extreme, all agents could be in charge of small pieces of the overall OSD task. For example, Gasser and Ishida (1991) consider OSD as more of an emergent effect of many local actions of individual agents. In their work, an agent uses what it knows locally about the organization's performance in its neighborhood. If the agent determines that it is being a bottleneck (that it is accomplishing its tasks too slowly relative to its neighbors), then it can unilaterally decide to "divide" itself into two agents, where each takes on roughly half of the load. Or, if it determines that it is being underutilized, it can "combine" with an underutilized neighbor to avoid resource waste. Thus, in their system, Gasser and Ishida's agents demonstrate all of the features of the process in our list. The monitoring is simple and local, the design is simply a matter of choosing to divide or combine, the evaluation and selection occurs by actually doing the reorganization (and undoing it if it fails to work out), and the implementation is a matter of partitioning or uniting tasks following a predefined format.

The disadvantage of an emergent approach to OSD is that wholesale changes to the organization may require quite a long propagation time to come about, if they ever do, because there are no agents getting the "bigger" picture that could result in making multiple changes simultaneously that contribute to the organization's improvement. For example, organizational structures like those described previously in the tree organization subsection come about because of some degree of top-down structuring. This notion, in fact, has appeared in the distributed AI literature in several forms, of which the first and probably most well known is the Contract Net (Davis and Smith 1983). Contract Net assumed that tasks originate at particular agents, and that those agents enlist the aid of others by announcing subtasks, collecting bids for them, and awarding subtasks to the highest bidders. The hierarchical decomposition of tasks into subtasks and subsubtasks and so on and the allocation of these to agents leads to an inherent hierarchical organization to accomplish the task. The top-down decomposition of the task leads to an organization that is tailored for the task, but the ability of agents to bid (or not) based on their current environmental circumstances also means that the individual agents have some say in the structure of and their participation in the organization.

Organizations formed through the influences of task needs and environmental constraints can potentially be very effective. Yet they remain effective only as long as the task-environment characteristics do not change drastically. Under such circumstances, it might be necessary to completely reorganize the agents. However, when environmental factors change while task characteristics remain unchanged, it might be possible for the agents within an organization to perform a subset of the OSD tasks: the agents could monitor for such changes and then reimplement the existing organization, in terms of reconfiguring themselves so that all of the organizational roles are accomplished. This reconfiguration problem was addressed in our work in distributed network monitoring.

The Distributed Network Monitoring System

Consider a distributed network monitoring (DNM) system where a set of nodes in a large network are endowed with the capability to communicate and cooperate in monitoring the network. The wide area can be divided into several regions or subnetworks and one or more agents can be employed to be responsible for each subnetwork. Within each subnetwork, a set of agents may be jointly responsible for maintaining up-to-date models of host performance and availability. Monitoring, or more generally network management, agents may have disjoint functions or potentially overlapping responsibilities for increased reliability. Since network monitoring involves polling information about each component in the network, each agent may be responsible for monitoring a subset of those components.

If we assume that each network monitoring or management node is a process on a host that might simultaneously be processing other tasks, the processing load of each manager's host can vary as well as the communication load in a subarea of the network. Depending on the computational and communication load distribution in the network, one or more management nodes may potentially be in a better position to do the work. Thus, when such load distributions change, a work redistribution may well result in better performance (for example, response time). An extreme case will be a node failure, where a substitute must be found or its function must be taken over by another agent. For the network managers to be capable of such OSD processes, they must be able to monitor the performance and availability of each node, and when one or more nodes become a performance bottleneck either because of computational overload or because of communication link congestion, they must be able to agree upon an alternative organization which would redistribute the task to more idle nodes or further decompose the task into subtasks and lessen the burden of the overloaded nodes. On the other hand, too many small subtasks distributed among many nodes may incur large communication bandwidth consumption, which may decrease performance when there is much traffic on the communication links. In such cases, composition of subtasks into a higher granularity task and assignment of the task to a single node may decrease the amount of communication and improve overall performance of the organization.

Reconfiguration of Stable Organizations. Our previous work on a distributed network monitoring system called Distributed Big Brother (DBB) (So and Durfee 1992) solved the OSD subproblem called the reconfiguration problem (Pattison, Corkill, and Lesser 1987), where broken organizations were repaired by reallocating the organizational roles and responsibilities to new nodes when the nodes previously responsible for particular tasks were unable to perform them effectively. In other words, reconfiguration involves the first and the fourth of the OSD tasks we listed: the nodes monitor the performance of the current implementation of the organization (making sure that every node is doing what it is supposed to be doing), and when some failure is detected, the agents reimplement the organization within the current operating conditions (reassigning roles and tasks of the organization to compensate for the loss or failure of some node[s]). DBB provides mechanisms for the agents themselves to solve the reconfiguration problem at run time.

DBB uses a static organizational structure to decompose the management

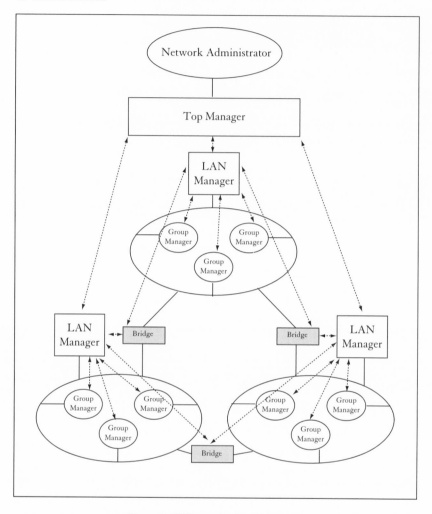

Figure 2. DBB organizational structure.

task, and within that structure uses contracting to assign specific tasks to nodes. A contracting protocol is also used to assign, and reassign, roles within the static organizational structure. The basic organizational structure, shown in figure 2, identifies several management roles in a hierarchical structure. The top manager provides information to the network administrator and oversees multiple LAN managers, which are responsible for providing the top with summaries of performance of their respective LANs. A LAN manager, similarly, oversees one or more group managers, which are responsible for directly monitoring a subset of hosts on the LAN and periodically reporting back to the LAN manager.

This type of organization is only effective if all the roles are filled—if a LAN manager disappears, the TOP loses touch with an entire LAN; if a GROUP manager fails, then a LAN manager loses track of a subset of hosts. The reconfiguration problem, within DBB, thus involves having managers at the various levels monitor each other to detect breakage of the organizational hierarchy and having the managers reimplement the hierarchy by reassigning roles among themselves to restore the functionality.

Monitoring within DBB has taken two forms. One type of monitoring is implicitly achieved through the assignment of tasks from above to below, such as when the TOP requests an update from a LAN manager, or a LAN manager expects reports about a group of hosts from a group manager. In these cases, a problem can be detected when expected messages or reports fail to arrive. However, having subordinate managers detect when their superiors are nonfunctional requires explicit messages for this purpose within DBB. Diagnostic "are you alive?" messages from subordinates to superiors are periodically sent out, and failure to receive a response indicates that something is wrong with the current implementation of the organization.

When monitoring has detected a problem, DBB skips issues of organizational design and evaluation and instead assumes that the predetermined organizational structure is still the best choice, but it needs to be reimplemented. Reimplementation strategies depend on where in the organization the break has occurred. If LAN managers detect that the top manager is unreachable, for example, reimplementation is fairly passive: the LAN managers will continue to perform their monitoring tasks and will periodically try to reconnect to the TOP manager. If a LAN manager detects that a group manager is not responding, on the other hand, the LAN manager can be much more proactive; it can determine which tasks (host monitoring) the failed group manager was responsible for and can reallocate those tasks among the remaining group managers.

The most interesting case is when a LAN manager fails. When the top manager detects such a failure, it discontinues assigning tasks to that manager and waits for a manager for that LAN to recontact it. The new LAN manager comes about because of the activities of the group managers that are now left without a LAN manager. These group managers over time come to a consensus that they are without a LAN manager, and as each comes to believe this it reverts to a "roleless manager" designation (called a "John Doe" role in DBB). When all managers within a LAN have individually adopted this designation, they then initiate an election procedure, selecting among themselves a node to temporarily act as the election chairman and then each submitting their qualifications for the role of LAN manager. The chairman names the best-suited manager as LAN manager, at which point the remaining nodes readopt the group manager status. The new LAN manager then introduces itself to the TOP manager, and the organization is reestablished.

Toward Redesigning the Organizational Structure. Solving the reconfiguration problem will allow only limited adaptation to changing task environments because it always assumes that the organizational structure is appropriate and is only concerned with maintaining it. But in a task like distributed network monitoring, what happens as the number of LANs increases to tens or hundreds? Is only one top manager going to be able to keep up, or should there be new layers of management in between? Or, conversely, if few managers are available such that only one group manager is available in a LAN, does it still make sense to have one LAN manager supervising only a single group manager? For these kinds of situations, we need full-fledged OSD so that a new organizational structure can be generated and implemented.

In our analysis of DBB performance, we have found that the performance (response time) of DBB is dependent on the number of hosts in a LAN (N_i), the unit task execution time (τ), and the task assignment rates (σ). In the analysis, we ignored the transmission delay (δ) because it was much smaller than τ or σ. However, depending on the amount of network traffic, the communication link technology, and the distance between the agents, δ may well vary and become a significant factor affecting the performance of the system. Likewise, depending on the computational power of the hardware of each agent and the current load of the processor in multitasking situations, the value of τ may vary. Finally, there may be long-term changes in the number of hosts (i.e., size of tasks) in one or more subnets, which will also change the performance graph as well. Thus, a configuration or an organizational structure that maximizes the overall utility in one task and resource environment may not be optimal in a different environment.

Therefore, if the DBB agents are not only to recover from failure but also to adaptively reconfigure themselves as the task and resource environment changes—that is, to be genuinely capable of OSD—they must be able to continuously monitor the changes in the environment (for example, values of N, τ, δ) and determine whether a change in the organizational structure (e.g., span of control) can lead to higher payoff. In order to do that, there must be a way to generate the possible changes in organization and a way to evaluate each possible organization given the current set of environmental parameter values or the predicted future values of those parameters.

Summary and Future Work

We have presented a model of organizations for computational agents and have described an approach for designing organizations based on a concrete understanding of their task environments and the performance metrics. The distinguishing feature of this model. compared to other models of distributed hierarchical problem solving such as Montgomery's (1992), is that this model takes into account the effect of task assignment overhead. Although parallel asynchronous communication is not uncommon, in many applications synchronous communication such as TCP/IP is common. When we think of human organizations, because of the biological limitation of a single agent, task assignment to other agents is often a sequential process. However, the assumption that the task assigner has to wait for an acknowledgment before he or she can start assigning the next task to another individual may be unrealistic. People often do continue doing other things after sending off a task but before it arrives at the destination.

The specific results reported here focus on tree-structured organizations and how to design such an organization (balance its height and width) depending on the nature of the task environment (characterized by task size and granularity) and the performance measure (we considered only response time here). We concluded that it is possible to predict the performance of an organization given such parameters, and thus to perform organizational design and evaluation. We also laid out the foundations for organizational self-design within our model and described how our DBB system currently performs a subset of the OSD functionality. Finally, we brought together our modeling framework with our DBB system to show that our framework can be used to build models whose predictions about DBB's performance correspond to actual experience.

There is much that can be done to extend this work. Certainly, we have to consider how the task of OSD, in its fullest sense, can be integrated within a system such as DBB. Key concerns involve the overhead of OSD. How much effort should agents within an organization devote to monitoring and reorganizing themselves? How do we avoid spending all the time reorganizing and never getting anything done? Should only a subset of the members of an organization be responsible for OSD?

In our most recent work, however, we are extending the range of task-environment, performance, and organizational parameters that we are considering. In particular, a common sense notion of an organization often implies some kind of resilience. People tend to come and go, while organizations often persist. We are trying to capture this notion in our model by considering the design of organizations that can reliably accomplish tasks even in environments where individuals might fail to perform their functions. This in turn leads us to organizational structures that involve some redundancy and begins to emphasize notions of coordination intelligence on the parts of the agents that populate these organizations. It is our hope that by pushing on our models in these ways, we can begin to provide prescriptive guidelines for designing organizations that succeed in complicated task environments and for constructing agents that are sophisticated enough to populate such organizations.

Notes

1. Practically speaking, this means that the programs running on the different computing processes capture, to some extent, the state-of-the-art techniques available within artificial intelligence.

2, The concept of reliability for distributed systems, however, is a little tricky because they may involve redundant components for improving reliability and therefore failure of some part of the overall system may degrade the performance of the system along other dimensions (such as response time) rather than making the entire system fail.

Organizations and External Conditions

4

The Choice Between Accuracy and Errors

A Contingency Analysis of External Conditions and Organizational Decision Making Performance

Zhiang Lin

Organizational decisions often have significant consequences. In order to succeed, organizations strive to maintain a high level of performance while minimizing the occurrence of mistakes, due either to underestimating or overestimating the environment. Often, success is not guaranteed by the existence of a complex organizational design nor by the existence of high-quality information alone. In this chapter, I examine the effect of external conditions, (i.e., task environments) on organizational decision-making performance. My focus is on conditions under which organizations make fewer type-1 (underestimating) or type-2 (overestimating) errors while achieving a high level of accuracy. This analysis is carried out using a computational model, which allows the researcher to examine various factors affecting the performance of organizations operating in dynamic task environments. The results suggest that an organization's ability to achieve a high level of decision accuracy is often done at the risk of committing more errors, particularly type-1 errors. Further, the occurrence of these errors is directly associated with the task environment the organization is in, the structural form the organization takes, and the time pressure the organization is under. Organizational design becomes a strategic decision between how accurate the organization's decisions should be and what type of errors the organization wants to minimize under different conditions.

This research builds on the basic idea of contingency theories and focuses on operationalizing variables in specific settings that can actually be tested, so that precise and consistent conclusions can be drawn. The following issue are addressed: how should organizations be designed to make high accuracy decisions while committing few errors, either due to underestimating or overestimating, given different conditions? Specifically, this chapter examines the effect of task environment on organizational decision making, studies the relationships among different types of decision errors, organizational design, and task environments, tests the proposition of contingency theories that an organization should have its design matched to the task environment to ensure better performance, and explores the value of computational techniques in advancing organization theories.

Because of the complex nature of the interrelationships and the difficulty in manipulating actual organizations, this uses the computational model DYCORP (Lin and Carley 1995) to address these issues. DYCORP can be used to systematically explore the contingencies underlying organizational decision making outcome as well as various conditions including task environment and organizational design. The model allows for the examination of crucial factors that can be interrelated and the agents' adaptiveness in the organization (and hence, the adaptiveness of the organization). The use of a computational framework such as DYCORP is similar to the expert systems approach of Baligh, Burton, and Obel (1990), as well as many other researchers in the field of computational organizational theory (such as Carley and Prietula 1994 or Masuch and LaPotin 1989).

In the following sections, the DYCORP framework is briefly described with specific attention to the task environment and organizational design model. A virtual experiment is run using DYCORP. The remainder of this chapter discusses the results of that virtual experiment.

Model Description

The DYCORP framework allows researchers to examine the decision making behavior of organizations under dynamic task environments. The DYCORP framework encompasses aspects of organizational design, task environment, and stress, with a focus on organizational information processing and decision making (figure 1). DYCORP is a general purpose framework for studying organizational performance. In this chapter, only limited aspects of that framework are discussed.

Stylized Radar Task

In DYCORP, the task has been operationalized as a stylized radar task. The organization faces a sequence of radar-detection problems (see also Lin and Carley 1995 and Carley and Lin 1995). Each problem is defined as a single aircraft moving through the airspace. Each aircraft is characterized by nine indicators or parameters. The organization acquires information on those parameters. The organization has nine analysts, each having access to some of the nine parameters

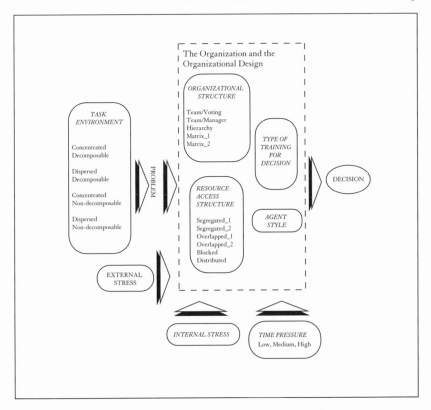

Figure 1. An overview of the DYCORP framework.

through the resource access structures. This is a distributed task. The indication of a specific parameter may not reflect the true state of the whole aircraft. For example, a plane emitting signals indicating it is carrying weapons may not necessarily be hostile. The organization has three choices—it must decide whether the aircraft in the airspace is friendly, neutral, or hostile. This aircraft has a true state; i.e., it is actually either friendly (marked as "1"), neutral (marked as '2"), or hostile (marked as "3"). To solve the problem, the organization must decide whether the organization "thinks" the observed aircraft is friendly, neutral, or hostile before the aircraft reaches the red zone. The red zone is either the point at which the aircraft enters the danger zone (the range is less than 1 mile or the altitude is less than 5,000 feet) or the point at which the time limit on making a decision (set by the organization) has been met, whichever occurs first. After the problem is over (i.e., the aircraft has hit the red zone) the organization's final decision is recorded. A new problem (aircraft) then occurs.

Some of the characteristics of the aircraft may change during the flight, but the true state of the aircraft, as is defined at the starting state, does not change.

Since this is a dynamic task, the amount of time pressure faced by the organization will vary. Time pressure in DYCORP is represented by the number of time units the organization has to make the decision. The lower the number of time units, the faster the organization must make its decision and the greater the time pressure. Time pressure is one divided by the number of time units. The number of time units is determined by two factors—the number of time units assigned to the problem and the number of time units required for decision before the aircraft enters the danger zone. For each aircraft, the number of time units assigned can vary from one to sixty, with the actual number being randomly assigned. For each aircraft, the number of time units required before entering the danger zone depends on its speed, direction, angle, and altitude.

Modeling the Organization

Within DYCORP's organizational decision-making process, no one agent has access to all the information needed to make a decision. Further, the task does not require consensus. For a particular alternative to be chosen, it is sufficient that the CEO or a majority of the agents in the organization choose that alternative. Because each agent in the organization has access (directly or indirectly) to only some of the nine parameters, the final organizational decision requires communication and coordination among organizational members. Which analyst reads what information depends on the resource access structure. How members of the organization communicate depends on the organizational structure. What style of decision each agent uses depends on the type of training the agent receives. The distribution of possible problems (aircraft) constitutes the task environment. The organizational operation can be disrupted by sub-optimal operating conditions.

The artificial organizations examined in DYCORP have procedures for providing and receiving feedback, communicating recommendations, combining recommendations to create an organizational decision, and training. In all organizations, agents during their training phase receive accurate and immediate feedback regarding the correct organizational decision. There is also no time constraint during training. Each agent's memory includes information only on task categorization experience, not time pressure, although agents may be trained to work faster. The focus in this research is on performance after training.

In all organizations, agents communicate their decisions only to their immediate supervisor(s). In a team using voting as a means to reach a decision, a majority rule procedure is used. In all other organizational structures, the procedure for combining subordinates' recommendations is determined by the supervisor. Training procedures can be systematically varied across all organizations.

In the DYCORP framework, the organization can track the moving aircraft and make a series of (not just one) decisions about the state of the aircraft. The number of decisions made by the organization for each aircraft is recorded in the simulation output, although the organization only reports its final decision.

There are many options available to the researcher for examining organizational performance within DYCORP. In this chapter, the analysis will be limited to cases where the incoming information is correct and complete, all agents are always available, and all communication channels are always open. Feedback is also complete and timely. Further, each agent in the organization has a proactive style and engages in the organizational decision-making process whenever possible (Lin and Carley 1993). That is, each agent asks for information according to his or her position, reads the information if there is information available, makes a decision based on the information, and then passes that decision to a superior. This process repeats itself until time expires. Time expires when the aircraft enters the red zone. Each agent's process (except the top-level manager's) can be interrupted when he or she receives a request from a superior for a decision. The agent will respond to the request by passing up an already-made decision. If the agent has not previously made a decision, he or she will take a guess and pass that along as his or her decision. There are minor differences among the top-level manager, middle-level managers, and analysts. The top-level manager cannot be interrupted (since there is no superior), and an analyst cannot ask for information (since there is no subordinate), but a middle-level manager can be interrupted as well as ask for information. Further, the top-level manager has the power to decide which decision will be used as the final organizational decision.

Variable Description

To examine the effects of different factors on organizational decision making performance, we consider three dependent variables and four independent variables.

Dependent Variables

The dependent variables chosen address not only how organizations make accurate decisions, but also how they may make different types of errors (table 1).

Percentage of Correct Decisions

In DYCORP, the percentage of correct decisions is the accuracy of the organizational response. It is measured as the number of correct decisions made by the organization over the total number of problems presented to the organization.

Percentage of Type-1 Errors

Percentage of type-1 errors represents the extent to which the organization misperceives problems as friendlier than they are. It is measured as the number of neutral or hostile problems incorrectly recognized as "friendly" over the total number of problems presented to the organizations.

		True State		
		Friendly	Neutral	Hostile
Decision	Friendly	Accurate	Type-1	Type-1
	Neutral	Type-2	Accurate	Type-1
	Hostile	Type-2	Type-2	Accurate

Table 1. Definitions of performance measures.

Percentage of Type-2 Errors

Percentage of type-2 errors represents the extent to which the organization misperceives problems as more hostile than they are. It is measured as the number of friendly or neutral problems incorrectly recognized as "hostile" over the total number of problems presented to the organization.

Independent Variables

The independent variables examined include task environment, time pressure, organizational structure, and resource access structure. These control variables are examined because organizational survival, to a large extent, depends on how the organization adjusts to its task environment and how the organizational design (organizational and resource access structure) mitigates time stress.

Task Environment

Task environment is the collection of all possible aircraft, each of which has its own true nature of being either friendly (marked as "1"), neutral (marked as "2"), or hostile (marked as "3"). The true state of the world is a feature of the task that is external to the organization and cannot be manipulated by the organization, at least in the short run, even though the organization can try to infer the true state of an aircraft through examining its radar characteristics.

The manipulation of the task environment determines which of the possible states (friendly, neutral, or hostile) is the true state for each unique aircraft. Referring to the literature, two types of manipulations of the task environment were built into DYCORP: (1) the extent to which the task is decomposable (Roberts 1990, Simon 1962) and (2) the extent to which it is concentrated (Aldrich 1979, Hannan and Freeman 1977).

A task environment is decomposable if there are no complex interactions among components that need to be understood in order to solve a problem. In contrast, when the task is nondecomposable, the pieces of information do not contribute equally to the final decision, and portions of the information interact to determine the true nature of the aircraft.

A task environment is concentrated if the possible outcomes are not equally likely. In a concentrated environment, this inequality of outcome biases perception. Concentrated environments, or niches, are quite common. In a dispersed environment, approximately one-third of the 19,683 aircraft (6,568) are hostile and one-third of the aircraft are friendly. This environment can be thought of as an uncertain environment because the chances of each of the three outcomes are almost identical—33.33 percent.

Based on the two manipulations (decomposability and concentration), four different realities or environmental situations can be examined in DYCORP, which, listed in order from simple to complex, concentrated decomposable, dispersed decomposable, concentrated nondecomposable, and dispersed nondecomposable. These four environments define, for any aircraft in that environment, the true state of that aircraft.

Time Pressure

Recall that the organization must make a decision before the aircraft reaches the red zone. The longer it takes the aircraft to reach the red zone, the less the time pressure. Within DYCORP, the researcher can examine three levels of time pressure: low, medium, and high. A low time pressure (no less than forty-one time units) puts little or no time constraint on the organization. In this case, the organizational decision making process is least affected by time. A high time pressure (no more than twenty time units) puts great pressure on an organization to respond quickly and so constrains the organization's decision-making process. A moderate time pressure (more than twenty but less than forty-one time units) places some constraint on the decision process. As DYCORP is a dynamic model, interactions among agents are affected by the time pressure. Time pressure can affect whether agents communicate, how they communicate, and which decision procedure they choose. These agent choices are dependent on the agent style (Lin and Carley 1993).

Organizational Structure

Organizational structure determines how organizations coordinate and control the activities of members, which in turn can greatly impact how effective and efficient organizations can be. Organizational structure (who communicates with whom), together with resource access structure (who has access to what), which will be further described later, also reflects how complex an organization is, and thus how costly the organizational design, is (Malone 1987).

Five structures can be examined in DYCORP: team with voting, team with a manager, hierarchy, matrix_1, and matrix_2. Each structure consists of nine analysts. In addition, some structures employ middle- and/or top-level managers. Studies on these typical organizational structures have not been few. These structures are listed in terms of increasing complexity.

1. Team with voting—This is a totally decentralized structure in which the or-

ganizational decision is the majority vote and each analyst in the organization gets an equal vote. Each analyst examines information and makes a recommendation. This recommendation is the analyst's vote.

2. Team with a manager—This is a flat hierarchy in which all analysts report to a single manager. Each analyst examines information and makes a recommendation. The manager examines these recommendations and makes the organizational decision.

3. Hierarchy—This is a multilevel structure in which each analyst reports to his or her immediate middle-level manager, and the middle-level managers report to the top-level manager. Each analyst examines information and makes a recommendation. Each middle-level manager examines the recommendations from his or her subordinates and makes a recommendation. The top-level manager examines the middle-level managers' recommendations and makes the organizational decision.

4. Matrix_1—This is a multilevel structure in which six of the nine analysts report to two middle-level managers, and the middle-level managers report to the top-level manager. Each analyst examines information and makes a recommendation. Each middle-level manager examines the recommendations from his or her subordinates, as well as the other analysts' reports, and then makes a recommendation. The top-level manager examines the middle-level managers' recommendations and makes the organizational decision.

5. Matrix_2—This is a multilevel structure in which each analyst reports to two middle-level managers, and the middle-level managers report to the top-level manager. Each analyst examines information and makes a recommendation. Each middle-level manager examines the recommendations from his or her subordinates, as well as the other analysts' reports, and makes a recommendation. The top-level manager examines the middle-level managers' recommendations and makes the organizational decision.

Resource Access Structure

The resource access structure determines the distribution of raw (unfiltered) information to analysts in the organization. The resource access structure has also been referred to as the information access structure (Carley 1991, Carley 1992), the task decomposition scheme (Carley 1990), or the task process structure (Mackenzie 1978). The term *resource access structure* is used first to emphasize the role of task environment in organizational performance and second to clearly differentiate the ties between people and data (the task decomposition scheme) and the ties between people and people (the organizational structure). In DYCORP the resource access structure determines which analyst has access to which type of radar or surveillance equipment. Each type of equipment allows that analyst to garner information on a particular or a particular set of characteristics. Using DYCORP the researcher can examine six resource access structures, listed in order of increasing complexity: segregated_1, segregated_2, overlapped_1, overlapped_2, blocked, and distributed. Note that both segregated structures have the same level of complexity. Overlapped_2, blocked, and distributed, are equally complex in terms of direct links (each analyst sees three pieces of information), but they vary in terms of indirect links (i.e., mid-level managers ultimately have access to different amounts of information).

1. Segregated_1—In this structure each analyst has access to one task component.

2. Segregated_2—In this structure each analyst also has access to only one task component, but it differs from that in Segregated_1.

3. Overlapped_1—In this structure each analyst has access to two task components. Each task component is accessed by two analysts.

4. Overlapped_2—In this structure each analyst has access to three task components. Each two task components are accessed by two analysts.

5. Blocked—Each analyst has access to three task components. Three analysts see exactly the same three task components, i.e., they have the same mental model. If these analysts are in a hierarchy or a matrix, then they all report to the same middle-level manager (i.e., they are in the same division).

6. Distributed—Each analyst has access to three task components. No two analysts see exactly the same information. Thus each analyst has a slightly different mental model. If these analysts are in a hierarchy or a matrix, then each middle-level manager has indirect access to all nine pieces of information.

As with the organizational structures, these resource access structures were chosen as they represent unique, albeit stylized, patterns of distributing the task information among analysts. In other words, these schemes represent a range of ways in which task-based information can be differentially accessed by the agents in the organizational structure. These structures vary in two dimensions—how much information overlap exists and where the overlap occurs. The impact of where the overlap occurs between the organizational structure and the resources access structure depends on who reports to whom. The teams do not have divisions, so the impact the resulting from the differences in resource access structures should be different from that those in a hierarchy where the personnel divisions are usually lined up with the resource divisions. By comparing these variations, DYCORP can be used to examine how different resource access structures affect organizational performance.

Virtual Experiment

Using DYCORP, the researcher systematically varies each of the following items: type of task environment (four types), level of time pressure (three levels), type of organizational structure (five types), and types of resource access structure (six types), while averaging across all other factors. Again, internal operating conditions are optimal, and all agents are proactive agents. Type of training is not controlled (for the effect of training see Lin and Carley [1995]). For each combination of the above items, the number of problems presented to the organization is 1,000. Each of the three dependent variables is recorded: percentage of correct decisions, percentage of type-1 errors, and percentage of type-2 errors, as is the organizations performance and decision for each task. Through this virtual experiment, the impact of task environment and/or organizational design on organizational performance when the level of time pressure can change is examined.

Results

In this section, first the impact of task environment on organizational performance will be considered. Then, the focus will shift to the impact of organizational design on organizational performance. Finally, the impact of a complexity match on organizational performance will be examined.

Task Environment

Task environment has a massive impact on organizational performance (figure 2). Organizations that have the highest percentage of accurate decisions are working under low time pressure in a concentrated nondecomposable task environment. Under the same task environment, organizations make the fewest type-2 errors but no type-1 errors, which are relatively high compared with other task environments. Under the other three types of task environments, organizational performance in terms of accuracy of decision making is close, but organizations tend to commit the most type-2 errors, while at the same time the fewest type-1 errors, under a concentrated nondecomposable task environment. This result suggests that there does not exist a task environment in which organizations will be both the most accurate and the least likely to commit errors (of either type). Organizations should recognize that their likelihood of error and their achievable performance are both a function of the task environment. For example, all else being equal, organizations operating in a concentrated nondecomposable task environment are simply going to make more type-1 errors than are other organizations.

When the time pressure increases to a moderate level, the patterns, although similar to those under low time pressure, become much flatter across different task environments. Percentages of correct decisions decrease, while percentages of type-1 errors increase significantly for organizations in all four task environments. In the meantime, percentages of type-2 errors remain less affected. This suggests that time pressure has a strong moderating effect on the impact of task

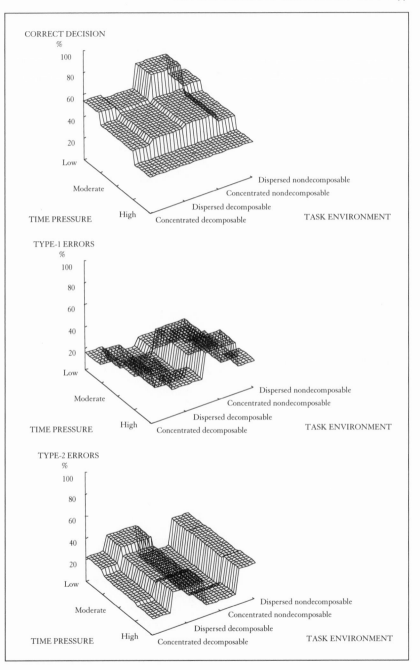

Figure 2. The impact of task environment on performance.

environment on performance and that the accuracy of decision making may be at the expense of committing type-1 errors.

When the time pressure increases to a high level, all the percentages are close to 33percent, which indicates that organizations have been reduced to simply guessing. In the meantime, the percentage of type-1 errors has increased significantly, especially for organizations in concentrated decomposable and concentrated nondecomposable task environments. Percentages of type-2 errors are less affected. This suggests that as time pressure increases, the impact of the task environment on accuracy decreases, but its impact on the likelihood of type-1 errors increases.

In summary, the above analyses demonstrate that task environment can have a major impact on accuracy, type-1 errors, and type-2 errors, although such impact is moderated by time pressure. Additionally, these results suggest that accuracy of decision making can often be achieved at the expense of committing more errors.

Organizational Design

I will now examine which organizational design fares best as time pressure increases.

Low Time Pressure

When there is little time pressure, organizational design has little impact on performance (figure 3). In terms of the percentage of correct decisions, there is little difference due to organizational design. The highest percentages of correct decisions are made by those organizations that are composed of teams with a voting structure and a simple resource access structure (overlapped_1, overlapped_2, and blocked). Organizations with a matrix_2 organizational structure and a distributed resource access structure (which happens to be the most complex form) make the fewest correct decisions. This fact suggests that structural complexity may not be effective in decision making.

For type-1 errors, the pattern is also relatively flat. Only the matrix_2 organizational structure with the distributed resource access structure stands out, with almost twice the percentage of type-1 errors. With regard to type-2 errors, percentages across most organizational designs are flat. However, most organizations have a higher percentage of type-2 errors than type-1 errors.

The analyses suggest that the organizational structure and resource access structure have less impact on performance than does the task environment under low time pressure. Additionally, these results indicate that complex designs may be less accurate and make more errors.

Moderate Time Pressure

Now let us look at the results under moderate time pressure (figure 4). As time

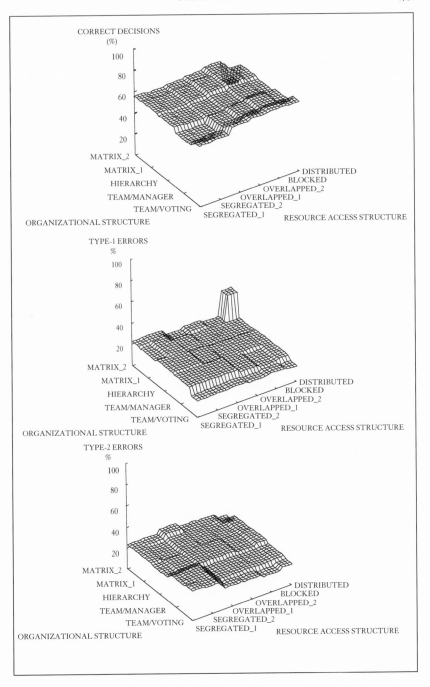

Figure 3. The impact of organizational design on performance under low time pressure.

pressure increases, the relative advantage of different organizational designs becomes apparent. Simple organizational designs (particularly in resource access) are now the most accurate and are the least likely to make type-1 errors. At moderate time pressure, there is still little relation between design and type-2 errors. Further, in general organizations are now less likely to make type-2 than type-1 errors.

High Time Pressure

The results under high time pressure are displayed in figure 5. Under extreme time pressure, there is no advantage to any organizational design in terms of accuracy or errors.

In summary, the above analyses suggest that the value of organizational design depends on the amount of time pressure. When there is either little or extreme time pressure, organizational design has little impact. However, under moderate time pressure, simple organizational designs perform best.

Match of Task Environment and Organizational Design

I now turn to examining how the match between organizational structure/resource access structure and task environment affects organizational decision making. Contingency theorists often argue that if there is a match between the complexity of the organization's design and the complexity of the environment, then the organization's performance should be high. If this theory is correct, then a higher match means higher performance, regardless of what the agents in the organization have learned or how they have been trained. To test this theory, the concept of complexity match needs to be operationalized. Organizational design complexity is defined as being either simple, complex, or moderate.

An organization with simple design complexity has an organizational structure of either team with voting or team with a manager paired with a resource access structure of either segregated_1, segregated_2, or overlapped_1

An organization with complex design complexity has an organizational structure of either hierarchy, matrix_1, or matrix_2, paired with a resource access structure of either overlapped_2, blocked, or distributed

An organization with moderate design complexity consists of all other organizations

Task environment complexity is defined by its decomposability and concentration. A concentrated task environment is simpler than a dispersed one, and a decomposable task environment is simpler than a nondecomposable one. There are three levels of complexity for the task environment: simple, complex, and moderate.

1. Simple task environment—a concentrated decomposable task environment

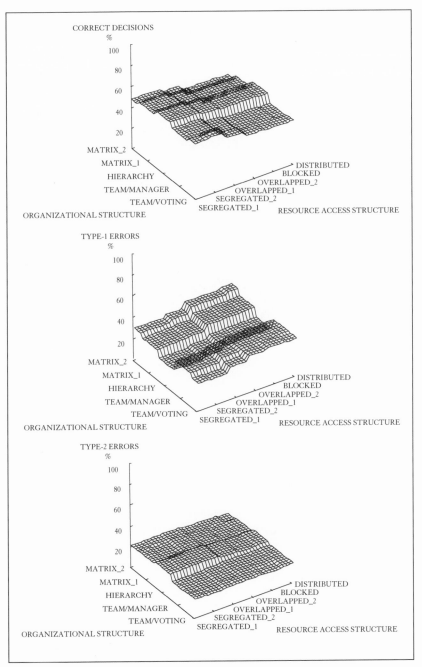

*Figure 4. The impact of organizational design on
performance under moderate time pressure.*

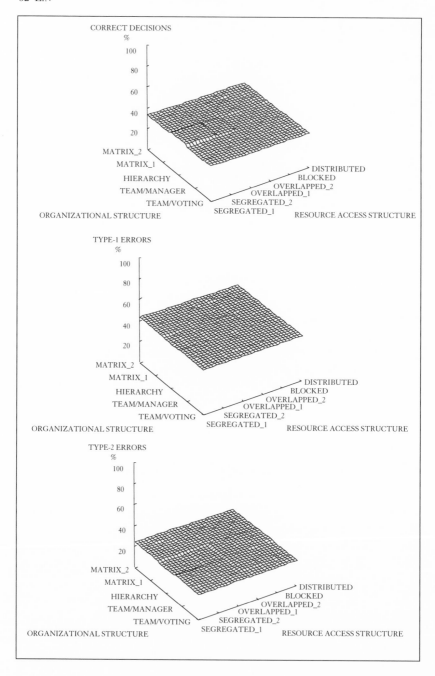

Figure 5. The impact of organizational design on performance under high time pressure.

2. Complex task environment—a dispersed nondecomposable task environment

3. Moderate task environment—all other task environments.

Using these measures, it is possible to determine whether there is a match between the organizational complexity and task environment complexity. A low match occurs if an organization is complex and a task environment is simple or if an organization is simple and a task environment is complex; a high match occurs if an organization is simple and a task environment is simple, if an organization is complex and a task environment is complex, or if an organization is moderate and a task environment is moderate; and a moderate match occurs in all other cases. The complete set of definitions for complexity match between task environment and organizational design is shown in table 2.

The results for the effect of the match between organizational design and task environment on performance are depicted in figure 6. A better match increases the accuracy of decision making, and it also increases the percentage of type-2 errors. Match has little impact on type-1 errors.

A further analysis using regression also shows that the impact of complexity match on correct decisions, type-1 errors, and type-2 errors is mixed (table 3). A high match significantly increases the percentage of correct decisions, even after controlling for the level of time pressure. However, as time pressure increases, the impact of such complexity match decreases. With regard to type-1 errors, an increase in the complexity match significantly decreases the percentage of errors, regardless of the level of time pressure. For type-2 errors, the model does not explain any relationship, suggesting that complexity match may not matter to type-2 errors.

The analyses presented indicate that the benefit of a match between task environment and organizational design may be limited to enhancing the accuracy of organizational decision making and limiting the occurrence of type-1 errors. This finding restricts contingency theory's argument that a good match between organizational design and task environment will help organizational performance to specifying which aspects of performance are improved by a match. Further, this result adds the restriction that the value of the match decreases as time pressure increases.

Discussion and Conclusion

These results suggest that making an organization more accurate may increase the risk of errors, particularly type-1 errors. The likelihood of errors is a function of the task environment, the organizational design, and the time pressure the organization is under. Researchers concerned with predicting and explaining organizational performance should consider both accuracy and error. Thus,

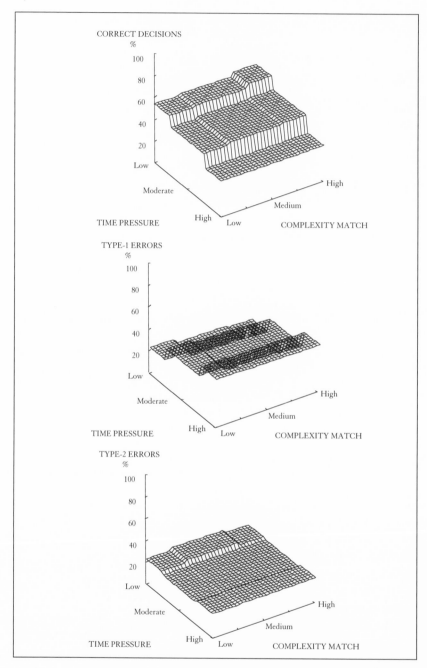

Figure 6. The impact of complexity match on performance.

Organizational Form		Task Environment		
Organization Structure	Resource Access Structure	Concentrated Decomposable	Dispersed Decomposable; & Concentrated Non-decomposable,	Dispersed Non-decomposable
	Segregated_1	High Match	Medium Match	Low Match
	Segregated_2	High Match	Medium Match	Low Match
Team/Voting	Overlapped_1	High Match	Medium Match	Low Match
	Overlapped_2	Medium Match	High Match	Medium Match
	Blocked	Medium Match	High Match	Medium Match
	Distributed	Medium Match	High Match	Medium Match
	Segregated_1	High Match	Medium Match	Low Match
	Segregated_2	High Match	Medium Match	Low Match
Team/Mgr	Overlapped_1	High Match	Medium Match	Low Match
	Overlapped_2	Medium Match	High Match	Medium Match
	Blocked	Medium Match	High Match	Medium Match
	Distributed	Medium Match	High Match	Medium Match
	Segregated_1	Medium Match	High Match	Medium Match
	Segregated_2	Medium Match	High Match	Medium Match
Hierarchy	Overlapped_1	Medium Match	High Match	Medium Match
	Overlapped_2	Low Match	Medium Match	High Match
	Blocked	Low Match	Medium Match	High Match
	Distributed	Low Match	Medium Match	High Match
	Segregated_1	Medium Match	High Match	Medium Match
	Segregated_2	Medium Match	High Match	Medium Match
Matrix_1	Overlapped_1	Medium Match	High Match	Medium Match
	Overlapped_2	Low Match	Medium Match	High Match
	Blocked	Low Match	Medium Match	High Match
	Distributed	Low Match	Medium Match	High Match
	Segregated_1	Medium Match	High Match	Medium Match
	Segregated_2	Medium Match	High Match	Medium Match
Matrix_2	Overlapped_1	Medium Match	High Match	Medium Match
	Overlapped_2	Low Match	Medium Match	High Match
	Blocked	Low Match	Medium Match	High Match
	Distributed	Low Match	Medium Match	High Match

Table 2. Definitions of complexity match between organizational design and task environment.

choice of organizational design becomes a strategic decision between how accurate the organization's decisions should be and what type of errors the organization wants to minimize under different conditions. The results suggest that compared with task environment, organizational design has a smaller impact on performance and that accuracy of decision making often has an inverse relationship with the occurrence of type-1 errors.

This research has examined one of the fundamental propositions in contingency theory: for an organization to achieve high performance, it should adopt an organizational design matched to the task environment. The results support the idea that the best design is contingent. Additionally, this research has gone beyond traditional contingency theory by operationalizing and testing different organizational designs under different specific conditions. The results restrict the contingent argument to just those cases where time pressure is moderate and performance is thought of in terms of either accuracy or type-1 errors. In

Independent Variables	Dependent Variable		
	CORRECT DECISIONS (%)	TYPE-1 ERRORS (%)	TYPE-2 ERRORS (%)
INTERCEPT	59.778*** (15.893)	14.846*** (3.597)	25.376*** (6.036)
TIME PRESSURE	-8.651*** (-4.969)	10.029*** (5.248)	-1.377* (-0.708)
MATCH	4.842** (3.019)	-3.709* (-2.107)	-1.134 (-0.632)
TIME PRESSURE * MATCH	-1.564* (-2.106)	1.065 (1.307)	0.499 (0.601)
R2	0.368	0.334	0.000

Note: Number of cases is 1080 for each dependent variable. T-statistics are in parentheses.
TIME PRESSURE is for level of time pressure in which 1 = low time pressure, 2 = moderate time pressure, and 3 = high time pressure.
MATCH is for level of complexity match between organizational design (organization structure and resource access structure) and task environment in which 1 = low match, 2 = moderate match, and 3 = high match.
*p < .05, **p < .01, ***p < .001.

Table 3. The impact of complexity match between organizational design and task environment on performance: A regression analysis.

this sense, this analysis demonstrates that computational models can be effectively used to place conditions on when a specific design is most effective and to extent organizational theories.

Future work should consider how suboptimal operating conditions may influence the outcome of decision-making accuracy as well as different types of errors. Additionally, researchers should consider other forms of adaptation, particularly focusing on how organizations adapt to a continually shifting task environment as reflected in today's world.

The utility of computational modeling has already been shown in many fields. Computational analysis as a developing methodology has many unique advantages. While the common misconception is that computers are just machines and so do not represent human beings, one thing being overlooked is that computational analysis actually allows us to complement or even go beyond conventional mathematical equations, laboratory experiments, or field studies. For example, compared with mathematical equations, computational models permit less quantified relationships among different factors and enable the researcher to examine different relationships under dynamic situations. Thus, computational analysis allows researchers to analyze complex adaptive systems (Carley and Lin 1995) and to create sophisticated models that are much closer to the real world (Lant and Mezias 1992). Also, compared with experiments using human subjects or field studies, virtual experiments are easier to control, more flexible, more objective, and can examine more factors in less time and with less cost. Many human experiments or field studies are not permitted in the real world because of either the cost of data collection or the impossibility of controlling the environment. At these times, virtual experimentation using computational models becomes not only useful but also necessary in developing organizational theories that can be tested in future empirical settings (Carley and Prietula 1994; Cohen, March, and Olsen 1972; Stasser 1988).

Although computational techniques have many merits, proper caution should still prevail when viewing the results of virtual experiments. Like any other research methodology, computational analysis has its limitations. One of them is that, like mathematical modeling, computational modeling often involves simplified assumptions, because of the relatively recent development of computer software and hardware technologies. Also, like laboratory experiments, computational models are often run for very specific and sometimes narrow settings. Because of these limitations, researchers should take care when trying to generalize the results to a larger or a different setting.

Given the pros and cons of computational analysis, there is no doubt that the pros far outweigh the cons. With the further sophistication of computational modeling techniques and understanding of organizational phenomena, the organizational theorist can be confident that the future of computational analysis in the field of organization is very bright.

5

Fluctuating Efforts and Sustainable Cooperation

Bernardo A. Huberman and Natalie S. Glance

When individuals confronted with a social dilemma contribute to the common good with an effort that fluctuates in time, they can make the group generate an average utility that actually decreases in time. This paradoxical behavior takes place in spite of the fact that typically individuals are found to be contributing at any given time. This novel phenomenon, which we verified in a number of computer experiments, is the result of an intermittent effect, whereby unlikely bursts of defection determine the average behavior of the group. Besides providing a dynamic theory for the lognormal distribution found in some sociological data, these results show that the typical behavior of individuals comprising a group can be inconsistent with its average properties.

Social dilemmas are at the heart of the problem of generating cooperation among individuals confronted with conflicting choices. As such they have been studied for a number of years within the context of rational choice theory. As shown originally by Olson (1965), individuals having to choose between producing a public good and free riding on the effort of others face a dilemma when the benefit to be accrued by overall cooperation offsets individual costs, since rationality on the part of each individual leads to failure in achieving the common good (Hardin 1968, Schelling 1978, Hardin 1982, Glance and Huberman 1994). The resolution of such dilemmas underlies successful attempts at ongoing collective action, such as the functioning of large organizations (Bendor 1987, Glance 1993), the mobilization of political movements (Taylor 1976, Oliver 1988), and the adoption of new technologies.

Beliefs and expectations are at the core of human choices and preferences. They arise from the intentional nature of people and reflect the way the future as well as the past enter into decisions that are made at present. Thus, individuals acting within the context of a larger group may take into account the effect of their actions both on their personal welfare and on the welfare of the group.

In other words, individuals form their own models of how the group dynamics works based on some set of beliefs that color their preferences. Within this context, we have recently shown that for a broad set of beliefs and group characteristics, cooperation can appear spontaneously in noncooperative and diverse groups after long periods of time if delays in information are not important (Huberman 1996). Moreover, cooperation or defection appear suddenly and unexpectedly, with diversity acting as an additional source of uncertainty, thus shortening the time to an outbreak (Huberman 1993).

Traditionally, studies of social dilemmas have made assumptions that do not always reflect the behavior of realistic groups of people, such as the existence of a utility function that is the same for all individuals, or the constancy of the benefits and costs over long periods of time. Concerning the latter, it is well known that since cooperation is based on a person's effort, one never implements precisely the amount of cooperation that one intends to. There are always a number of reasons for this to be the case. An individual may be late returning from a meeting and so can give less time for a cooperative endeavor than he or she had planned. Or, in situations where the production of the collective good demands some physical effort, it is reasonable to expect that individual contributions will vary over time. The same applies to cases where intellectual effort is required, such as clerical work in an organization. In those circumstances, it can be safely assumed that the benefit from cooperation will fluctuate around a mean value, with a dispersion determined by the variance of the appropriate distribution.

In, this chapter, we study the effects of such fluctuating benefits on the possibility of obtaining sustained cooperation from a group of individuals confronted with a social dilemma. In spite of the fact that this is the optimal case for either small groups or for individuals with long outlooks even in equilibrium, some members of a cooperating group will occasionally choose to defect because of misinformation as to what the other members are doing (Glance 1993). If in addition individual efforts also fluctuate, the benefit obtained by members of the group during those switchings could either encourage or discourage further switchings. Nevertheless, since these fluctuations lower the utility of the group, one expects that after a short period of time the group will revert to spontaneous cooperation.

If variations in individual output are normally distributed around an average value, fluctuations away from the fixed point should lead to a small and random modulation of the group's utility in time. Moreover, if the fluctuations have a vanishing time average, the average value of the utility to the group might be expected to remain constant over time. A careful study of the resulting dynamics, however, shows that this is not the case. Instead, variability in effort has a dramatic effect on the overall behavior of the system. We will show that a cooperating group of individuals can generate an average utility that decreases in time, even though the fluctuations in effort are small and with zero mean. This striking and paradoxical behavior is the result of a social intermittency effect, whereby unlikely bursts of defection determine the average behavior of the group, in spite of the fact that individuals are typically found to be cooperating at any given time. These predictions will then be verified through a number of computer experiments.

This effect, although exhibited here within the context of social dilemmas, is likely to be encountered in many other social situations characterized by equilibria punctuated with fluctuations. In certain cases, it might even be possible for a large group of defectors to generate a utility that increases in time. Intermittency implies that in situations where the only available data is some average utility or other productivity measure, the inference that the individuals constituting the group act in ways consistent with the average behavior might be incorrect. If one had to summarize these findings in a simple vernacular sentence, it would read: "what you see is not what you get."

At a different level, these results provide a dynamic theory for the lognormal distribution found in some sociological data (reference), while showing that the typical behavior of individuals constituting a group can be inconsistent with its average properties.

Social Dilemmas

In a general social dilemma, each individual can either contribute to (cooperate with) the production of a common good, or not (defect). While no individual can directly observe the effort of another, each member observes instead the collective output of the group or organization and can deduce overall group participation using knowledge of individual and group functions. In this process, there is an amount of uncertainty in the relation between members' efforts and group performance. There are many causes for this uncertainty; for example, a member may try but fail to contribute because of unforeseen obstacles. Another type of uncertainty might arise from the fact that individuals act with bounded rationality, occasionally making suboptimal decisions.

In a simple but general limit, collective benefits increase linearly in the contribution of the members, at a rate b per cooperating member. Each contributing individual bears a personal cost, c. If k_i denotes whether member i is cooperating ($k_i = 1$) or defecting ($k_i = 0$), then the utility at time t for member i of a group of size n is given by Bendor (1987)

$$U_i(t) = b \frac{\hat{n}_c(t)}{n} - ck_i \tag{1}$$

From knowledge of the functional form of the utility function, each individual can deduce the number of individuals effectively cooperating at some time t by inverting this equation and obtaining an estimate of the value of $\hat{n}_c$, or, alternatively, by evaluating $\hat{f}_c(t) = \hat{n}_c(t)/n$, the fraction of individuals effectively cooperating at time *t*. Since the information available is not perfect, this estimate will differ from the actual number of individuals intending to cooperate.

When all members contribute successfully, each individual receives net benefits $b / n - c = b - c$, independent of the group's size. The production of the collective good becomes a social dilemma when $b > c > b / n$. Thus, although the good of all is maximized when everybody cooperates ($b - c > 0$), the dominant strategy in a one shot interaction is to defect since additional gains from personal participation are less than the private cost ($b / n - c < 0$).

This logic changes when the interaction is ongoing, since future expected utility gains will join present ones in influencing the rational individual's decision to cooperate or not in the production of the collective good. In particular, individual expectations concerning the future evolution of the game can play a significant role in each member's decisions. The barest notion of expectations comes from the economic concept of horizon length. The horizon length is how far an agent looks into the future or how long the agent expects to continue interacting with the other members of the group. Within this framework, agents believe that their present actions will affect those of others in the future. In particular, individuals expect that defection encourages defection and cooperation encourages cooperation (Quattrone and Tversky). But the degree to which this belief holds depends on the size of the group and the present level of production.

In earlier work, we stated the benefits and costs to the individual associated with the two actions of cooperation and defection, i.e., contributing or not to the social good. We also allowed for diverse beliefs and expectations about other individuals' actions in the future to influence each member's perception of which action, to cooperate or defect, to take (Glance 1993). Using those preference functions, we showed that if α is the rate at which individuals reevaluate their choices, and H is the horizon length that determines the discount of future returns, there is a strategy such that an individual will cooperate if the observed fraction cooperating exceeds a value f_{crit}, which is given by

$$f_{crit} = \frac{nc - b}{H\alpha(b - c)} \tag{2}$$

Thus, individuals engage in conditional cooperation, cooperating when the fraction perceived as cooperating is greater than a critical amount, and defecting when it is lower than the critical amount. Although the precise functional form of f_{crit} can depend on specific sets of beliefs, there is a wide range of preference functions for which a critical fraction appears as the determinant of cooperation (Huberman 1994).

The dynamics of cooperation is determined by the equation governing the fraction of agents cooperating at a given time. This equation was derived earlier, and it is given by Glance (1993)

$$\frac{d\hat{f}_c(t)}{dt} = -\alpha\left\{\hat{f}_c(t) - \frac{1}{2}\left[1 + \mathrm{erf}\left(\frac{\left(<\hat{f}_c(t)> - f_{crit}\right)}{\sigma\sqrt{2}}\right)\right]\right\} \tag{3}$$

where erf denotes the error function, $<\hat{f}_c> = p\hat{f}_c + (1-p)(1-\hat{f}_c)$, p is probability that an agent intending to cooperate does so successfully, and σ determines the level of uncertainty in the system. This uncertainty is made up of two parts. One is related to the connection between intent and action that we just stated. The other refers to the variance in individual characteristics that make individuals have a diversity in their outlooks or in their benefit-cost ratios (Huberman 1993).

The fixed points of this equation, which are obtained by setting the right hand to zero, give the critical sizes beyond which cooperation can no longer be sustained. In our earlier work, we showed that there is a sharp upper limit, n^*, to the size of a group which can support cooperation. Even if all members of a group larger than this size started cooperating, after a long time the whole group would switch to defection. Moreover, the outbreak of cooperation is sudden and unpredictable, taking place over a very short period of time. These predictions were observed in a number of computer experiments simulating social dilemmas.

Fluctuating Efforts

Although in the equilibrium state the number of cooperating agents does not change in time, occasional fluctuations take place whereby individuals might switch from cooperation to defection for short periods of time. These random events are due to the uncertainty that individuals have about the behavior of the others. This uncertainty can cause an individual to perceive the amount of cooperation to be different than it actually is. Because of this misperception, an individual might act against the equilibrium condition of mutual cooperation or defection, causing the system to move away from the fixed point. The more uncertainty there is in the system, the more likely it is that there will be fluctuations away from the equilibrium state.

The situation becomes more complicated if one allows for the fact that individual efforts at contributing to the common good vary from time to time. This implies that superimposed on the occasional switchings from cooperation to defection and from defection to cooperation, there is an extra source of randomness stemming from the fact that benefits fluctuate in time, thus potentially creating a complex dynamic scenario.

When fluctuations take place, the group recovers in time according to an equation that governs the dynamics of fluctuations away from the equilibrium state. This equation can be obtained by performing a linear stability analysis of eq. (3) around the fixed point, which we will denote by $\hat{f}_o$. For the sake of simplicity, in what follows we will consider the case where the equilibrium corresponds to overall cooperation, so that $\hat{f}_o \cong 1$. That is the optimal situation for the case of small groups or for individuals with long horizons. The opposite case, that of a large group of defectors, can be treated by similar methods. Denoting a small deviation from the fixed point by δ_c, the fraction of individuals cooperating at any given time will be given by

$$\hat{f}_c(t) = \hat{f}_o - \delta_c(t)$$

(4)

with $\delta_c << \hat{f}_o$. Replacing this expression in equation 3 and performing a linear stability analysis around the fixed point yields an equation for the dynamics of fluctuations around the cooperative equilibrium. As shown in the linear stability analysis of equation 3 section that follows, in the case of large uncertainties due to diversity, one obtains

$$\frac{d\delta_c(t)}{dt} = -\alpha \delta_c(t) \left[A' - \frac{2}{\sigma^3 \sqrt{2\pi}} f_{crit} \right]$$

(5)

with

$$A' = 1 + \frac{1}{\sigma \sqrt{2\pi}} \left(\frac{1}{2\sigma^2} - 1 \right).$$

If the parameter values do not change with time, the expression inside the bracket of equation 5 becomes a constant and the solutions of this equation correspond to exponential relaxation of any initial fluctuation to the state $\delta_c = 0$, i.e., overall cooperation. The characteristic relaxation time is given by the inverse of this constant bracket times the evaluation rate, α. The situation changes drastically, however, when the cooperative output that an individual can produce fluctuates in time, making the utilities change accordingly. In what follows, we will assume that the cooperative output is given by

$$b(t) = \bar{b} + \beta(t)$$

(6)

where $\bar{b}$ is the time independent benefit that results from cooperating, and the fluctuating component, $\beta(t)$, is a Gaussian random variable such that

$$\langle \beta(t) \rangle = 0$$

$$\langle \beta(t)\beta(t') \rangle = 2\sigma\delta(t - t')$$

(7)

where σ' denotes the variance in effort. Notice that the Gaussian character of the fluctuations implies that for all practical purposes the probability of observing an individual contributing a benefit above or below $\bar{b}$ by an amount exceeding three standard deviations is vanishingly small.

As shown in a later section, fluctuations in benefits translate into a time-dependent critical fraction that is given by

$$f_{crit}(t) = f_{crit} - \frac{\beta(t)}{H\alpha(b - c)}$$

(8)

with f_{crit} given by equation 2, but with b replaced with $\hat{b}$. Substituting this expression in equation 5, we obtain the equation governing the dynamics of fluctuations away from the cooperative fixed point. It is given by

$$\frac{d\delta_c(t)}{dt} = -A\delta_c(t) + B(t)\delta_c(t) \tag{9}$$

where $A = \dfrac{\alpha A' - \alpha f_{crit}}{\sigma^3 \sqrt{2\pi}}$ and $B(t) = \dfrac{\beta(t)}{\sqrt{2\pi} H\sigma^3(b-c)}$.

It also follows that $B(t)$ is a Gaussian random variable with zero mean and with autocorrelation equal to

$$\langle B(t)B(t')\rangle = \overline{\sigma}\delta(t-t'), \text{ with } \overline{\sigma} = \frac{\sigma'}{\sqrt{2\pi} H\sigma^3(b-c)} .$$

With these properties of the random function $B(t)$, equation 9 is a stochastic differential equation. In what follows we will obtain an exact solution of this equation and calculate the behavior of all the moments of δ_c.

Bursts of Defection

In order to study the role of fluctuations around the overall cooperative state, we now solve the stochastic differential equation given by equation 9 by standard methods (Arnold 1992). Since the fluctuations in $B(t)$ are Gaussian, we can use the Stratonovich formalism (Stratonovich 1967) to find the time evolution of δ_c. It is given by

$$\delta_c(t) = \delta_c(0)e^{-At+w_t} \tag{10}$$

where $\delta_c(0)$ is the initial value of the fluctuation and w_t is a Wiener process such that

$$B(t) = \frac{dw_t}{dt} ,$$

and with the property that

$$\langle w_t\rangle = 0$$
$$\langle w_t^2\rangle = \overline{\sigma}t \tag{11}$$

As can be seen from equation 10, typical fluctuations away from the cooperative state relax exponentially fast to the fixed point, a result to be expected in the case of small groups and large horizons.

A paradox appears, however, when computing the moments of $\delta_c(t)$, which are given by

$$\langle [\delta_c(t)]^m\rangle = [\delta_c(o)]^m \langle e^{-(At+w_t)m}\rangle \tag{12}$$

where m is the mth moment and $\delta_c(0)$ is the initial configuration of the fluctuating system. Using the fact that

$$\left\langle e^{mw_t} \right\rangle = e^{m^2 \sigma t},$$

this equation becomes

$$\left\langle \left[\delta_c(t)\right]^m \right\rangle = \left[\delta_c(o)\right]^m e^{-Amt + m^2 \bar{\sigma}t} \tag{13}$$

From this expression, it is clear that the higher moments grow in time with increasing order, at a rate given by $m(\bar{m\sigma} - A)$. This happens while typical realizations of the fluctuations relax exponentially fast, as indicated by equation 10. In particular, the average fraction of defecting agents, which is given by the first moment ($m = 1$) of $\delta_c(t)$, increases in time when the fluctuations in individual efforts exceed the value of A, which amounts to the condition

$$\bar{\sigma} > \alpha \sigma^2 H(b-c)\left(\sigma\sqrt{2\pi} - 1\right) \tag{14}$$

This behavior takes place in spite of the fact that typical fluctuations decay to zero, as shown by equation 10. Even more striking, the average utility to an individual, which is given by

$$\left\langle U_i(t) \right\rangle = \left\langle b\hat{f}_c(t) \right\rangle - ck_i$$

decreases in time as

$$\left\langle U_i(t) \right\rangle = \bar{b}\left[1 - \delta_c(0)e^{(\bar{\sigma}-A)t}\right] - ck_i \tag{15}$$

Therefore, a measurement of the utility over a given time interval would lead to the wrong inference that defection is the prevalent strategy, for most individuals are cooperating, as follows from equation 10. Conversely, an increasing average utility might not necessarily signal increasing levels of cooperation in a large group.

In order to understand this paradox, it is useful to remember that the higher moments of $\delta_c(t)$ are related to the probability of very unlikely events. The fact that the moments grow in time indicates that the behavior of the system is dominated by occasional bursts in which the number of individuals suddenly found to be defecting is very large, so large that the probability of their occurrence would be practically zero if the fluctuations were Gaussian in nature. These intense peaks of defection happen in spite of the fact that fluctuations in effort are normally distributed around a mean value b.

If these intermittent bursts are non-Gaussian, we need to compute the quasi-stationary distribution of fluctuations that results from their evolution over a long time period. In order to so, divide both sides of equation 9 by δ_c and integrate over a time interval T to obtain, up to a constant,

$$\ln\frac{\delta_c(T)}{\delta_c(0)} = \sum_0^T B_n \tag{16}$$

where the integral of $B(t)$ over time has been replaced by a sum over discrete time steps, at each of which the random quantity $B(t)$ acquires the value B_n.

Since the values of B_n are normally distributed random quantities with zero mean and variance $\overline{\sigma}^2$, the sum of the right hand side can be evaluated by invoking the Central Limit Theorem. Therefore, the logarithm of δ_c will be normally distributed with zero mean and variance $\overline{\sigma}^2$. In other words, δ_c is log-normally distributed according to

$$\text{Prob}[\delta_c] = \frac{1}{\delta_c \overline{\sigma} \sqrt{2\pi}} e^{-\left(\frac{(\log \delta_c)^2}{2\overline{\sigma}^2}\right)}$$

(17)

with the mean value of δ_c, μ, given by

$$\mu = e^{\overline{\sigma}^2}$$

and its variance by

$$\mu^2 \left(e^{\overline{\sigma}^2} - 1\right) .$$

This probability density function, with mean 1.0 and standard deviation 1.0, is shown in the figure, along with the Normal one with the same mean and standard deviation.

As can be seen, the log normal distribution differs from the Gaussian one in two important aspects. The first one has to do with the fact that, unlike the normal distribution, the log-normal is quite asymmetric. Thus, typical realizations of the system do not coincide with its average behavior. Second, the tail of the log-normal distribution extends much farther out than that of a normal distribution with comparable mean and variance. This can seen by the fact that for the parameters used in the figure, the ratio of the log-normal to the normal distribution at six standard deviations is 33,000, implying a finite probability for events which, when described by a normal distribution would have vanishing probability of occurring.

If fluctuations around the fixed points of the cooperative solution to social dilemmas are distributed in a log-normal fashion, they should be observable in computer simulations. But since in this case the average is dominated by rare intermittent events, care has to be exercised in the analysis of such simulations. If the simulation runs for a relatively short time, it would sample only a small fraction of the total number of possible states of the system. Thus, one would then detect the typical, or most probable, value of the observable. It is only when simulations run for long enough times to sample a finite fraction of all the states of the system that the measurements will converge to the true average of the observable.

Computer Experiments

We now describe a number of computer experiments that were performed to test the theoretical predictions made above.

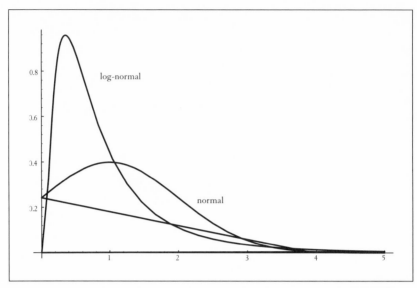

Figure 1. Probability densities for both the lognormal distribution and the normal distribution.
They were computed for the case of mean 1.0 and standard deviation 1.0.

The theory presented in this chapter predicts that the distribution of the number of individuals cooperating over time is lognormal in certain domains. In order to test this prediction, we ran experiments on the evolution of cooperation in a number of different groups characterized by different sizes, horizon lengths, uncertainty levels, and magnitudes of time fluctuations in the efforts.

The experiments consisted of event-driven Monte Carlo simulations that were conducted in asynchronous fashion, with each agent reevaluating its choice to cooperate or defect at a rate α. The agent decides whether to cooperate or defect based on the fraction f_{crit}, it observes cooperating and the choice criterion given by equation 2. That is, when the fraction observed cooperating is greater than f_{crit}, the agent will choose to cooperate; otherwise it will defect. As we pointed out above, the fraction observed cooperating differs from the actual fraction intending to cooperate in a way that depends on the amount of uncertainty in the system. Because the benefit of cooperation fluctuates stochastically in time, f_{crit} does so as well. As a result, the condition for cooperation becomes more or less severe each time an agent reevaluates its decision to cooperate or defect. The algorithm that we used is described in the section on algorithms used in the simulations.

For each experiment we recorded the number of individuals cooperating at discrete intervals. These data were then binned to yield the distribution of the number of cooperating individuals over the course of the recorded run. We then used the chi-squared probability distribution to test how well the experi-

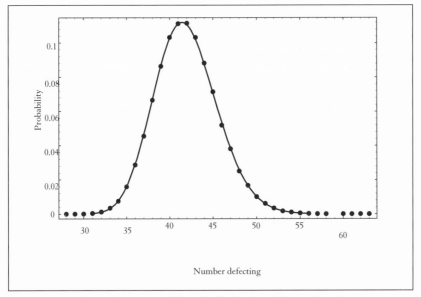

*Figure 2. Lognormal fit to the distribution of the number of
individuals defecting, sampled 5000 times at regular intervals.*

The parameters are group size n = 100, benefit for cooperation b = 2.5, standard deviation in
b due to fluctuations = 0.25, cost of cooperation c = 1, horizon length H = 69, probability of
error p = 0.9. The points represent the experimental data, while the curve is a lognormal fit to
the data. The chi-squared test, used for testing the difference between the binned data and a
continuous probability function, yields the probability 99.4% that the predicted distribution
can explain the experimental data.

mental data could be described by either a lognormal distribution or a normal
distribution.

For a number of experimental conditions, we found that a lognormal distribution could account for the observed data much better than a normal distribution could. Figure 2 shows the fit to a lognormal of the distribution of the number of individuals defecting for an experiment in which the group size was n =
100, the benefit for cooperating was b = 2.5, the standard deviation in b due to
fluctuations = 0.25, the cost of cooperation c = 1, the horizon length H = 69, and
the probability of error p = 0.9. In this case, the chi-squared test yields the probability 99.4 percent that the predicted distribution explains the experimental data, while a normal fit to the data yields a chi-squared statistic of only 4.6 percent.

While it is impossible to prove a theory statistically, these results show that
our predictions have a significantly higher probability of being correct than a
theory which would yield a normal distribution of fluctuations in the number of
individuals cooperating.

Lineal Stability Analysis of Equation 3

We now present the linear stability analysis of equation 3 around its fixed points. Equation 3 can be written as

$$\frac{d\hat{f}_c(t)}{dt} = F(\hat{f}_c) \tag{18}$$

with $F(\hat{f}_c) \equiv -\alpha[\hat{f}_c - \rho(\hat{f}_c)]$ \hfill (19)

and $\rho(\hat{f}_c) = \frac{1}{2}\left\{1 + \operatorname{erf}\left[\dfrac{\left(\langle\hat{f}_c\rangle - f_{crit}\right)}{\sigma\sqrt{2}}\right]\right\}$ \hfill (20)

with $<\hat{f}_c> = p\hat{f}_c + (1-p)(1-\hat{f}_c)$, and $0 \le p \le$.

The fixed points of this equation are determined by $F(\hat{f}_{eq}) = 0$ and their stability can be studied by performing a linear stability analysis of equation 18 around them. For the sake of simplicity, we will study the fluctuations around the cooperative fixed point $\hat{f}_o$, which obtains in the limit of small groups or individuals with long horizons. Writing

$$\hat{f}_c(t) = \hat{f}_0 - \delta_c(t) \tag{21}$$

where $\delta_c \ll \hat{f}_0$

is the deviating fraction of individuals away from the fixed point, replacing this expression in equation 18 and performing a Taylor series expansion of $F(\hat{f}_c)$ around its fixed point, we obtain

$$\frac{d\delta_c(t)}{dt} = \delta_c(t)(F'(\hat{f}_o) \tag{22}$$

where $F'(\hat{f}_o)$ denotes the derivative of $F(\hat{f}_c)$ with respect to $\hat{f}_c$ evaluated at $\hat{f}_o$. Using equations 19 and 20, and assuming $p \approx 1$, this equation can be written as

$$\frac{d\delta_c(t)}{dt} = \alpha\delta_c(t)\left\{1 - \frac{2}{\sigma\sqrt{2\pi}}\exp\left[-\frac{\left(\hat{f}_o - f_{crit}\right)^2}{2\sigma^2}\right]\right\} \tag{23}$$

where, since $p \approx 1$, the uncertainty is mostly determined from diversity of outlooks among the members of the group.

For the case of a cooperative equilibrium with long horizons, $f_o \approx 1$, and f_{crit} is small. Expanding the exponential in a power series and assuming a large uncertainty gives, to lowest order in f_{crit},

$$\frac{d\delta_c(t)}{dt} = -\alpha\delta_c(t)\left[A' - \frac{f_{crit}}{\sigma^3\sqrt{2\pi}}\right] \tag{24}$$

where $A' \cong 1 + \dfrac{1}{\sigma\sqrt{2\pi}}\left(\dfrac{1}{2\sigma^2} - 1\right)$.

How Fluctuations in Effort Affect Time Dependence

We now establish how fluctuations in effort affect the time dependence of f_{crit}. As shown in equation 2, the critical fraction is given by

$$f_{crit} = \frac{nc - b}{H\alpha(b - c)} \tag{25}$$

In the case of time-dependent benefits, $b(t) = \bar{b} + \beta(t)$, so that equation 25 becomes

$$f_{crit} = \frac{nc - \bar{b} - \beta(t)}{H\alpha(\bar{b} - c)\left(1 + \dfrac{\beta(t)}{\bar{b} - c}\right)} \tag{26}$$

For fluctuations small enough that $\beta << (\bar{b} - c)$, this can be written as

$$f_{crit} \cong \frac{nc - \bar{b} - \beta(t)}{H\alpha(\bar{b} - c)} \tag{27}$$

Or equivalently

$$f_{crit}(t) = f_{crit} - \frac{\beta(t)}{H\alpha(\bar{b} - c)} \tag{28}$$

with f_{crit} given by equation 25 but with b replaced with $\bar{b}$.

Algorithm Used in the Simulations

The algorithm used in the simulations consisted of the following steps.
1. Initialize individual actions.
2. While *current_time t* < *final_time*:

Step forword Δt in time (an exponential random deviate) to next agent re-evaluation:

Δt = 1n *(random number)* / αn—this simulates asynchronous reevaluation.

current_time t = *final_time* +Δt

Pick an agent at random for reevaluation.

Evaluate time fluctuation in benefits:

Evaluate $f_{crit}(t) \equiv \dfrac{1}{H\alpha} \dfrac{nc - b(t)}{b(t) - c}$

Evaluate number observed cooperating by individual at *current_time* as a function of the number intending to cooperate and the uncertainty h parameter, p:

$\hat{n}_c$ = binomial deviate (n_c, p) +

binomial deviate $(1 - n_c, 1 - p)$

If the fraction observed cooperating, $\hat{f}_c > f_{crit}(t)$ then individual cooperates; if $\hat{f}_c < f_{crit}(t)$ then individual defects; if $\hat{f}_c = f_{crit}(t)$ the agent cooperates with probability 0.5 and defects with probability 0.5.

Summary

In this chapter we have shown how fluctuations in the effort to produce a public good can lead to a new social phenomenon characterized by rare and intense bursts of defection superimposed on a background of overall cooperation. This phenomenon is stochastic in nature. It leads to a paradoxical behavior of the average utility accrued by any individual, for it decreases in time in spite of the fact that typically all individuals are found to be contributing the same average amount of effort. Conversely, there can be cases where an equilibrium group of defectors can generate a utility that *increases* in time, although the conditions are more restrictive than in the case of cooperation.

This paradox was observed in computer simulations of social dilemmas and should also appear in real social settings corresponding to equilibria punctuated by fluctuations. If costs or benefits fluctuate, then one would observe the fact that typical, most probable, behavior is not the same as the average. This is also reflected in the nature of the statistical distribution of the data. Rather than obtaining the familiar bell-shaped curve corresponding to a normal distribution, one would observe an asymmetric distribution with a long tail. We emphasize that the detailed form of the critical fraction used in equation 2 is not important for the existence of this effect. If the utility function has the general form given by equation 1, then fluctuations in benefits will lead to intermittent bursts in cooperation and defection.

For the purpose of verifying these predictions, computer simulations have the advantage over social experiments that the variables and parameters can be precisely specified. Although computer simulations are no substitute for real social dynamics, their relative simplicity and clear outcomes can be used as a sign that this phenomenon can appear in real social settings, in particular those situations where the average behavior of quantities reflecting collective action seems at odds with what typical members of a group are doing.

An interesting application of these results is to provide a possible explanation for the so-called paradox of group size in political movements (Oliver 1988). It has been documented that in certain cases (Marwell 1970) the larger the group, the more likely it is to engage in collective action, a result that seems at odds with the common resolution of social dilemmas. This apparent paradox was explained by Oliver and Marwell (Oliver 1988) by invoking the simple statistical fact that if what is needed to trigger a political movement is a minority of highly motivated individuals, a large group will be more likely to have such individuals than a smaller one.

This chapter presents a dynamic alternative to that view. If large temporal variations in effort exist in a social group, rare bursts of extreme cooperation could lead to an average utility that increases in time, so that individuals confronted with a social dilemma might construe a level of cooperation which is at odds with what typically everybody is doing. A test of this hypothesis could be performed by measuring the distribution of levels of effort in large political groups. Whereas the theory of Oliver and Marwell would predict that it is normally distributed around some mean value, our theory would lead to an asymmetric, log-normal type, distribution. If this were the case, it would provide a theoretical underpinnig to the folk observation that in volunteer organizations, ten percent of the people do fifty percent of the work.

On a normative vein, these results suggest that in order to secure cooperation within a group or organization, the requirements of long, diverse outlooks and small groups might not be enough. Since fluctuations in the effort of individuals are unavoidable, a group of individuals with small variance in their outputs will be more successful at generating cooperative behavior than a group of the same size made up of individuals with large temporal variations in effort. If that were not possible, the solution would then have to rely on either making controls and monitoring more efficient, or organizing the production of the common good in such a way that the overall utility due to cooperation increases faster than linear with the number of individuals in the organization. This can be the case when cooperation is used in the solution of complex problems (Clearwater 1991, Huberman 1996).

Finally, this chapter produces a dynamic derivation of the lognormal distribution, which has been used to fit data ranging from distributions of income in diverse populations to the size distributions of cities. Even for situations where one has apriori expectations of normal distributions of data, these results also suggest that outliers that are routinely rejected might actually signal a deeper regularity, that of an asymmetric distribution with a long tail underlying the phenomenon being studied. In such cases, it is warranted not only to include those extreme events in analysis of the data, but also to arrive at average measures that depart from typical behavior, one of the signatures of intermittent bursts of activity.

Acknowledgments

This work profited from useful discussions with Jon Bendor and Mette Huberman. Part of the theoretical work was done while one of the authors, BAH, was a visiting professor at CONNECT, which is part of the Niels Bohr Institute, University of Copenhagen. The warm hospitality provided by Dr. B. Lautrup and his staff is gratefully acknowledged.

6

Task Environment Centered Simulation

Keith S. Decker

The design of organizations or other coordination mechanisms for groups of agents depends in many ways on the agent's task environment. Two important dependencies are the structure of the tasks and the uncertainty in the task structures. The structure of a task includes the scope of the problems facing the agents, the complexity of the multiple choices facing the agents, and the particular kinds and patterns of interrelationships that occur between tasks. A few examples of environmental uncertainty include uncertainty about the a priori structure of any particular problem-solving episode, in the actions of other agents and in the outcomes of an agent's own actions. These dependencies hold regardless of whether the system comprises just people, just computational agents, or a mixture of the two. For example, the presence of both uncertainty and high variance in a task structure can lead a system of agents to perform better by using coordination algorithms that adapt dynamically to each problem-solving episode (Decker and Lesser 1993b, 1993c). Designing coordination mechanisms also depends on nontask characteristics of the environment such as communication cost, and properties of the agents themselves. Representing and reasoning about the task environment must be part of any computational theory of coordination.

Task analysis, environment modeling, and simulation (TÆMS) was developed as a framework with which to model and simulate complex, computationally intensive task environments at multiple levels of abstraction and from multiple viewpoints. It is a tool for building and testing computational theories of coordination. TÆMS is compatible with both formal computational agent-centered approaches and experimental approaches. The framework allows us to both mathematically analyze (when possible) and quantitatively simulate the behavior of multiagent systems with respect to interesting characteristics of the computational task environments of which they are part. By *quantitative simulation* I mean that changes are simulated and recorded in the quantitative values of task characteristics, such as duration and quality, that affect performance. I believe that TÆMS provides the correct level of abstraction for meaningfully evaluating centralized, parallel, and distributed control algorithms, negotiation strategies, and organizational designs.

This chapter will briefly describe the TÆMS modeling framework for representing abstract task environments, concentrating particularly on its support for simulation. I will describe how to model each of several different multiagent problem-solving environments, such as distributed situation assessment, hospital patient scheduling, multiphysician consultation, airport ground services management, and multiagent information retrieval. I will also discuss the generation of episodes within environments for simulation.

Background

Artificial intelligence (AI), growing as it has from the goal of modeling *individual* intelligence, or at least replicating or augmenting it, has focused primarily on representations of individual choice and action. A large effort has gone into describing the principled construction of agents that act rationally and predictably based on their beliefs, desires, intentions, and goals (Cohen and Levesque 1990, Shoham 1991). Fairly recently, researchers concerned with real-world performance have also realized that Simon's criticisms and suggestions about economics (Simon 1957, March and Simon 1958, Simon 1982) also hold for many realistically situated individual agents—perfect rationality is not possible with bounded computation (Horvitz 1988, Boddy and Dean 1989, Russell and Zilberstein 1991, Garvey, Humphrey, and Lesser 1993). Distributed AI has too often kept the individualistic character of its roots, and focused on the principled construction of individual agents. It hasn't even, so far, really concerned itself with the questions of bounded rationality in real-time problem solving when it comes to the principled construction of individual agents. Worst of all, it has failed yet to bring the environment to center stage in building and analyzing distributed problem-solving systems.

In contrast, the organizational science community has since the 1960s (e.g. Lawrence and Lorsch [1967]) regarded the task environment as a crucial, central variable in explaining complex systems, and a whole branch of research has grown up around it (contingency theory). Representations in this community are rarely mathematically formal in nature but rather try to present very rich descriptions using terms such as *uncertainty*, *decomposability*, or *stability*.

TÆMS, as a framework to represent coordination problems in a formal, domain-independent way, is unlike any existing computational representation that is focused on coordination issues. The form of the framework is more detailed in structure than many organizational-theoretic models of organizational environments, such as Thompson's notions of pooled, sequential, and reciprocal processes (Thompson 1967), Burton and Obel's linear programs (Burton and Obel 1984), or Malone's queuing models (Malone 1987), but is influenced by them and by the importance of environmental uncertainty and dependency that appear in contingency-theoretic and open systems views of organizations (Lawrence and Lorsch 1967, Galbraith 1977, Stinchcombe 1990, Scott 1987). As a problem representation for computational tasks, it is richer and more expressive than game theory (Rosenschein and Genesereth 1985; Zlotkin and Rosenschein 1991; Gmytrasiewicz, Durfee, and Wehe 1991) or team theory (Ho 1980) representations. For example, a typical game or team theory problem statement is concerned with a single decision; a typical TÆMS objective problem-solving episode represents the possible outcomes of many sequences of choices that are interrelated with one another (such as schedules). TÆMS can represent a game theoretic problem, and a single decision made by an agent faced with a TÆMS task structure could be boiled down into a game theoretic problem. (TÆMS does not say how agents make their decisions. It is perfectly reasonable for an agent to use game-theoretic reasoning processes.) Because TÆMS is more expressive, it can be used to operationalize some of the rich but informal concepts of organizational science (such as decomposability, described later in this chapter). Another difference between TÆMS and traditional distributed computing task representations is that TÆMS indicates that not all tasks in an episode need to be done.

As a tool for building and testing computational theories of coordination, the TÆMS framework can, for example, support the construction of ACTS theory instances (Carley and Prietula 1994). In ACTS theory, organizations are viewed as collections of intelligent agents who are cognitively restricted, task oriented, and socially situated. TÆMS provides ways to think about and represent environmental constraints (task characteristics and social characteristics involving communication links and what information and what possible actions are available to what agents). While simple models can sometimes be solved analytically (Decker and Lesser 1993b, 1993c), many complex models require simulation techniques. Compared to other organizational simulations (such as Lin and Carley 1993, Levitt et al. 1994), TÆMS provides a much more detailed model of task structures, and does not provide a fixed agent model.

Features of TÆMS

There are many unique features of TÆMS. TÆMS allows the explicit, quantitative representation of task interrelationships. Both hard and soft, positive and negative relationships can be represented. When relationships in the environment extend between tasks being worked on by separate agents, they are called *coordination relationships*. Coordination relationships are crucial to the design and analysis of coordination mechanisms. The set of relationships is extensible.

An example of a hard relationship is *enables*. If some task *A* enables another task *B,* then *A* must be completed before *B* can begin. An example of a soft relationship is *facilitates.* If some task *A* facilitates a task *B,* then completing *A* before beginning work on *B* might cause *B* to take less time, or cause *B* to produce a higher-quality result, or both. If *A* is *not* completed before work on *B* is started, then *B* can still be completed, but might take longer or produce a lower quality answer than in the previous case. In other words, completing task *A* is not necessary for completing task *B,* but it is helpful. For example, imagine that your task is to find a new book in a library, and you can do this either before or after the new books are unpacked, sorted, and correctly shelved.

TÆMS also represents the structure of a problem at multiple levels of abstraction. The highest level of abstraction is called a *task group* and contains all tasks that have explicit computational interrelationships. A *task* is simply a set of lower-level subtasks and/or executable methods. The components of a task have an explicitly defined effect on the quality of the encompassing task. The lowest level of abstraction is called an *executable method.* An executable method represents a schedulable entity, such as an instance of a human activity at some useful level of detail, for example, "take an x-ray of patient 1's left foot." For a computational agent, a method could also be a blackboard knowledge source instance, a chunk of code and its input data, or a totally-ordered plan that has been recalled from memory and instantiated for a task.

TÆMS makes very few assumptions about what an agent is like cognitively. TÆMS defines an agent as a locus of subjective beliefs (or state) and actions (executing methods, communicating, and acquiring subjective information about the current problem-solving episode). This is important because the study of principled agent construction is a very active area. By separating the notion of agency from the model of task environments, one does not have to subscribe to a particular agent architecture (which one would assume will be adapted to the task environment at hand). This separation also allows a user to ask questions about the inherent social nature of the task environment at hand (allowing that the concept of society may arise before the concept of individual agents [Gasser 1991]). Such a conception is unique among computational approaches.

TÆMS also represents the task structure from three different viewpoints. The first view is a *generative* model of the problem-solving episodes in an environment—a statistical view of the task structures. The second view is an *objective* view of the actual, real, instantiated task structures that are present in an episode. The third view is the *subjective* view that the agents have of objective reality. The subjective view is derived from the social situation, i.e., the organizational role of an agent may partly determine what part of the whole task structure that agent sees (and with what certainty).

For example, in this chapter I will discuss a hospital scheduling environment. The generative model describes how to generate a hospital scheduling episode (perhaps one day's worth of work). The generative model will describe how often new patients arrive at the hospital, and what procedures need to be done on them (for instance, patient 12 needs a foot x-ray and physical therapy). The resulting objective task structure episode describes, from Nature's global omniscient point-of-view, what tasks are possible as time goes forward, and how those tasks are related (perhaps the physical therapy must come after the x-ray). Finally, the generative model also generates a subjective model that describes what portions of the task structures become available to the agents and at what time. For example, only the nurse in charge of the patient's nursing unit will initially have access to the tests prescribed by the doctor for that patient; the nurse must explicitly inform ancillary hospital units such as the x-ray unit about the need for x-ray tasks on the patient.

The TÆMS representation of an objective task structure is *not* intended as a schedule or plan representation, although it intentionally provides and relies on much of the information that would go into such uses.

TÆMS allows us to clearly specify concepts and subproblems important to multiagent and AI scheduling approaches. For example, the difference between *anytime* (Boddy and Dean 1989) and *design-to-time* (Garvey 1993) algorithms in TÆMS can be clearly represented.

This chapter will focus mostly on *computational* task environments, where agents do not require shared physical resources. However, I will also describe extensions of TÆMS to represent shared physical resource constraints.

As I have mentioned, TÆMS provides a system for simulating environments: generating random episodes, providing subjective (socially situated) information to the agents, and tracking their performance. The TÆMS simulator is written in the portable common Lisp object system (CLOS) and uses CLIP (Westbrook et al. 1994) for data collection. Simulation is a useful tool for learning parameters to control algorithms, for quickly exploring the behavior space of a new control algorithm, and for conducting controlled, repeatable experiments when direct mathematical analysis is unwarranted or too complex. The simulation system that has been built for the direct execution of models in the TÆMS framework supports, for example, the collection of paired response data, where different or ablated coordination or local scheduling algorithms can be compared on identical instances of a wide variety of situations. For example, simulation has been used to explore the effect of exploiting the presence of facilitation between tasks in a multiagent real-time environment where no quality can be achieved after a task's deadline (Decker and Lesser 1993a). The generative environmental characteristics there included the mean inter-arrival time for tasks, the likelihood of one task facilitating another, and the strength of the facilitation (see the next section).

The TÆMS framework was validated by building a detailed model of the complex distributed sensor networks (DSN) environment of the distributed vehicle monitoring testbed (DVMT). Simulations of simplified DSN models show many of the same characteristics as were seen in the DVMT (Durfee et al. 1987c). I have also described models of many other environments: hospital patient scheduling, the prisoners' dilemma, airport resource management, multiagent Internet information gathering, and the pilot's associate. Some of these will be summarized in this chapter. Finally, the framework has been validated by allowing others to use it in their work—on design-to-time scheduling, on parallel scheduling, on the diagnosis of errors in local area networks, on Internet information gathering, and on learning when to apply particular coordination mechanisms. I encourage its use in exploring computational theories of human or mixed human–computer organizations as well.

Building a TÆMS Model

In this section I will give a brief example of the construction of a TÆMS objective-level model for a single episode. Typically a TÆMS user will begin with a set of representative episodes (problem instances) to model at the objective level. At this point the user decides at what level of detail he or she will model the tasks and methods (this depends on the questions being asked); what the performance measures will be (TÆMS provides duration and quality, but quality may mean different things in different environments—or even be a vector); and what task interrelationships are needed (TÆMS currently has definitions for enables, facilitates, bounded facilitates, simple facilitates, hinders, precedes, causes, shares-results, cancels, uses, limits, consumes, consumable, replenishes, full, inhibits, and requires-delay [Decker 1995]).

After building several episodes, it is easier to move on to specifying a generative model and a subjective model. The generative model deals with the question of how those episodes might actually come about, and what parts of them are routine and what parts are extraordinary. Being able to generate a large number of reasonable episodes is important especially when using simulation so that one does not jump to conclusions about only a few hand-picked examples. A generative model needs to generate both objective and subjective information for each episode. The subjective information describes, for example, what parts of the task structure are seen by agents with different organizational roles, and what information those agents can access about the task structure they perceive. Examples of some of this sort of information are the task decomposition schemes defined by Lin (1994).

Let's build a very small example using a post-office task (von Martial 1992) (I'll give much larger examples later in the chapter). A TÆMS task structure is specified at various levels of abstraction. Figure 1 shows a task structure for going to the post office to buy stamps. A directed acyclic graph of tasks connected by subtask relationships (here, it is a tree) is called a *task group*. Each task group has an identified root task (here, it is T1). Often agents know about many task groups simultaneously. A common performance measure is for the agents to at-

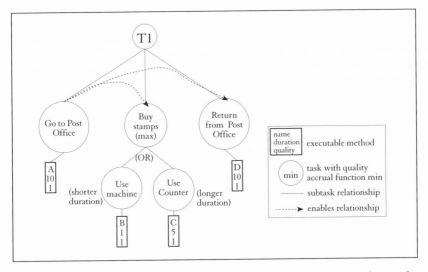

Figure 1. One possible instance of an objective task structure for buying stamps at the post office. Unless otherwise indicated, all quality accrual functions are min (AND).

tempt to maximize the sum of qualities achieved for all known task groups. Of course, not all task groups need to have equal importance, not all agents will know about all task groups, not all agents need to have the same performance criteria, task groups can have deadlines, and new task groups might appear at any time—I'll give some more complex examples later, and keep this one simple. At the leaves of the task group are tasks called *executable methods*. These are the only possible actions represented directly in the task structure. Two other classes of actions that agents can take are *communication actions* and *information-gathering actions*. Communications can be at both the domain level (of partial results of tasks) or at a meta level (communications about tasks, such as commitments to do things by a certain time). Information gathering trades off an agent's time for better or newer information about the objective problem solving structure.

Each executable method has an initial duration and an initial maximum quality. When there are no interrelationships, if an agent chooses the action of executing a method, it will take the amount of time as specified by the initial duration and produce the initial maximum quality. Quality of a nonexecutable task is some function of the qualities of the subtasks (typically max (OR), min (AND), sum, or mean). Task groups may have hard or soft deadlines—no quality can accrue for a task after a hard deadline. A good example of the difference between generative, objective, and subjective views is the specification of "duration." From the generative view, the duration of a task is often a statistical distribution, and different classes of tasks can have different duration distributions.

From the objective view, the duration of some specific task instance is a single value. From the subjective view, the agent usually doesn't know that precise value; all that it knows is the original distribution from which the objective duration was drawn.

In figure 1 the objective task group associated with buying stamps has the following structure: the root task T1 to buy stamps at the post office; subtasks to go to the post office, buy the stamps, and return from the post office; and two ways to buy the stamps at the post office that include using the stamp machine in the lobby or waiting in line to buy them at the post office counter. Each of these lowest level tasks have executable methods associated with them, and each method has an initial duration and maximum quality. On top of this basic task–subtask structure, there can be task interrelationships (nonlocal effects, or NLEs) such as *enables*. The *enables* NLE from "go to post office" to "buy stamps" is a shorthand that indicates that the enabling task *enables* all the executable methods below the enabled task (in figure 1, these are methods B and C). Every NLE has a precise quantitative definition which describes changes in duration and/or quality of the effected method. For example, the definition of the *enables* effect on maximum quality looks like this:

$$\text{enables}_Q(T_a, M, t, d, q, \theta) = \begin{cases} 0 & t < \Theta(T_a, \theta) \\ q & t \geq \Theta(T_a, \theta) \end{cases}$$

enables$_Q$ indicates that this is the effect on maximum quality, T_a is the enabling task, M is the method being enabled, t is the current time, d the current duration of M, q the current maximum quality of M, and θ is a threshold parameter only for *enables*. The definition states that the current maximum quality of the enabled method M is 0 until such time as the quality of T_a rises above the threshold θ. The helper function $\Theta(\mathbf{T}, \theta)$ returns the earliest time that the quality of T is greater than θ. I have built a large collection of these relationship definitions that are often reused, and I add to the collection whenever I find new relationships while modeling new environments.

Now let's look at an episode where there are two task groups: one (T1) to buy stamps, and another (T2) to mail a package at the post office (figure 2). Once an agent waits in line to get to the counter, the agent may both buy stamps and mail a package, so these two tasks facilitate one another. The formal definition of *facilitates* (Decker et al. 1993d, Decker 1995) takes two parameters, one for the change in duration, and one for the change in quality. In the postal example, there is no change in quality, but a large change in duration (once you wait in line to buy stamps at the counter, it is a short time to also mail a package, and vice versa). This particular episode is used by von Martial to illustrate a favors relationship, where the agent who needs to mail a package can reasonably offer to buy stamps for another agent. Note that it might not be reasonable for an agent who needs to buy stamps to offer to mail another agent's package, because the stamp-buying agent has the option of a much quicker method of buying stamps (using the ma-

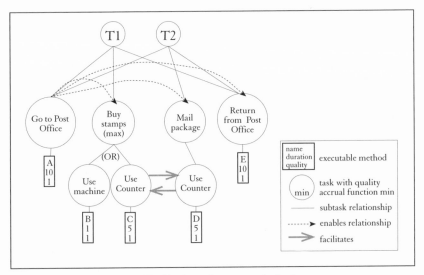

Figure 2. Possible objective task structures for buying stamps
(T1) and mailing a package (T2) at the post office.

chine) than waiting in line (which is required for mailing the package).

This has been a very simple example; I often work with much larger structures and many more agents. Note that both structures can be represented where the agents have a considerable number of choices in their actions (and need fairly complex agent models) as well as task structures where the agents are highly constrained in their actions (Carley and Prietula 1994). It is also possible to represent when an agent's capabilities or organizational role does not allow the agent to take certain actions by not creating an executable method for that agent (see the more complex examples later in this chapter).

Example TÆMS Models

The most detailed and analyzed TÆMS models are the simple and complex models of DSN and DVMT. These models include features that represent approximate processing, faulty sensors and other noise sources, low-quality solution errors, sensor configuration artifacts, and vehicle-tracking phenomena such as training and ghost tracks. This work represented the first detailed analysis of a DSN, and the first quantitative, statistical analysis of any distributed AI system outside Sen's work on distributed meeting scheduling for two agents (Sen and Durfee 1994). This was important because much of the earlier work in the area had been ad hoc, anecdotal, or based on a small number of hand-constructed examples. The details of this work have been reported elsewhere (Decker and Lesser 1993b, 1993c, Decker 1995). I have been working on models of several other, quite different, task environments.

Hospital Scheduling

This description is from an actual case study:

> Patients in General Hospital reside in *units* that are organized by branches of medicine, such as orthopedics or neurosurgery. Each day, physicians request certain tests and/or therapy to be performed as a part of the diagnosis and treatment of a patient. [...] Tests are performed by separate, independent, and distally located *ancillary departments* in the hospital. The radiology department, for example, provides x-ray services and may receive requests from a number of different units in the hospital. (Ow 1989)

Furthermore, each test may interact with other tests in relationships such as *enables*, *requires-delay* (must be performed after), and *inhibits* (test A's performance invalidates test B's result if A is performed during a specified time period relative to B). Note that the unit secretaries (as scheduling agents) try to minimize the patients' stays in the hospital, while the ancillary secretaries (as scheduling agents) try to maximize equipment use (throughput) and minimize setup times.

A generative level model of this environment would focus on the mean time between patient arrivals and the number and distribution of patient tests. Other generative parameters would include the specification of the "agents" in this environment: the number of nursing units and the number and type of ancillaries and their associated resources (e.g. how many x-ray machines can be used in parallel by ancillary 1). Thus an episode generator for Ow's hospital would have a fixed number of nursing units and ancillaries, and a fixed set of test templates corresponding to taking x-rays, physical therapy, blood tests, and so on. These templates would also contain duration distributions on how long it takes to take the x-ray, etc. Then, an arrival rate for patients and a distribution of tests (instantiated from the set of templates) for each patient would be postulated. Thus when each patient arrives, linked to that patient is a unique task structure of what needs to be done to that patient.

Figure 3 shows a hand-generated example objective TÆMS task structure corresponding to an episode in this domain and the subjective views of the unit and ancillary scheduling agents after four tests have been ordered. I use *min* (AND) to represent quality accrual because in general neither the nursing units nor ancillaries can change the doctor's orders—all tests must be done as prescribed. This figure explicitly represents the patient as a nonsharable resource (*resource-constrains* represents the pair of NLE's *uses-resource* and *resource-limits*). Note that the patient is not needed for all portions of all tests (e.g. the blood work after the blood samples have been drawn). Also note that I have not represented the patient's travel times in any way—this is an important difference from the

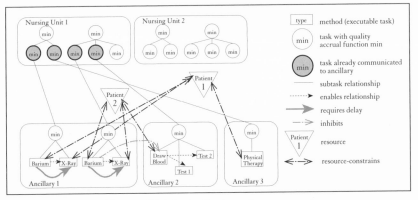

Figure 3. High-level, objective task structure and subjective views for a typical hospital patient scheduling episode.

The top task in each ancillary is really the same objective entity as the unit task it is linked to in the diagram.

airport environment described in the next section. The reason for not representing this is that the scale of the problem is such that patient travel time can be fixed beforehand (auxiliaries can assume that the patients will be delivered from their rooms rather than from other auxiliaries). I will go so far as to point out the future implications of this downplay of travel times—this hospital will have to change its organization, i.e. its coordination and scheduling mechanisms, if it has to face significant travel delays with *more than one ancillary*. This could happen if, for example, it is a smaller hospital and cannot afford its own MR scanner or CAT scanner and doctors take to prescribing MR and CAT scans at another hospital. Patients requiring *both* MR and CAT scans now have a significant *facilitates* effect in their task structures to do both scans nearly consecutively (potentially affecting the coordination structures of *both* hospitals).

The *requires-delay* relationship says that a certain amount δ of time must pass after executing one method before the second is enabled:

$$\text{requires}-\text{delay}_q\left(T_a M, t, d, q, \delta\right) = \begin{cases} 0 & \text{Start}(M) < \text{Finish}\left(T_a\right) + \delta \\ q_0(M) & \text{Start}(M) \geq \text{Finish}\left(T_a\right) + \delta \end{cases}$$

Examining the hospital's current coordination structure is enlightening because it shows a mismatch between the structure and the current hospital environment (this mismatch having triggered the study in the first place). From this mismatch it is possible to guess at how the environment has changed over time, assuming that the current hospital structure was in fact a good structure when it was originally put into place (Ow calls this the *sympathetic structure* [Ow 1989]).

The current hospital structure is described by Ow as follows:

After receiving a request from a physician, the unit secretary conveys the test request to the secretary of the relevant ancillary department. In turn, the ancillary secretary determines the appropriate time for the test to be run. The unit secretary is notified immediately prior to that scheduled time slot and not sooner. The actual time the patient is scheduled is known only to the ancillary secretary (i.e., it is not relayed back to the requesting unit). Since each ancillary schedules independently (and without knowledge) of all other ancillaries, conflicts arise when a patient is scheduled in overlapping (or nearly overlapping) time slots in different ancillaries. Such conflicts must be resolved by the unit secretaries. However, as the unit secretaries are made aware of the scheduled ancillary times only when the request to "deliver" the patient comes from the ancillary, little slack time remains to resolve scheduling conflicts and delays. This can disrupt the care of the patient (Ow 1989).

Additional problems may also ensue. For example, in some cases the *sequence* of multiple tests are important—a wrong sequence can result in patient stay delays as the residual effects of one test may influence the earliest start time of another test.

While this structure seems sorely lacking when compared to the current environment, it may at one time have been a reasonable, low overhead arrangement. It may be that in the past doctors ordered fewer tests on less complex ancillary equipment (there has been quite an explosion in medical technology in the last decade) and (concomitantly) interfering relationships between these technologies. The structure is adapted for a different task environment.

Ow and his colleagues describe a new set of coordination mechanisms using computer support that are better adapted to the hospital's current task environment. Two types of computer agents are defined—a *unit subsystem* that collects, disseminates, and monitors the test requests and resulting schedules for the patients in a unit, and an *ancillary subsystem* that receives test requests from the unit subsystems and schedules them. Two communication protocols rest on this structure:

Primary: The unit subsystems inform the appropriate ancillary about the test request (transmitting part of the task structure). The request includes a soft deadline (the "flow due date") for the task. The ancillary will schedule the test immediately, using a shared primary performance criteria of not missing the deadline and secondary local criteria such as minimizing setups, maximizing throughput, etc. All other criteria being equal, the ancillary picks the earliest slot. As soon as the slot is chosen, the scheduled slot (what generalized partial global planning [GPGP] [Decker and Lesser 1995] terms a *commitment*) is communicated back to the unit subsystem.

Secondary: As soon as a slot is scheduled for a patient at an ancillary, the slot (commitment) is *broadcast* to all other ancillaries, thus effectively blocking that slot from consideration by the other ancillaries for any tests on that patient (as indicated in the diagram by the *resource-constrains* relationships).

One thing to note about this new system is that it does not explicitly handle interactions between tests at different ancillaries. The GPGP family of coordination algorithms could be configured to respond to these interactions as well as eliminate broadcast communication.

Airport Resource Management

The airport resource management (UMASS ARM) (Hildum 1994) and Dis-ARM (Neiman et al. 1994) systems solve airport ground service scheduling problems. The function of such systems is to ensure that each airport flight receives required ground servicing (gate assignment, baggage handling, catering, fuel, cleaning, etc.) in time to meet its arrival and departure deadlines:

The supplying of a resource is usually a multistep task consisting of setup, travel, and servicing actions. Each resource task is a subtask of the airplane servicing supertask. There is considerable parallelism in the task structure: many tasks can be done simultaneously. However, the choice of certain resource assignments can often constrain the start and end times of other tasks. For example, selection of a specific arrival gate for a plane may limit the choice of servicing vehicles because of transit time from their previous servicing locations and may limit refueling options because of the presence or lack of underground fuel tanks at that gate. For this reason, all resources of a specific type cannot be considered interchangeable in the airport ground service scheduling domain (Neiman et al. 1994).

The generative model for this environment includes the nominal flight schedule, a model of the errors in this schedule (i.e., late arrival times), and the airport's resources (assuming all planes will need the same set of services). An episode is a twenty-four-hour time period including the initial, nominal flight schedule. Another possible addition to the generative model is failure rates for the servicing resources. Because the nominal flight schedule for the airport is fixed ahead of time, generating an episode mostly concerns variations in arrival time (usually delays) and equipment breakdowns. Each arriving flight spawns a task group to service that flight.

Figure 4 shows the objective task structure for a small episode with two gates, two fuel trucks, and two baggage trucks. Gate 2 has an underground fuel tank and thus allows local fuel delivery without a fuel truck. Slightly unusual relationships hold between using a gate and servicing the plane, because the gate must be held for the entire time of servicing (as opposed to a strict sequencing like *enables*). The subjective information available to any agent is the same, except for the arrival times of task groups (flights) in the future, which are only tentative.

Notice the differences between this structure and the hospital structure. Resources are much more important here and connect many more of the substructures to one another. Much of this comes out of the need to represent the effect of equipment travel times that are not represented in the hospital case (the point is not that "equipment doesn't travel in the hospital" but that the travel times of the patients can be *standardized*—an important classical coordination technique). Travel times, however, cause every action taken by a resource (such as a fuel truck) to be related to every other action in a complex way, changing the effects at each potential successive action. This strongly connected structure thus impacts

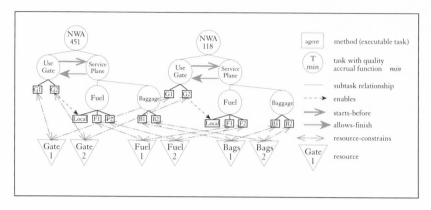

Figure 4. Objective task structure for a small airport resource management episode.

the potential coordination mechanisms used. For example, in ARM, and in real airports, this scheduling is done in a centralized manner for a fixed set of resources (although one might consider resources such as baggage trucks as "agents," in such a system these agents are slaves that only obey the commands of the central coordinator—similar to the bulldozers in Phoenix [Cohen et al. 1989]).

Such a centralized scheduling process is obviously expensive and complex in terms of computation. The Dis-ARM project (Neiman et al. 1994) looks to provide performance improvements over a centralized system by using multiple schedulers. The subjective view of the problem for each scheduler is considerably simplified by assigning each scheduler exclusive control of certain resources (for example, each scheduler could get one airport concourse of gates and a commensurate number of fuel and baggage trucks). Each scheduler tries to schedule the services locally for planes arriving in its concourse. The problem for each agent then becomes considerably simpler because it has been separated from the similar problems at other agents' concourses, and the agents can solve the problems in parallel as well. The downside is that the totally separate solutions are potentially more wasteful of resources. To combat this, the Dis-ARM system allows agents to lend resources to one another—note, however, that each lending act will connect initially unrelated task groups through resource relationships and make each agent's scheduling that much harder.

Other solutions are also suggested by the task structure. For example, since the services provided to each plane are already standardized, one could schedule the services at a constant headway (or one keyed to the business pattern, i.e., closer headway during the morning and evening rush times). Thus prescheduled and fixed slots would be established, and when a plane arrives (or soon before), it would be assigned to the next available slot (and associated gate). This technique removes the uncertainty in plane arrivals from the system (but is probably not used by airports because they wish for gate assignments to be made as early as possible, both for customers and for automated baggage handling). Another solution would be similar to the Dis-ARM structure; basically the corporate division organizational form—rather than direct negotiation, each scheduler (division) would apply for resources through a centralized "front office" (which in turn centralizes all the rapidly changing information about the resources). A modification to this structure is a matrix organization in which separate agents keep track of each class of resources (i.e., a baggage truck agent, a fuel truck agent, etc.), and then other agents are responsible for servicing the flights, drawing resources from the resource-class pools (Sycara et al. 1991).

Internet Information Gathering

Another task environment mentioned at the start of this chapter was distributed information gathering. The Internet, as well as several popular commercial services, grows by leaps and bounds daily, providing rich and varied sources of information. Fast and efficient retrievial of this information can be viewed as a set of interrelated tasks in an uncertain and dynamic environment. The same piece of data can be available via many different methods and at many different locations; at any point in time only some of those locations are accessible through some subset of methods. It is extremely common nowadays for one to know precisely where a certain answer can be found but have to undertake a time-consuming sequential search to find a currently available resource and access method. Within a single query, multiple agents could search in multiple locations in parallel and coordinate their actions when it is useful. For example, the results of work by one agent may suggest the need for some of the existing agents to gather additional information, or it might suggest the need for a new division of tasks among the agents (Oates 1994).

Generative-level information in this task environment includes the frequencies and types of queries (are the agents beholden to individuals, or are they available to the network, which would result in very different usage patterns?). It also includes information about the dynamics of the environment: how frequently do connections or links to physical information sources change, how often are the physical sources available, how often does the information on those sources change, and how often are new physical sources being added?

Figure 5 shows part of an objective level description of an example episode. Here two queries are being made—one about Macintosh information and one about movies. The Macintosh query might encompass several general sources of Macintosh information—the *TidBits* electronic newsletter, Info-Mac and other electronic file archives, Usenet newsgroups, and even standard library article searches. This particular query might be constructed by the interaction of a human user and a persistent Macintosh query intelligent agent. The task of searching each information source can be broken down into the different possible access methods for that source (for example, WAIS, FTP, HTTP, or a special-

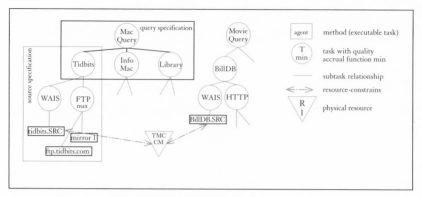

Figure 5. High-level, objective task structure for
two independent queries that resolve at one point to a single machine.

purpose agent that can use telnet to access a class of library databases). Each access method may still imply multiple physical resources (for example *TidBits* back issues can be found both at the mother site, ftp.tidbits.com, and at various mirrors of that site. Work done by retrieving from mirror sites is redundant in the TÆMS sense—but which sites are likely to be operating at all? How fast will they be? Are they accepting connections? Note that these are all TÆMS generative-level questions. One can imagine the enforcement of user performance criteria on the agents carrying out these tasks. One user might want a (not necessarily complete) answer immediately; another might be willing to wait for the agents to find the "best" answer they can find. Queries might be continuous "profiles" for information to be retrieved now and in the future as it becomes available.

Another point to note about figure 5 is the presence of shared resources linking otherwise unrelated queries. In this example, the shared physical resource is Thinking Machines' CM5 WAIS server, which stores many example WAIS databases. Other similar examples include popular mirror and archive sites like uunet.uu.net and wuarchive.wustl.edu.

Figure 6 shows more detail from a particular Macintosh query episode for a review of some Macintosh software product. Such reviews can be found both in online forms and in what were originally published paper forms (but which may now be online as well). A user may perhaps view truly published product information as being of higher quality. Online product information might be found in the review portion of the *TidBits* newsletter, or in collected product information in the Info-Mac archives, or in exchanges about a product in *Usenet News*. Finding paper reviews of a product can be reduced to locating a citation and then the actual article itself. *TidBits* contains the table of contents of the popular Macintosh magazines; some magazines are indexed by free periodical indices such as *Uncover*; sometimes the seller of a product will have both infor-

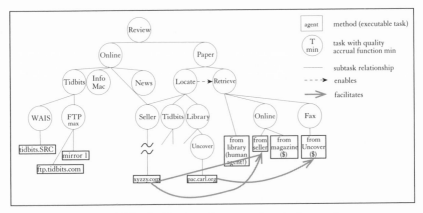

Figure 6. Midlevel, objective task structure for a single query for a review of a Macintosh product showing intraquery relationships.

mation available on the net and citations of reviews of their product. Once a citation is found, retrieval can be by hand or from online sources (but almost all of these will cost money). Note that some parts of this structure facilitate others; e.g., having used *Uncover* to come up with a citation, you can very easily have the article faxed to you at a price.

The task structure of this environment lends itself to a great deal of parallelism since a lot of work can be done in parallel and the interrelationships are relatively few and fixed. On the other hand, efficient planning for search according to a user's preferences (such as quick response? or best answer?) makes the coordination problem more one of intelligent task decomposition.

The Pilot's Associate

The global coherence problems I would like to address occur in many systems other than the DVMT, such as the pilot's associate (PA) system (Smith 1987), where situations occur that cause potentially complex and dynamically changing coordination relationships to appear between goals that are spread over several agents. Each agent in the PA system has subtasks that other agents must fulfill and receives tasks from other agents that only it can fulfill.

For example, assume a tactical situation, so the tactical planner is in control (see figure 7). It has two ordered subtasks: turn on the active sensors (request to situation assessment), and get a detailed route of the plane's movements during the tactical maneuver (request to the mission planner). Turning on active sensors causes a plane to become a transmitter and thus become easily detected (most of the time the plane uses passive sensors). Since this is dangerous, the situation assessment agent will ask the pilot-vehicle interface (PVI) to ask for pilot confirmation of the use of active sensors. The pilot, upon seeing the request,

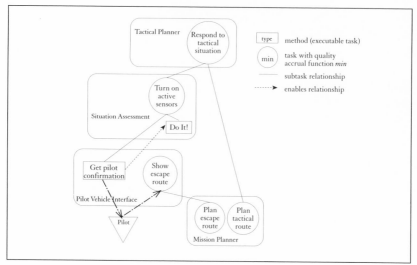

Figure 7. Dynamic situations in PA. All tasks accrue quality with Min (AND).

asks the PVI to plot the escape route of the plane on the screen in case things go wrong. The PVI passes this task to the mission planner.

Meanwhile, the tactical planner has asked the mission planner to produce the detailed route for the tactical maneuver. Which task does the mission planner act on first? From a local view, it may perhaps do the tactical planner request first because the tactical planner tasks are a high priority. But from a global perspective, unless the mission planner plans the escape route, which the pilot needs in order to authorize turning on the active sensors, which are needed for the tactical planner to do its job, the whole system performance goal of handling the tactical situation is in jeopardy. Hence, the mission planner should do the escape route plan first.

Although I do not discuss GPGP in detail here, let me briefly describe this scenario with respect to GPGP. There will be an overall deadline on the "respond to tactical situation" task, which will be inherited by the "plan tactical route" subtask. The *enables* relation between "get pilot confirmation" and "do it" (pinging the active sensors) could trigger a GPGP coordination mechanism to place an earlier deadline on the "get pilot confirmation" task when it is communicated to the PVI. The task "show escape route," based on this, would also have an earlier deadline, and thus "plan escape route" would have an earlier deadline (earlier than "plan tactical route") as well. Thus the mission planner obtains the necessary information with which to schedule the two tasks. If the time to do both tasks is more than the earlier deadline and less than the later deadline, then the scheduler can only rationally choose to do "plan escape route" first.

Support for Simulation

In order to test coordination and scheduling algorithms in general environments, the TÆMS simulator has a random task structure generator. This generator does *not* generate structures from a real application environment; the structures it generates are quite abstract. When working with TÆMS on a particular application such as those described above, I do not use this random generator, but rather one crafted to match the specific environment. Of course, components of the random task structure generator can be reused for building environment-specific generators. The random, abstract environments are useful for general experimentation and performance analysis of coordination mechanisms and organizations.

The random environment generator has three parts: specifying general environmental parameters such as the interagent communication delay, specifying a generative subjective template, and specifying the potential classes of task groups (generative objective templates).

The default generative subjective template takes a list of agent names and a simple probability $p_{overlaps}$ for the chance of overlapping methods. For each objective method generated and for each other agent, there is a $p_{overlaps}$ chance that the agent will have an overlapping method. If there is no overlapping method, then the method is unique to a single agent's capabilities or role.

All objective values are passed unchanged to the agents. Agents who execute information-gathering actions will receive information on all methods executable by them, and all parents of those methods, recursively. The default generative subjective template guarantees no other subjective properties. The level of expressiveness of the subjective model is where much of my current work on TÆMS is occurring—adding both organizational roles and better uncertainty representations.

A random environment will consist of one generative subjective template and a list of generative objective templates (one for each potential class of task groups). Each generative objective template takes parameters that indicate the average depth, branching factor, duration, max-quality, quality accumulation function distribution, deadline tightness, interarrival-time, and how redundant work should be valued.

The TÆMS random structure generator also allows the specifications of certain "patterns" of relationships on top of this basic structure. These patterns have parameters that are in addition to the generative objective template parameters just mentioned. Some patterns allow the expression of hard and soft task interrelationships (NLEs), the presence of cleanup methods (a single method that must be done to complete a task group), and the presence of fast-fallback methods (versions of regular methods that take less time but produce a lower quality).

Current Work

The TÆMS simulator has been used for several projects, some of them ongoing. Besides the verification of the analytical model of the distributed sensor network environments such as the DVMT (Decker and Lesser 1993b, 1993c), researchers at the University of Massachusetts have used TÆMS to develop new scheduling algorithms (Garvey 1993) that help a computational agent to choose what actions to take, in what order to take them, and when to take them. Ongoing work includes the development of scheduling algorithms for scheduling the work of groups of agents.

Another area of work has been the development and evaluation of the GPGP family of coordination algorithms. GPGP both generalizes and extends Durfee's partial global planning (PGP) algorithm (Durfee 1991). My approach has several unique features:

First, each mechanism is defined as a response to certain features in the current subjective task environment. Each mechanism can be removed entirely, or parameterized so that it is active for only some portion of an episode. New mechanisms can be defined; an initial set of five mechanisms has been examined. These are micro-mechanisms when compared to, for example, Mintzberg's macro-mechanisms (Mintzberg 1983), but they too can be clustered into archetypical forms (Decker 1995).

Second, GPGP works in conjunction with an existing agent architecture and local scheduler. My experimental results were achieved using a "design-to-time" soft real-time local scheduler developed by Garvey (Garvey 1993, Wagner et al. 1997). GPGP thus makes assumptions about the internal architecture of an agent (unlike TÆMS). In the GPGP approach, an agent's local scheduling component develops several possible courses of actions (the schedules), and an agent's decision-making component chooses one course to follow for some period of time. The GPGP coordination component, then, works by supplying information and constraints to the local scheduler and to other agents coordination components. The most common constraint is a *commitment* to achieve a certain level of quality for a task by a certain time.

Third, GPGP, unlike PGP, is not tied to a single domain. GPGP also allows more agent heterogeneity than PGP with respect to agent capabilities.

Finally, GPGP mechanisms in general exchange less information than the PGP algorithm, and the information that GPGP mechanisms exchange can be at different levels of abstraction. PGP agents generally communicate complete schedules at a single, fixed level of abstraction. GPGP mechanisms communicate scheduling commitments to particular tasks, at any convenient level of abstraction.

An example of a GPGP coordination mechanism is one that handles simple method redundancy. If more than one agent has an otherwise equivalent method for accomplishing a task, then an agent that schedules such a method will commit to executing it and will notify the other agents of its commitment. If more than one agent should happen to commit to a redundant method, the mechanism takes care of retracting all but one of the redundant commitments. The fact that most of the GPGP coordination mechanisms use commitments to other agents as local scheduling constraints is the reason that the GPGP family of algorithms requires cooperative agents. Nothing in TÆMS, the underlying task structure representation, requires agents to be either cooperative, antagonistic, or simply self-motivated. Details about GPGP and evaluations of the mechanisms can be found elsewhere (Decker 1995, Decker and Lesser 1995).

A Simulation Example

Let's look at a small example (from Decker and Lesser [1993d]) in which TÆMS is used as a simulator to explore hypotheses about the interactions between environmental and agent-structural characteristics. I use as an example a question explored by Burton and Obel: is there a significant difference in performance due to either the choice of organizational structure or the decomposability of technology? Technology is used here in the management science sense of "the physical method by which resources are converted into products or services" or a "means for doing work" (Burton and Obel 1984, Scott 1987).

I equate a technology with a TÆMS task structure instead of a linear program. Task structures allow me to use a clear interval measure for decomposability, namely the probability of a task interrelationship (in this example enables, facilitates, and overlaps). I define a nearly decomposable task structure to have a base probability of 0.2 for these three coordination relationships and a less decomposable task structure to have a base probability of 0.8 (see figure 8).

Burton and Obel were exploring the difference in M-form (multidivisional) and U-form (unitary-functional) hierarchical structures; here I will analyze the GPGP family of team-oriented coordination algorithms. For the structural variable, I will vary the communication of nonlocal views (just one of the GPGP coordination mechanisms). Informally, I will be contrasting the situation in which each agent makes commitments and communicates results based only on local information (no nonlocal view) with one in which the agents freely share task structure information with one another precisely when there are coordination relationships (partial nonlocal view). Figure 9 shows an example—note that in neither case does the agent have the global view of figure 8.

Burton and Obel used a profitability index as their performance measure, derived from the percentage of optimal profit achieved. In general, scheduling an arbitrary TÆMS task structure is an NP-hard problem, and so there is no access to optimal solutions. Instead performance is compared directly on four scales: the number of communication actions, the amount of time spent executing meth-

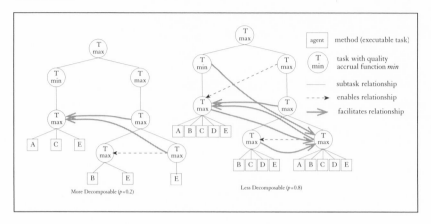

Figure 8. Example of a randomly generated objective task structure.

ods, the final quality achieved, and the termination time. Simulation runs for each of the four combinations of nonlocal view policy and level of task decomposability were done in matched sets—the randomly generated episode was the same for each combination with the exception of more coordination relationships (including more overlapping methods) being added in the less decomposable task structures. Following Burton and Obel, I used the nonparametric Friedman two-way analysis of variance by ranks test for my hypotheses. The assumptions of this test are that each block (in this case, randomly generated episode) is independent of the others and that each block contains matched observations that may be ranked with respect to one another. The null hypothesis is that the populations within each block are identical.

I generated forty random episodes of a single task group; each episode was replicated for the four combinations in each block. I used teams consisting of five agents; the other parameters used in generating the task structures are summarized in table 1, and a typical randomly generated structure is shown in figure 8. Figure 9 shows the difference in the local view of one agent with and without creating partial nonlocal views. I first tested two major hypotheses:

Hypothesis 1: There is no difference in performance between agents with a partial nonlocal view and those without. For the communication and method execution performance measures, the null hypothesis was rejected at the 0.001 level. I cannot reject the null hypothesis that there is no difference in final quality and termination time. Teams of computational agents that exchange information about their private, local views consistently exchange more messages (in this experiment, a mean increase of seven messages) but do less work (here, a mean decrease of twenty time units of work, probably due mostly to avoiding redundancy).

Hypothesis 2: There is no difference in performance due to the level of decomposability of technology. For the communication and method execution

Parameter	Value
Mean Branching Factor (Poisson)	1
Mean Depth (Poisson)	3
Mean Duration (exponential)	10
Redundant Method QAF	max
Number of Task Groups	1
Task QAF Distribution	(50% min) (50% max)
Decomposition Parameter	$p = 0.2$ or 0.8
Hard CR Distribution	(p enables) ((1-p) none)
Soft CR Distribution	(p facilitates) (10% hinders) ((0.9-p) none)
Chance of Overlaps (binomial)	p

Table 1. Parameters used to generate the forty random episodes.

performance measures, we reject the null hypothesis at the 0.001 level. I cannot reject the null hypothesis that there is no difference in final quality and termination time. Teams of computational agents, regardless of their policy on the exchange of private, local information, communicate more messages (in this experiment, a mean increase of forty-seven messages) and do more work (here, a mean increase of twenty-four time units) when faced with less decomposable computational task structures (technology).

Again following Burton and Obel, I next test for interaction effects between nonlocal view policy and level of technology decomposability by calculating the differences in performance at each level of decomposability, and then testing across nonlocal view policy. This test was significant at the 0.05 level for communication, meaning that the difference in the amount of communication under the two policies is itself different depending on whether task decomposability is high or low. This difference, however, is small (two communication actions in this experiment) and was not verified in a second independent test.

Conclusions and Future Work

In this chapter I have given an overview of the TÆMS framework with which to model and simulate complex, computationally intensive task environments at multiple levels of abstraction and from multiple viewpoints. TÆMS is a tool for building and testing computational theories of coordination and organization. Such theories can relate environmental features (such as a large variance in work-

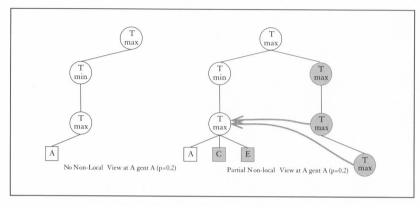

*Figure 9. Example of the local view at Agent A when the team shares
private information to create a partial nonlocal view and when it does not*

load) to useful behaviors (load-balancing metalevel communication [Decker and Lesser 1993b]). A TÆMS model provides information about the structure and other characteristics of tasks in an environment and about what task information is known and what actions can be taken by agents in certain organizational roles or with certain capabilities. TÆMS models of task environments are compatible with many popular models of agents' internal structure—evaluating a computational theory requires putting these two parts together during the simulation.

So far, TÆMS has been used primarily to computationally operationalize various aspects of textual organizational theory and to examine its impact on the design of distributed computing systems. GPGP derives some of its structure from elementary contingency theory; I am looking into a computational version of Williamson's transaction cost economics theories. I intend to apply these results to the organization of a multiagent, distributed information gathering system. Here transaction-specific investments are not physical equipment but costly metainformation about network information sources and alternatives. Other work is focusing on extending the set of GPGP coordination mechanisms and studying how agent organizations can learn to adapt their coordination mechanisms to new task environments.

Acknowledgments

This work was supported by DARPA contract N00014-92-J-1698, Office of Naval Research contract N00014-92-J-1450, and NSF contract IRI-9321324. The content of the information does not necessarily reflect the position or the policy of the Government, and no official endorsement should be inferred.

Organizations and Information Technology

7

An Organizational Ontology for Enterprise Modeling

Mark S. Fox, Mihai Barbuceanu,
Michael Gruninger, & Jinxin Lin

What is an organization and how do we model it in an information system? Many disciplines have explored the former and every information system built has created a version of the latter. The purpose of this chapter is to explore modeling of organizations in information systems from the perspective of artificial intelligence.

As information systems play a more active role in the management and operations of an enterprise, the demands on these systems have also increased. Departing from their traditional role as simple repositories of data, information systems must now provide more sophisticated support to manual and automated decision making; they must not only answer queries with what is explicitly represented in their enterprise model, but must also be able to answer queries with what is *implied* by the model. The goal of the TOVE enterprise modeling project is to create a next generation common sense enterprise model. By *common sense* we mean that an enterprise model has the ability to deduce answers to queries that require relatively shallow knowledge of the domain.

We are taking what can be viewed as a "second-generation knowledge engineering" approach to constructing our common sense enterprise model. Rather than extracting rules from experts, we are "engineering ontologies." An *ontology* is a formal description of entities and their properties, relationships, constraints, and behaviors. Our approach to engineering ontologies begins with a definition of the ontology requirement. We create this definition by asking questions that an ontology must be able to answer. We call this process the *competency* of the ontology. Next, we define the terminology of the ontology—its objects, attributes, and relations. In our third step, we specify the definitions and constraints on the terminology, if possible. Our specifications are represented in first order logic and implemented in Prolog. Finally, we test the competency of the ontology by proving the competency questions with Prolog axioms.

Our initial efforts have focused on ontologies to support reasoning in industrial environments. The tasks that we have targeted to support are in supply chain management, which extends MRP to include logistics and distribution;and concurrent engineering, which looks at issues of coordination of engineering design. Our efforts have been focused on the creation of representations of organizational behavior, such as activity, state, causality, and time; and the objects they manipulate, including resources (Fadel 1994, Fadel et al. 1994), inventory, orders, and products. We also have efforts underway in formalizing knowledge of ISO 9000 quality (Kim and Fox 1993), activity-based costing (Tham et al. 1994), and organizational agility. This chapter describes the organizational ontology being developed as part of the TOVE project. In particular, it focuses on organizational structure, roles, authority, and empowerment.

What Is an Organization?

We consider an organization to be a set of constraints on the activities performed by agents. This view follows that of Weber (1987), who views the process of bureaucratization as a shift from management based on self-interest and personalities to one based on rules and procedures.

Mintzberg (1983) provides an early, informal analysis of organizational structure. He isolates the five basic parts of an organization and the five distinct organizational configurations that are encountered in practice. His ontology includes several mechanisms that together achieve coordination, such as goals, work processes, authority, positions, and communication. The various parts of an organization are distinguished by the specific roles they play in achieving coordination with the above means.

The "language and action perspective" (Winograd 1987) on cooperative work in organizations provides an ontology that emphasizes the social activity by which agents generate the space of cooperative actions in which they work, rather than the mental state of individuals. The basic idea of Winograd's perspective is that social activity is carried out by language and communication. The pragmatic nature of communication as the way of creating commitments among participants is exploited in Flores's Coordinator system (Flores et al. 1988).

In the same vein, Auramaki and his colleagues (1988) present a method for modeling offices as systems of communicative action through which people engage in actions by creating, modifying, and deleting commitments that bind their current and future behaviors.

Lee (1988) looks at language acts in the bureaucratic office, viewing language not as a mechanism for information transfer but as a mechanism for social interaction and control. He presents a logic-based representation of deontic notions—authorization, permission, and prohibition—and shows how this can be used to model cooperative work in the office.

More recently, Yu and Mylopoulos (1994) have proposed a framework for modeling organizations made of social actors that are intentional (with motivations, wants, and beliefs), and strategic (evaluating their opportunities and vulnerabilities with respect to each other). This formal model is used to explore alternative process designs in business reengineering.

Ontology Competence

A problem in the engineering of ontologies is their evaluation. A number of criteria have been proposed (Fox et al. 1993; Gruber 1993), including functional completeness, generality, efficiency, perspicuity, precision and granularity, and minimality. We will discuss these criteria briefly in the following paragraphs.

To determine *functional completeness,* we must ask the question: Can the ontology represent the information necessary to support some task?

To determine *generality,* we must ask to what degree is the ontology shared between diverse activities such as engineering design and production, or design and marketing? Is the ontology specific to a sector such as manufacturing, or applicable to other sectors such as retailing or finance?

Efficiency is determined by asking: Does the ontology support efficient reasoning, i.e., space and time, or does it require some type of transformation?

Perspicuity is determined by asking: Is the ontology easily understood by the users so that it can be consistently applied and interpreted across the enterprise? Does the representation document itself?

Precision or *granularity* is determined by asking: Is there a core set of ontological primitives that are partitionable, or do they overlap in meaning? Does the representation support reasoning at various levels of abstraction and detail?

Finally, *minimality* is determined by asking: Does the ontology contain the minimum number of objects (i.e., terms or vocabulary) necessary (Gruber 1993)?

The criterion we have found most useful is *competence.* Tasks in which the ontology is to be employed impose a set of requirements on the ontology. These requirements can be specified as a set of queries that the ontology should be able to answer, if it contains the relevant information. Such requirements, which we call *competency questions,* are the basis for a rigorous characterization of the information that the ontology is able to provide to the task. Competency questions are benchmarks in the sense that the ontology is necessary and sufficient to represent the tasks specified by the competency questions and their solution. They are also those tasks for which the ontology finds all, and only, the correct solutions. Tasks such as these can serve to drive the development of new ontologies and can also justify and characterize the capabilities of existing ontologies.

This characterization of competency raises an important issue: Where does the representation end and inference begin? If no inference capability is to be assumed, then query processing is reducible to looking up an answer that is represented explicitly. In contrast, object and semantic network representations assume at least inheritance as a deduction mechanism. In defining an ontology, a key question then becomes: should we be restricted to just a terminology? Should the terminology assume an inheritance mechanism or some type of theorem-proving capability as provided, say, in a logic programming language with axioms restricted to Horne clauses (i.e., Prolog)? What is the deductive capability that is to be assumed by an ontology? In the TOVE project, we assume a theorem prover of the power of Prolog.

The basic entities in the TOVE ontology are represented as objects with specific properties and relations. These objects are structured into taxonomies, and the definitions of objects, attributes, and relations are specified in first-order logic. The ontology is defined in the following way. First, we identify the objects in our domain of discourse. They will be represented by constants and variables in our language. Next, we identify the properties of the objects and the relations that exist over them. The properties and relations will be represented by predicates in our language. Third, we define a set of axioms in first-order logic to represent the constraints over the objects and predicates in the ontology. This set of axioms provides a declarative specification for the various definitions and constraints on the terminology. Then we prove the competency of the ontology. The ontology must contain a necessary and sufficient set of axioms to represent and solve our questions, thus providing a declarative semantics for the system. It is in this sense that we claim to have a competent ontology, and it is this rigor that is lacking in previous approaches to ontology engineering.

Competency questions are generated because the ontology must be able to support the various tasks in which it is employed. Within our applications of activity and time ontology, these tasks include planning and scheduling, temporal projection, execution monitoring and external events, hypothetical reasoning, and time-based competition. We will explore these tasks in greater detail in the following paragraphs.

Planning and scheduling: What sequence of activities must be completed to achieve the goal? At what times must these activities be initiated and terminated?

Temporal projection: Given a set of actions that occur at different points in the future, what are the properties of resources and activities at arbitrary points in time? These actions include the management of resources and activity-based costing (where we are assigning costs to resources and activities).

Execution monitoring and external events: How do external and unexpected events (such as machine breakdown or the unavailability of resources) effect the enterprise model?

Hypothetical reasoning: What will happen if we move one task ahead of schedule and another task behind schedule? How will orders be affected if we buy another machine?

Time-based competition: We want to design an enterprise that minimizes the cycle time for a product (Blackburn 1991). This is essentially the task of finding a minimum duration plan that minimizes action occurrence and maximizes concurrency of activities.

We propose the following set of competency questions for the organizational ontology. (These questions are not meant to be complete, but simply indicative of what is needed.)

Structure Competency

Representative structure competency questions include the following:
- What role does an agent play?
- Which division does the agent belong to?
- Who must the agent communicate with?
- What kinds of information does the agent communicate?
- Who does the agent report to?
- Is a role a generalization of another role?

In linking the structure of an organization with the behavior of agents within that organization, we must define how the organizational ontology is integrated with the activity ontology. If we consider an organization to be a set of constraints on activities performed by agents, then competency questions for the organizational ontology are extensions of the temporal projection and plan existence problems, incorporating the abilities and obligations of agents. The temporal projection problem is used to characterize the constraints that agents must satisfy to perform activities. Plan existence characterizes the set of achievable goals.

Behavior Competency

Behavior competency questions include the following:
- What are the goals of the organization?
- What are the goals of a role?
- What are the goals of person X?
- What activities are available for a role to achieve its goal?
- What resources are available to achieve a goal?

Authority, Empowerment and Commitment Competency

Finally, the questions concerning authority, empowerment, and commitment include:
- What resources does the person have authority to assign?

- In order to perform a particular activity, whose permission is needed?
- What activities may a person execute under his or her own authority?

Activity and Time Ontology

In this section we define the ontology of time and action that is used to represent the behavior of the organization. An important component of behavior representation is the ability to temporally project—that is, to determine the possible set of future states given a current state. Temporal projection induces a number of requirements on the ontologies.

First, temporal projection requires the evaluation of the truth value of a proposition at some point in time in the future. We must therefore define axioms that express how the truth of a proposition changes over time. In particular, we need to address the frame problem and express the properties and relations that change or remain constant as the result of an activity.

Second, we must define the notion of a state of the world, defining what is true of the world before and after performing different activities. This definition is necessary to express the causal relationship between the preconditions and effects of an activity.

Third, the time interval over which the state has a certain status is bounded by the times when actions that change status occur. This interval defines the duration of an enabled state, and is essential for the construction of schedules.

Fourth, we want a uniform hierarchical representation for activities (aggregation). Plans and processes are constructed by combining activities. We must define precisely how activities are combined to form new ones. The representation of such combined activities should be the same as the representation of the subactivities. Thus, aggregate activities (sets of activities or processes) should themselves be represented as activities.

Finally, the causal and temporal structure of states and subactivities of an activity should be explicit in the representation of the activity.

Situation Calculus Specification

We represent time as a continuous line. On this line, time points and time periods (intervals) are defined as the domain of discourse. We define a relation $<$ over time points with the intended interpretation that $t < t'$ iff t is earlier than t'.

One important property must be represented to define what holds in the world after performing an action that captures the notion of causality. How do we express these notions if we have a continuous time line? The extended situation calculus of Pinto and Reiter (1993) allows us to incorporate the notions of situations and a time line by assigning durations to situations.

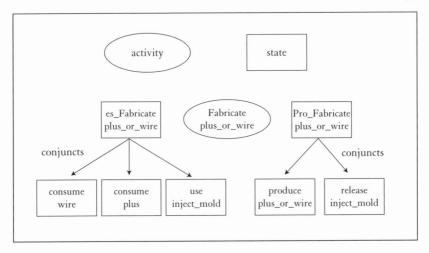

Figure 1. Activity-state cluster.

The intuition behind the situation calculus is that there is an initial situation and that the world changes from one situation to another when actions are performed. There is a predicate Poss (a, σ) that is true whenever an action a can be performed in a situation σ.

The structure of situations is that of a tree; two different sequences of actions lead to different situations. Thus, each branch that starts in the initial situation can be understood as a hypothetical future. The tree structure of the situation calculus shows all possible ways in which the events in the world can unfold. Therefore, any arbitrary sequence of actions identifies a branch in the tree of situations.

Further, we impose a structure over situations that is isomorphic to the natural numbers by introducing the notion of successor situations (Reiter 1991). The function do (a, σ) is the name of the situation that results from performing action a in situation σ. We also define an initial situation denoted by the constant σ^0.

Situations are assigned different durations by defining the predicate *start*(σ, t) (Pinto and Reiter 1993). Each situation has a unique start time that begins at 0 in σ^0 and increases monotonically away from the initial situation.

To define the evaluation of the truth value of a sentence at some point in time, we use the predicate holds (f, σ) to represent that ground literal f is true in situation σ. Using the assignment of time to situations, we define the predicate *holds* $_T(f, t)$ to represent the fact that some ground literal f is true at time t. A fluent is a predicate or function whose value may change with time.

Another important notion is that actions occur at points in time. The work of Pinto and Reiter (1993) extends the situation calculus by selecting one branch of the situation tree to describe the evolution of the world as it actually unfolds. This is done using the predicate actual. To represent occurrences, we introduce two predicates, *occurs(a, σ)* and *occurs*$_T$*(a, t)*, defined as follows:

occurs(a, σ) ≡ *actual(do(a, σ))*
occurs$_T$*(a, t)* ≡ *occurs(a, σ)* ∧ *start(do(a, σ), t)*

We now apply this formalism to the representation of activities in an enterprise.

Activity and Time Terminology

At the heart of the TOVE enterprise model lies the representation of an activity and its corresponding enabling and caused states (Sathi et al. 1985; Fox et al. 1993). In this section, we examine the notion of states and define how properties of activities are defined in terms of these states. An activity is the basic transformational action primitive with which processes and operations can be represented. Activities specify how the world is changed. An enabling state defines what has to be true of the world in order for the activity to be performed. A caused state defines what is true of the world once the activity is complete.

An activity, along with its enabling and caused states, is called an activity cluster. The state tree, linked by an *enables* relation to an activity, specifies what has to be true in order for the activity to be performed. The state tree, linked to an activity by a causes relation, defines what is true of the world once the activity has been completed. Intermediate states of an activity can be defined by elaborating the aggregate activity into an activity network (figure 1).

There are two types of states: terminal and nonterminal. In figure 1, es_fabricate_plug_on_wire is the nonterminal enabling state for the activity fabricate_plug_on_wire and pro_fabricate_plug_on_wire is the caused state for the activity. The terminal conjunct substates of es_fabricate_plug_on_wire are consume_wire, consume_plug, and use_inject_mold, since all three resources must be present for the activity to occur. The terminal states of pro_fabricate_plug_on_wire are produce_plug_on_wire and release_inject_mold.

In TOVE there are four terminal states. They are represented by the predicates *use(s, a)*, *consume(s, a)*, *release(s, a)*, and *produce(s, a)*. These predicates relate the state with the resource required by the activity. A resource is used and released by an activity if the properties of a resource remain unchanged when the activity is successfully terminated and the resource is released. A resource is consumed or produced if some property of the resource is changed after termination of the activity, including the existence and quantity of the resource or some arbitrary property such as color. Thus, *consume(s, a)* signifies that a resource is to be used up by the activity and will not exist once the activity is completed, while *produce(s, a)* signifies that a resource that did not exist prior to the performance of the activity has been created by the activity. We define use and consume states to be enabling states because the preconditions for activities refer to the properties of these states. We define release and produce states to be caused states because their properties are the result of the activity.

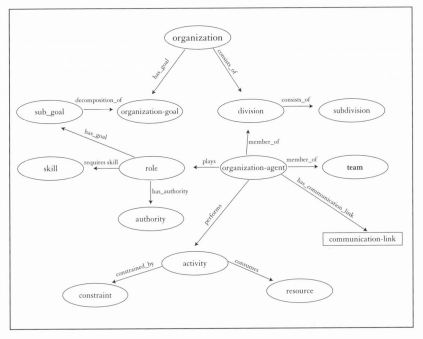

Figure 2. Organizational object taxonomy.

Terminal states are also used to represent the amount of a resource that is required for a state to be enabled. For this purpose, the predicate *quantity(s, r, q)* is introduced, where *s* is a state, *r* is the associated resource, and *q* is the amount of resource *r* that is required. Thus, if *s* is a consume state, then *q* is the amount of resource consumed by the activity; if *s* is a use state, then *q* is the amount of resource used by the activity; and if *s* is a produce state, then *q* is the amount of resource produced.

A state may have a status whose value is one of the constants *possible, committed, enabled, completed, disenabled,* or *reenabled*. The status of a state is changed by the actions *commit(s, a), enable(s, a), complete(s, a), disenable(s, a),* or *reenable(s, a)*. Note that these actions are parametrized by the state and the associated activity.

Similarly, activities have a status whose value is one of the constants *dormant, executing, suspended,* or *completed*. The status of an activity is changed by the actions *execute(a), suspend(a),* or *complete(a)*.

As part of our logical specification of the activity ontology, we define the successor axioms that specify how the aforementioned actions change the status of a state. These axioms provide a complete characterization of the value of a fluent after performing any action. Consequently, we can use the solution to the frame problem in Reiter (1991). If we are given a set of action occurrences, we can solve the temporal projection problem (determining the value of a fluent at any point in time) by first finding the situation containing that time point and then using the successor axioms to evaluate the status of the state in that situation. We present one of the successor axioms in the ontology:

> The status of a state is committed in a situation iff either a commit action occurred in the preceding situation or the state was already committed and an enable action did not occur.

$(\forall\ s,\ a,\ e,\ \sigma)\ holds(status(s,\ a,\ committed),\ do(e,\ \sigma)) \equiv (e = commit(s,\ a)\ \wedge$
$holds(status(s,\ a,\ possible),\ \sigma)) \vee (\neg(e = enable(s,\ a))\ \wedge\ holds(status(s,\ a,\ committed),\ \sigma))$

A more complete specification can be found in Gruninger and Fox (1994).

Organizational Terminology and Axioms

In this section we introduce the basic terminology and axioms of our organizational ontology. Figure 2 shows the basic elements of our organizational ontology.

We consider an organization to be a set of constraints on the activities performed by agents. In particular, an organization consists of a set of divisions and subdivisions (recursive definition), a set of organization agents (said to be members of a division of the organization), a set of roles that the members play in the organization, and an organization goal tree that specifies the goal (and its decomposition into subgoals) the members are trying to achieve. For example, the department of industrial engineering (IE) can be modeled as an organization having a number of goals related to education and research. Subdivisions include the enterprise integration laboratory (EIL); the human-computer interfaces laboratory; a number of organizational agents, consisting of individual faculty, research staff, and students; and roles such as professors, students, teaching assistants, and general-secretaries.

An organization-agent (or agent) plays one or more roles. Each role is defined by the goalset that it must fulfill. Each role is also given enough authority to achieve its goals. Agents perform activities in the organization and consume resources (such as materials, labors, or tools). The constraint set limits the agent's activities. An agent can also be a member of a team created to perform a special task. An agent has skill requirements and a set of communication links defining the protocol with which it communicates with other agents in the organization.

In the remainder of this chapter, we use o to denote organization, d to denote division, oa or agent to denote organization-agent, r to denote role, cl to denote communication link, g to denote goal, ath to denote authority, a to denote activity, s to denote state, sk to denote skill, tm to denote team, t to denote time, and con to denote constraints.

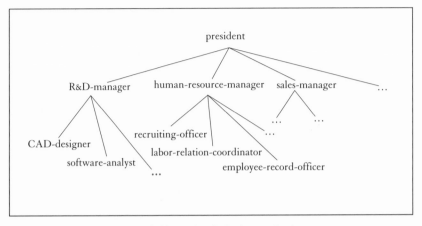

Figure 3. Hierarchy of roles in organization.

An organization consists of divisions with goals that the organization is actively pursuing:

consist_of(o, d)

has_goal(o, g)

Role

Roles define one or more prototypical job functions in an organization. Each role is associated with the following goals, processes, authority, skills, policies, and resources.

Goals include one or several goals that the role is intended to achieve.

has_goal(r, g)

Processes are activity networks that have been defined to achieve the goals.

has_process(r, a)

Authority is needed for the role to achieve its goals. Authorities include the right to use resources, the right to perform activities, and the right to execute status-changing actions (we will discuss activity and status changing action in a later section).

has_authority(r, ath)

Skills are required for the realization of the job functions.

requires_skill(r, sk)

Policies are constraints on the performance of the role's processes. Such constraints are unique to the organizational role.

has_policy(r, con)

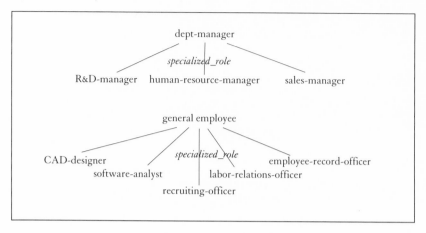

Figure 4. Role generalization and specialization.

Resources may be allocated to a role for disposition under its authority.

has_resource(r, rs)

Role Hierarchy

Within the organization, there is usually a hierarchy of roles. Figure 3 depicts one president role, several dept-manager roles, and many general employee roles, where general employees are subordinate to dept-managers.

For example, recruiting-officer is a subordinate of human-resource-manager, which, in turn, is a subordinate of president. We denote *subordinate_of(r, r′)* to mean role *r* is a subordinate of role *r′*. The *subordinate_of* relation establishes some kind of ranking of roles. A role higher in the hierarchy is of higher rank. It is obvious that subordinate relation is transitive:

subordinate_of(r1, r2)∧subordinate_of(r2, r3) ⊃ subordinate_of(r1, r3).

The relation is also nonreflexive and antisymmetric; no role is subordinate to itself, and no two roles can be subordinate to each other.

¬ subordinate_of(r, r).
subordinate_of(r, r′) ⊃ ¬ subordinate_of(r′, r).

If a role is subordinate to another role, then the latter is called the superior of the former:

subordinate_of(r, r′) ≡ superior_of(r, r′).

In an organization with centralized authority, authority increases up the role hierarchy based upon the subordinate relation. Therefore, the top executive (usually the president) has ultimate authority for everything in the organization. For this type of organization, we have:

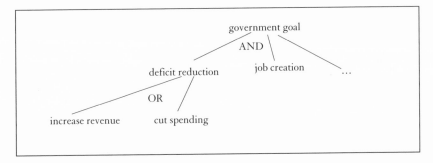

Figure 5. Subgoal tree.

$subordinate\_of(r, r') \equiv [(\forall \, ath)has\_authority(r, ath) \supset has\_authority(r', ath)]$
$\land \, (\exists \, ath')has\_authority(r', ath') \land \neg has\_authority(r, ath').$

That is, r is a subordinate of r' if r has strictly less authority than r'. In real life, organizations with decentralized authority are more common.

Role Generalization and Specialization

Besides the subordinate relation, different roles may also relate to each other through the concept of generalization and specialization (Sandhu et al. 1994). A role may be a generalized or specialized role of another. For example, R&D-manager, human-resource-manager, and sales-manager are all specialized roles of the dept-manager role, and CAD-designer and software-analyst are specialized roles of general-employee role (figure 4). In this case, dept-manager and general-employee are generalized-roles.

Clearly, specialization and generalization can be captured by class, subclass, and instance in object-oriented systems. However, because of the special characteristics of roles, we use a new relation, $specialized\_role(r, r')$ to mean r is a specialized role of r'. And the reverse relation $generalized\_role(r, r')$ is defined as:

$generalized\_role(r, r') \equiv specialized\_role(r', r).$

Specialized roles inherit all the authority from their generalized roles:

$(1)specialized\_role(r, r') \land has\_authority(r', ath) \supset has\_authority(r, ath).$

Thus, R&D-manager, human-resource-manager, and sales-manager inherit all the rights that belong to the dept-manager role., and software-analyst and recruiting-officer inherit the rights of general-employee. Axiom (1), the inheritance property, allows us to grant rights to a whole class of organization-agents without the need to do so one by one. For example, if the quarterly earning information of the company is made available to the dept-manager role, it is automatically available to the R&D-manager, human-resource-manager, and sales-manager roles. Daily news or report of the company is often directed to the general-employee role so every employee in the company can access it.

Goal

Our ontology models organizational goals can be decomposed into AND/OR sub-goal trees and are achieved by executing activity clusters. Figure 5 shows the goal of a government, which is decomposed into subgoals deficit reduction, job creation, and others, and where deficit reduction goal is decomposed into increase revenue or cut spending goal.

The nodes in the subgoal tree have dependency relations among them. Let achieved (g, t) mean the organizational goal g has been achieved at time t. Then it is clear that for a goal g, which is decomposed into several subgoals $g1, ..., gn$ with the AND relationship, we have

achieved(g, t) $\equiv$ achieved $(g1, t) \wedge ... \wedge$ *achieved(gn, t)*.

If the relationship is OR, we have

achieved(g, t) $\equiv$ achieved $(g1, t) \vee ... \vee$ *achieved(gn, t)*.

A goal $g1$ is said to depend on goal $g2$ if $g1$ can not be achieved unless $g2$ has been achieved previously:

depend_on(g1, g2) $\equiv$ $(\forall t)[achieved(g1, t) \supset achieved(g2, t)]$.

Let decomposition_of (g, g') mean that goal g is a node in the subgoal tree of g'. Then every goal of a role in an organization is a decomposition (subgoal) of some goal of the organization.

has_goal(r, g) $\supset$ $(\exists g')$ *has_goal(o, g')* $\wedge$ *decomposition_of(g, g')*.

Subgoaling ensures that everyone in the organization contributes to the overall goal of the organization, and enables us to say that the individual goal is consistent with the overall goal.

The goal of a subdivision is a goal or a subgoal of its parent division:

has_goal(d, g) $\wedge$ *subdivision_of(d, d')* $\supset$ *has_goal(d', g)* $\vee$ $(\exists g')$ *has_goal(d', g')*
$\wedge$ *decomposition_of(g, g')*.

Organization Agent, Division, Team

An organization-agent *(oa)* is an individual human member of an organization. The organization-agent concept can also be extended to include machine and software agents if needed. An organization-agent is a member of a division, plays one or more roles in the organization, can perform activities, and communicates with other *oas* using communication-links.

member_of(oa, d)
plays(oa, r)

has_communication_link(oa, cl)

If an agent is assigned to a role, then a commitment is created to achieve the goal(s) of the role. The goals of an agent are defined as the goals of the roles that the agent plays:

has_goal(oa, g) $\equiv$ $(\exists r)$ *plays(oa, r)* $\wedge$ *has_goal(r, g)*.

The authority of the agent is the authority of the roles that the agent plays:

$has\_authority(oa, ath) \equiv (\exists\, r)\, plays(oa, r) \wedge has\_authority(r, ath).$

Each organization-agent is a member of or is affiliated with a division (or sub-division) in the organization. In our model, each agent is a member of a division:

$(\forall\, oa)\, (\exists\, d) member\_of(oa, d).$

An agent can be a member of more than one division. This is shown by the following axiom, where $home\_div(oa, d)$ means that the home division of agent oa is d:

$home\_div(oa, d) \wedge home\_div(oa, d') \supset d = d'.$

An organization-agent may also be a member of some teams set up to pursue specific tasks in the organization. Compared to a division, which is usually a long-term setup within the organization, a team is temporary in nature and is usually set up when needed. Members of a team may be from different divisions and there may be many teams within the organization. The relationship between an agent and a team is member_of(oa, tm), which means agent oa is a member of team tm.

Only two or more members can form a team; hence we have:

$(\forall\, tm)\, (\exists\, oa, oa')\, oa \neq oa' \wedge member\_of(oa, tm) \wedge member\_of(oa', tm).$

A team, as a whole, can play a role in the organization. If everyone in a team plays a same role, we also say that the team plays the role

$(\forall\, r, tm)\, [(\forall\, oa)\, member\_of(oa, tm) \wedge plays(oa, r)] \supset plays(tm, r).$

Communication-Links

Communication-links are established among organizational agents in various roles. Communication-links capture the notion of benevolent communication in which agents who regard each other as peers volunteer information that they believe is relevant to other agents. This exchange does not create obligations for any agent.

The communication-link is a unidirectional link used to communicate information from one agent to another. It describes, for an agent in a given organizational role, the information the agent is interested in receiving as well as the information it can benevolently distribute to others.

For example, an agent in the C++ programmer role may distribute information about the state of the file server to other programmers, alerting them each time the server is down.

The communication-link specifies the following:

- Sending-Agent: the agent sending information along the link

  $has\_sending\_agent(cl, oa)$

- Receiving-Agent: the agent receiving information from the link

  $has\_receiving\_agent(cl, oa)$

- Sending-Role: the organizational role played by the sending agent

  has_sending_role(cl, r)

- Receiving-Role: the organizational role played by the receiving agent

  has_receiving_role(cl, r)

- Interests: the information interests of the receiving agent

  has_interest(cl, inf)

- Volunteers: the information the sending agent can supply to other agents

  will_volounteer(cl, inf)

It is understood that information distribution in the aforementioned case is noncommittal in the sense that it does not create obligations for either the sender or the receiver. Our axiomatization of the communication-link focuses on consistency, in particular, that the agent specified by a communication-link also has the role specified by the link.

has_sending_agent(cl, oa) ∧ *has_sending_role(cl, r)* ⊃ *has_role(oa, r)*
has_receiving_agent(cl, oa) ∧ *has_receiving_role(cl, r)* ⊃ *has_role(oa, r)*

Authority and Commitment

A special kind of authority is the control relationship between two organizational agents (*oa*). For *oa*1 to have authority over *oa*2 implies that *oa*1 is able to extract a commitment from *oa*2 to achieve a goal that is defined as part of *oa*2's organization-roles. In order to extract that commitment, *oa*1 has to be related directly or indirectly by a communication-with-authority (*cwa*) link relation.

communication_with_authority(cwa)
has_supervisor(cwa, oa)
has_supervisee(cwa, oa)

The communication-with-authority link, used when communication is intended to create obligations, specifies the two agents; one in the authority position (called supervisor) and the other in the controlled position (called supervisee), between which communication takes place. Because we model communication as an exchange of speech-acts, authority of an agent appears as the set of speech-acts the agent can use to create obligations for the other agent. For example, an agent may have authority to request another agent to perform action *a*1, but not to perform action *a*2. In this case, the second agent will have to commit to achieving *a*1 when requested by the first agent, but not *a*2.

We now introduce a set of four properties for the communication-with-authority relation that delineate the extent of authority that can be exercised by a supervisor.

The *has_goal* property defines the set of goals that the supervisor can assign to the supervisee.

has_goal(cwa, g)

The *has_resource* property defines the set of resources that the supervisor can allocate to the supervisee.

has_resource(cwa, rs)

The *has_empowerment* property defines the set of empowerment the supervisor can assign to the supervisee (more on empowerment later).

has_empowerment(cwa, em)

Finally, the *has_role* property defines the roles that the supervisor can assign to the supervisee.

has_roles(cwa, r)

The authority relationship is defined among agents in given organizational roles. An agent in a project-manager role can request another agent in a programmer role to write a program for a given function, but cannot request the second agent to (for example) deliver a mailpackage, because writing programs is a goal of the programmer role, while delivering mailpackages is not.

We now introduce the concept of an *oa*'s commitment to achieving a goal (Jensen 1993). The predicate

committed_to(oa, g)

signifies that agent *oa* is committed to the achievement of goal *g*. Consequently, the totality of activities performed by *oa* must include the achievement of *g*. Prioritization of goals is not considered here.

The next axiom states that any agent that fills an organizational role is committed to the goals associated with the role.

has_role(agent, role) ⊃ [*has_goal(role, goal)* ⊃ *commited_to(agent, goal)*]

An agent can allocate only resources that have been assigned to a role it plays.

has_resource(cwa, rs) ⊃ (∃ r) [*has_supervisor(cwa, oa)* ∧ *plays(oa, r)*
∧ *has_resource(r, rs)*]

Empowerment: Linking Structure and Behavior

With the introduction of organizational knowledge, we now have to address the problem of how to specify who can do what. That is, what is the set of activities that an *oa* is allowed to perform as a member of the organization? It would appear that by associating processes with *oas* through the has_process property, we have solved the problem. That is, an *oa* can perform any activities specified by the process in the roles that the *oa* plays. However, consider the following situation:

"Jill, in her role as a CNC machine operator, has a process she must perform in order to achieve the goal of producing a part. The process is composed of three activities: (1) machine-setup, (2) machine-run, and (3) machine-teardown. But before the machine-run activity can commence, she must receive permission from her supervisor."

The problem is that Jill has a process that specifies a sequence of activities that she must perform, but she cannot perform the second activity—machine-run—without permission. The implication is that within our activity ontology, she is not allowed to change the state of the machine-run activity to "execute."

An obvious way to solve the problem is to insert a fourth activity between machine-setup and machine-run, in which she seeks approval from her supervisor. If approval is obtained, then she can commence the subsequent machine-run activity. Again we have a problem. Who is allowed to change the status of this new approval activity to "completed"? If Jill is allowed to make any status changes she wants to the activities in her process, she can change the status of the approval activity regardless of whether she obtained approval or not.

The problem lies with who is allowed to make status changes to states and activities. When Jill goes to her supervisor for permission, is it Jill who changes the status of the approval activity to completed or her supervisor? The answer is not clear. Therefore, the only solution to the problem of permission to perform an action lies in stating precisely who is allowed to change the status of the activity, for example, from "dormant" to "executing."

We introduce the concept of empowerment as a means of specifying the status-changing rights of an *oa*. *Empowerment is the right of an oa to perform status-changing actions*, such as "commit," "enable," and "suspend." Empowerment naturally falls into two classes: state and activity empowerment.

State empowerment specifies the range of stati through which an *oa* may take a state by performing the appropriate actions, such as commit. State empowerment not only specifies allowable status changes but may be used to restrict the set of resources an *oa* is empowered to commit to a use/consume state. An *oa* may be empowered for any type of resource, including other *oa*s. The implication is the first *oa* may commit a second to a state.

state-empower(oa, s, c)

where *s* is a state, and *c* is one of the following: "commit," "enable," "complete," "disenable," or "reenable."

Activity empowerment specifies the range of stati through which an *oa* may take an activity by performing the appropriate actions, such as execute and suspend. Even though an activity may be enabled, the *oa* whose role contains the process that contains the activity may not be empowered to start its execution.

activity-empower(oa, a, c)

where *a* is an activity, and *c* is one of the following: "execute," "suspend," and "complete."

With the addition of empowerment, a second type of authority arises. That is, the supervising agent may alter what a supervisee is empowered to do.

The definitions of and constraints on the empowerment predicates follow:

For any activity *a* that requires that the agent be empowered, the status

changing actions for the activity require *holds(activity_empower(agent, a, c), σ)*
as a precondition.

For any state that requires that the agent be empowered, the status changing
actions for the activity require *holds(state_empower (agent, s, c), σ)* as a precondition.

It is possible for one agent to empower another agent for an activity if the
first agent supervises the second and the supervisor is empowered for that activity.

Poss(activity_empowers(agent, agent', a, c), σ) ≡ holds(supervises(agent, agent'), σ)
∧ holds(activity_empower(agent, a, c), σ)

It is possible for one agent to disempower another agent for an activity if the
first agent supervises the second and the supervisor is empowered for that activity.

Poss(activity_disempowers(agent, agent', a, c), σ) ≡ holds(supervises(agent, agent'), σ)
∧ holds(activity_empower(agent, a, c), σ)

An agent is empowered for an activity only as a result of the action
activity_empowers and is no longer empowered only as a result of the action *activity_disempowers.*

holds(activity_empower(agent, a, c), do(a', σ)) ≡ (∃ agent') a' =
activity_empowers(agent', agent, a, c) ∨ holds(activity_empower(agent, a, c), σ)
∧ ¬(∃ agent') a' = activity_disempowers(agent', agent', a, c)

It is possible for one agent to empower another agent to change the status of a
state if the first agent supervises the second and the supervisor is empowered to
change the status of that state.

Poss(state_empowers(agent, agent', s, c), σ) ≡ holds(supervises(agent, agent'), σ)
∧ holds(state_empower(agent, s, c), σ)

It is also possible for one agent to disempower another agent to change the
status of a state if the first agent supervises the second and the supervisor is empowered to change the status of that state.

Poss(state_disempowers(agent, agent', s, c), σ) ≡ holds(supervises(agent, agent'), σ)
∧ holds(state_empower(agent, s, c), σ)

An agent is empowered to change the status of a state only as a result of *actionstate_empowers* and is no longer empowered only as a result of the *actionstate_disempowers.*

holds(state_empower(agent, a, c), do(a', σ)) ≡ (∃ agent') a'
= activity_empowers(agent', agent, a, c) ∨ holds(state_empower(agent, a, c), σ)
∧ ¬(∃ agent') a' = state_disempowers(agent', agent', a, c)

Agent Interaction and Speech Acts

Agent interaction takes place at several levels. The first level is concerned with
the information content communicated among agents. A piece of information

communicated at this level might be a proposition (or fact) like "produce 200 widgets."

The second level specifies the intentions of agents. The same information content can be communicated with different intentions. For example, (*ask* (produce 200 widgets))—the sender asks the receiver if the mentioned fact is true; (*tell* (produce 200 widgets))—the sender communicates a belief of his to the receiver; (*achieve* (produce 200 widgets))—the sender requests the receiver to make the fact one of his beliefs; and (*deny* (produce 200 widgets))—the sender communicates that a fact is no longer believed.

The second level supports interaction through explicit linguistic actions, called speech-acts (Searle 1969). The speech-act framework has been developed by philosophers and linguists to account for human communication.

The third level is concerned with conventions (Jennings 1993) that agents share when exchanging messages. The existence of shared conventions makes it possible for agents to coordinate in complex ways, such as carrying out negotiations about their goals and actions. As an example, consider the supply chain of our TOVE virtual manufacturing enterprise as a multiagent system. The order acquisition agent interacts with a customer and acquires an order for 200 lamps. The order has a due date of 28 September. The order acquisition agent sends the order as a proposal to the logistics agent. The order acquision agent knows that the logistics agent's answer must be either an acceptance, rejection, or counter proposal. Thus, the order acquision agent can verify that the logistic agent's response is valid, and carry out a corrective dialogue with the logistics agent if the response is invalid or other events (such as delays or lost messages) occur. If the logistics agent sends a counter proposal (such as "200 lamps with a due date of 15 October"), the order acquisition agent may use knowledge about an acceptable trade-off to negotiate an amount and a due date with the logistics agent that can be achieved and is satisfactory to the customer. Then, the logistics agent will begin negotiations with the scheduling agent to determine the feasibility of scheduling the production of the order, and will determine feasibility of the delivery date with the transportation agent.

To model the complexity of the third level, the organization ontology includes a representation of foundation speech acts. This representation distinguishes between the performative (such as propose, accept, and reject), the sender (an agent initiating the communication), the receiver (an agent receiving the communication), the content being communicated (no commitment is made at this level), the language in which the content is expressed, and the ontology defining the context in which the content message must be interpreted.

Our solution for the third level of interaction is reported in Barbuceanu and Fox (1995).

Competency Revisited

In this section we repeat the competency questions and follow each with the query that would provide the answer. Note that parameters that are preceded with a question mark are variables. We also leave out the situational calculus predicates because all of the logical statements refer to the current situation.

Structure

What roles does agent *P* play?

> *plays(P, ?r)*

Which division does the agent belong to?

member_of(P, ?d)

- Who must agent *P* communicate with (*?rec* provides the answer)?

  plays(P, ?r) ∧ has_communication_link(?r, ?cl) ∧ has_receiving_agent(?cl, ?rec)

What kinds of information does agent *P* communicate (*?inf* provides the answer)?

plays(P, ?r) ∧ has_communication_link(?r, ?cl) ∧ will_volunteer(?cl, ?inf)

Who does *P* report to (*?p* provides the answer)?

subordinate_of(P, ?p).

Is role *r* a generalization of another role *r´*?

generalized_role(r, r´).

Behavior

What are the goals of the organization *o* (*?g* provides the answer)?

> *has_goal(o, ?g)*

What are the goals of the role *r* (*?g* provides the answer)?

> *has_goal(r, ?g)*

What are the goals of agent *P* (*?g* provides the answer)?

> *plays(P, ?r) ∧ has_goal(?r, ?g)*

What activities are available for a role *r* to achieve its goals (*?a* provides the answer)?

> *has_process(r, ?a)*

What resources are available to the agent *P* to achieve a goal *g* (*?rs* provides the answer)?

> *plays(P, ?r) ∧ has_goal(?r, g) ∧ has_resource(?r, ?rs)*

Authority, Empowerment, and Commitment

What resources does agent P have authority to assign ($?rs$ provides the answer)?

plays(P, ?r) ∧ has_resource(?r, ?rs) ∧ state_empower(P, ?s, commit)
∧ ((?s = use) ∨ (?s = consume))

Whose permission does an agent need to perform activity a ($?oa$ provides the answer)?

activity_empower(?oa, a, execute)

What activities may agent P execute without explicit permission ($?a$ provides the answer)?

activity_empower(P, ?a, execute)

Conclusions

Ontologies are shared views of domains. They provide conceptualizations that are agreed upon by participants in collaborative action and decision making. The explicit existence of such shared perspectives makes it possible for both people and programs to collaborate, by ensuring that everybody makes the same distinctions and uses the same terms with the same meaning.

This chapter presented our preliminary exploration into an organization ontology for the TOVE enterprise model. The ontology views organizations as agents playing roles and acting to achieve specific goals, according to various "rules of the game" constraints. A primary focus of this chapter has been in linking structure and behavior through the concept of empowerment. Empowerment is the right of an organizational agent to perform status changing actions. This linkage is critical to the unification of enterprise models and their executability. Further work is required to complete the axiomatization of the ontology and extend it to capture other concepts such as skill, intention, and access right to the information system of the organization.

Acknowledgments

This research is supported in part by the Natural Science and Engineering Research Council, Manufacturing Research Corporation of Ontario, Digital Equipment Corporation, Micro Electronics and Computer Research Corporation, Numetrix, Spar Aerospace, Carnegie Group, Quintus Corporation, Toyo Engineering, and BHP Research.

8

Modeling, Simulating, and Enacting Complex Organizational Processes

A Life Cycle Approach

Walt Scacchi

Workflow modeling, business process redesign, enterprise integration, and teamwork support are among the current generic goals for advanced information technology (IT) within organizations. Organizations are looking for ways to respond to competitive pressures and attain new performance levels by redesigning and continuously improving their production and operational processes. Organizations are also looking into IT as a strategy for establishing, sustaining, and expanding a presence in electronic markets for their goods and services. Such endeavors must therefore address complex organizational processes that entail tens, hundreds, or even thousands of organizational participants, as well as support the integration of a heterogeneous collection of both legacy and emerging ITs. Thus, we are faced with the problem of how to realize these goals in a coherent, scalable, and evolutionary manner.

In this chapter, I describe the approach and supporting mechanisms we have been investigating at the USC ATRIUM Laboratory in an effort to solve this problem and realize these goals. I describe our approach to modeling, enacting, and integrating complex organizational processes using an advanced knowledge-based computing infrastructure, as well as some of the associated technologies we have developed and deployed in large-scale business and government organizations.

The Process Engineering Life Cycle

In simplest terms, support for organizational processes entails more than the modeling and creation of process descriptions or representations. Our view at

USC is that the goal should be to support the engineering of organizational processes across the process life cycle. Much as the development of complex information systems entails more than programming, so does the development of complex organizational processes entail more than creating documents that describe them. As such, work at USC has led to the initial formulation of an organizational process life cycle that is founded on the incremental development, iterative refinement, and ongoing evolution of organizational process descriptions. In this way, the organizational process life cycle spiral includes activities that address process metamodeling, modeling, analysis, simulation, visualization, prototyping, walkthrough and training support, administration, integration, environment generation, instantiation and enactment, monitoring, recording, and auditing, history capture and replay, articulation, and evolution. In the following list, each of these activities will be defined.

- *Metamodeling*: constructing and refining a process concept vocabulary and logic (a resource ontology) for representing families of processes and process instances in terms of object classes, attributes, relations, constraints, control flow, rules, and computational methods

- *Modeling*: eliciting and capturing informal process descriptions and converting them into formal process models or process model instances

- *Analysis*: evaluating static and dynamic properties of a process model, including its consistency, completeness, internal correctness, and traceability, as well as other semantic checks. This process also addresses the feasibility assessment and optimization of alternative process models

- *Simulation*: symbolically enacting process models in order to determine the path and flow of intermediate state transitions in ways that can be made persistent, replayed, queried, dynamically analyzed, and reconfigured into multiple alternative scenarios

- *Visualization*: providing users with graphic views of process models and instances that can be viewed, navigationally traversed, interactively edited, and animated to convey process statics and dynamics

- *Prototyping, walkthrough, and training support*: incrementally enacting partially specified process model instances in order to evaluate process presentation scenarios through the involvement of end users prior to performing tool and data integration.

- *Administration*: assigning and scheduling specified users, tools, and development data objects to modeled user roles, product milestones, and development schedule.

- *Integration*: encapsulating or wrapping selected information systems, repositories, and data objects that are to be invoked or manipulated when enacting a process instance. This provides a computational workspace that binds user, organizational role, task, tools, input, and output resources into "semantic units of work."

- *Environment generation*: automatically transforming a process model or instance into a process-based computing environment that selectively presents proto-typed or integrated information systems to end-users for process enactment.

- *Instantiation and enactment*: performing the modeled process using the environment by a process instance interpreter that guides or enforces specified users or user roles to enact the process

- *Monitoring, recording, and auditing*: collecting and measuring process enactment data needed to improve subsequent process enactment iterations, as well as documenting what process steps actually occurred in what order.

- *History capture and replay*: graphically simulating the re-enactment of a process in order to more readily observe process state transitions or to intuitively detect possible process enactment anomalies.

- *Articulation*: diagnosing, repairing, and rescheduling actual or simulated process enactments that have unexpectedly broken down because of some unmet process resource requirement, contention, availability, or other resource failure.

- *Evolution*: incrementally and iteratively enhancing, restructuring, tuning, migrating, or re-engineering process models and process life cycle activities to more effectively meet emerging user requirements and to capitalize on opportunistic benefits associated with new tools and techniques.

While such a list might suggest that engineering a business process through its life cycle proceeds in a linear or waterfall manner, this is merely a consequence of its narrative presentation. In practical situations where these activities and associated process mechanisms have been initially tried out (at AT&T Bell Laboratories [Votta 1993], Northrop-Grumman Corporation, Naval Air Warfare Center, China Lake, California, and elsewhere [Scacchi and Mi 1993]), it quickly becomes clear that business process engineering is a dynamic team-based endeavor that can lead to mature processes only through rapid process prototyping, incremental development, iterative refinement, and the re-engineering of ad hoc process task instances and models. To no surprise, many of our efforts addressing these life cycle activities and supporting prototype mechanisms have been described in greater detail elsewhere (Mi and Scacchi 1990; Mi and Scacchi 1991; Noll and Scacchi 1991; Mi and Scacchi 1992; Mi and Scacchi 1993; Mi and Scacchi 1994; Scacchi and Mi 1993). Thus, I now turn to briefly describing our approach to some of these activities.

Modeling, Analysis, and Simulation

My colleagues and I have developed a knowledge-based computing environment for modeling, analyzing, and simulating complex organizational processes (Mi and Scacchi 1990). We call this environment the Articulator. It first became oper-

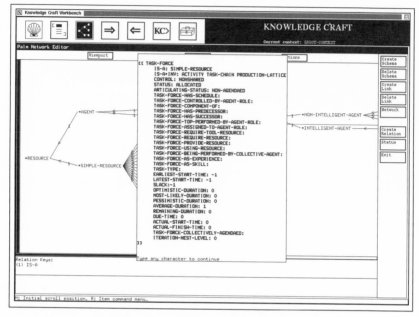

Figure 1. A generic business process model class hierarchy and schema example.

ational in 1988, and we have continued to use and evolve it since. The Articulator uses a rule-based object-oriented knowledge representation scheme for modeling interrelated classes of organizational resources. In this sense, the Articulator's knowledge representation ontology represents a resource-based theory of organizational processes (cf. Grant 1991). In this regard, its purpose and use is similar in spirit to that used in the TOVE system, as described in the chapter by Fox, Barbuceanu, and Gruninger. The Articulator's object classes characterize the attributes, relations, and computational methods associated with a taxonomy of organizational resources. Thus, using the Articulator, we can construct or prototype knowledge-based models of organizational processes. For example, figure 1 displays a hierarchy of object classes that characterize common business processes that we built using the Articulator. In turn, associated with each of these classes is a schema of attributes, relations, and rule-based computational methods that describe the named processes. Figure 2 then follows with a more detailed view of a model of a generic order-fulfillment process.

Modeling

The resource taxonomy my colleagues and I have constructed, explained in detail elsewhere (Garg and Scacchi 1989, Mi and Scacchi 1990, Mi and Scacchi 1994), serves as a process metamodel that provides an ontological framework

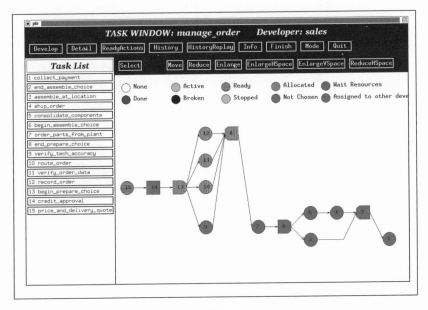

Figure 2. Top level of an order-fulfillment process model.

and vocabulary for constructing organizational process models (OPMs). In simplest terms, the process metamodel states that organizational processes can be modeled in terms of (subclasses of) agents that perform tasks using tools and systems that consume or produce resources. Further, agents, ITs, and tasks are resources—which means they can also be consumed or produced by other agents and tasks. For example, a project manager may produce staff through staffing and allocation tasks that consume departmental budgets, while this staff may then be assigned to other routine or creative production tasks using the provided resources (such as computer workstations, spreadsheet and desktop publishing packages, schedules, and salary) to construct the desired products or services (reports and documents). OPM instances can then be created by binding values of corresponding real-world entities to the classes of corresponding entities employed in the OPM. For instance, Mary may be the project manager who is responsible for getting a set of documents produced for an external client, and she is authorized to assign 2 or 3 individuals in her department to use their desktop PCs, which run Windows95, Lotus 1-2-3, and WordPerfect software, in order to get the reports produced by the end of the week.

The agents, tasks, product resources, tools, and systems are all hierarchically decomposed into subclasses that inherit the characteristics of their (multiple) parent classes, for economy in representation. Further, these resource classes and subclasses are interrelated in order to express relationships such as precedence among tasks (which may be sequential, iterative, conditional, optional, or concurrent), task/product pre- and post-conditions, authority relationships among agents in different roles, product compositions, IT tool/system aggregations, and others (Mi and Scacchi 1990, Mi and Scacchi 1994). Thus, in using these classes of process-modeling entities, we are naturally led to model organizational processes as a web of multiple interacting tasks that are collectively performed by a team of developers using an ensemble of tools that consume resources and produce composed products/artifacts (Kling and Scacchi 1982). In addition, it allows us to treat these models as a reusable information resource, which can be archived, shared, or transferred to other organizations (Leymann and Altenhuber 1994).

In addition, the metamodel enables us to model other complex phenomena associated with organizational processes, such as agents' resource sovereignties (i.e., the set of resources under the control of an agent), authority asymmetries (political relationships among agents), multiple belief systems, negotiation strategies, technology transfer strategies, etc. Accordingly, these relationships are defined in the metamodel, used, and then instantiated in the OPMs. Then we use the Articulator to query and simulate modeled processes as described below.

Analysis

As the process metamodel provides the semantics for OPMs, we can construct computational functions that systematically analyze the consistency, completeness, traceability, and internal correctness of OPMs (Choi and Scacchi 1989, Mi and Scacchi 1990). These functions represent batched or interactive queries to the knowledge base through its representational schemata. At present, we have defined a few dozen paramaterized query functions that can retrieve information through navigational browsing, direct retrieval, or deductive inference, as well as what-if simulations of partial or complete OPMs (Mi and Scacchi 1990). Further, most of these analysis functions incorporate routines for generating different types of reports (for example, raw, filtered, abstracted, or paraphrased into structured narrative) that can be viewed interactively or incorporated into Web-based or desktop publication documents.

Simulation

Since process models in our scheme are computational descriptions, we can simulate—or, symbolically execute—them using knowledge-based simulation techniques supported by the Articulator (Mi and Scacchi 1990). In simple terms, this is equivalent to saying that simulation entails the symbolic performance of process tasks by their assigned agents using the tools, systems, and resources to produce the designated products. Using the previous example, this means that in the simulation, Mary's agent would "execute" her project management tasks according to the task precedence structure specified in the OPM instance, con-

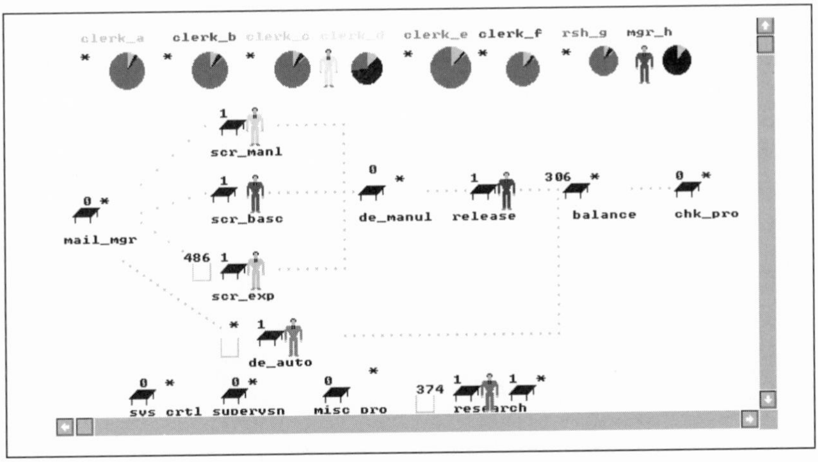

Figure 3. Visual display from an animated multiagent simulation.

suming simulated time and effort along the way. Because tasks and other resources can be modeled at arbitrary levels of precision and detail, the simulation makes progress as long as task preconditions or postconditions are satisfied at each step (for example, for Mary to be able to assign staff to the report production task, the staff must be available at that moment, otherwise the simulated process stops, reports the problem, then waits for new input or command from the simulation user).

Simulations also allow us to dynamically model different samples of parameter values. This in turn enables the simulated processes to function like transportation networks whose volumetric flow, traffic density, and congestion bottlenecks can be assessed according to alternative (heuristic or statistical) arrival rates and service intervals. When the simulation is used this way, which follows classic discrete-event simulation techniques, users find it is often easy to observe or discover process bottlenecks and optimization alternatives. Further, since commercially available discrete-event simulations now provide animated visual displays, users can watch process simulations under different scenarios as brief animated movies that can be modified, replayed, and viewed. Although we cannot conveniently show such animations in printed form, the following two snapshots captured from such an animated simulation may suggest what can be observed. In figure 3, we have modeled an eight person/agent activity for performing an "accounts payable" process. When an organization authorizes a purchase order to be fulfilled, payment for that purchase is provided by the accounts payable process. This figure depicts the structure of the workflow, which agents currently perform what tasks, and pending workload quantities (the backlog of invoices, bills, and checks). Following this, figure 4 displays a snapshot of an accompany-

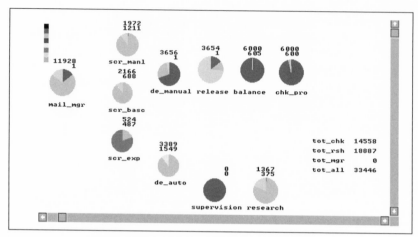

*Figure 4. Visual display of dynamic pie chart depicting
current workload, division of labor, and aggregate costs.*

ing pie chart depicting current workload, division of labor, and activity-based
cost figures (lower right) for a simulated workflow volume.

At USC, we have used the Articulator environment to model, analyze, and
simulate a variety of organizational processes. In this regard, we have constructed OPMs and instances for organizations within businesses and government
agencies, focused on activities involving team-based IT product design and review processes, as well as department- and division-wide IT production and
support processes that include tens to hundreds of participants. Such OPMs typically include dozens of classes of agents, tasks, resources, and products, but a
small number of IT tools and systems, while the OPM instantiation may include one to ten or more instances of each class. Our experience to date suggests
that modeling existing processes can take from one to three person-days to two
to three person-months of effort, and analysis routines can run in real-time or
acceptable near-real-time, while simulations can take seconds to hours (even
days!), depending on the complexity of the OPM, its instance space, and the
amount of nondeterministic process activities being modeled. Note, however,
that simulation performance is limited to available processing power and processor memory, thus suggesting better performance can be achieved with (clusters of) high performance computing platforms.

Visualization, Prototyping, and Enactment

As my colleagues and I improve our ability to construct and redesign plausible
models of different organizational processes, we have found that it is increas-

ingly important to be able to quickly and conveniently understand the structure and dynamics of complex OPM instances. To this end, we have developed a graphic user interface (GUI) for visualizing and animating OPM instances. This process-based interface (PBI) is coupled with another computational facility; OPM instances developed with the Articulator can be automatically translated into executable process programs that are then downloaded into a software program that serves as a process driver. In turn, the process driver and GUI enable OPM developers to develop or enact process-driven IT environments. These capabilities can be used to reflect, guide, try out, and support how users work with process-driven ITs. I will describe these capabilities next.

Visualization

PBI provides graphic visualizations of task precedence structure on a role-specific basis for each user (i.e., agent instance) (Mi and Scacchi 1992). For example, figure 2 shows a visual rendering of an order-fulfillment process that reveals precedence, iteration, and concurrency relationships among tasks. Since process tasks can be modeled and hierarchically decomposed into subtasks of arbitrary depths, PBI provides users with a subtask window and an associated (cached) workspace. Figure 5 shows an example of this presentation for a second-level decomposition of the order-fulfillment process model, followed by figure 6, which displays the third-level decomposition view. Since a subtask precedence structure appears as a directed graph, a development status value (none, allocated, ready, active, broken, blocked, stopped, finished) is associated with each subtask step. For ease of understanding, these status values are represented in the PBI as colors (not shown here), so that the current state of a process task can be observed as a color pattern in the direct graph. Further, as PBI also incorporates a facility for recording and replaying all changes in process task state, evolving process state histories can be maintained and visualized as an animation of changing task step status colors. Subsequently, we have found that project managers in industrial organizations can quickly browse such a PBI display to ascertain the current status of an arbitrarily complex organizational process to varying degrees of detail. (For examples, see Mi and Scacchi [1992]).

Prototyping

The process driver that backs PBI can also accept an OPM as its input. Since OPMs need not include instance details, it is possible to use these OPMs to create prototype mock-ups of process-driven environments. These prototypes show the user the look and feel of how the emerging process-driven environment would appear. That is, the OPM serves to provide role-specific views of process task precedence structure, which in turn guides users in their use of IT tools, systems, and data resources. Thus, since the Articulator accommodates

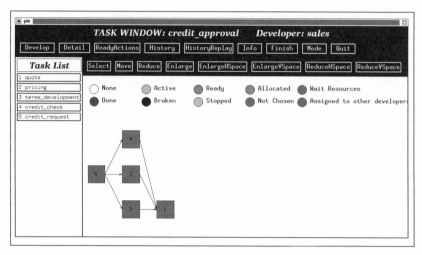

Figure 5. A second-level decomposition of the order-fulfillment process model.

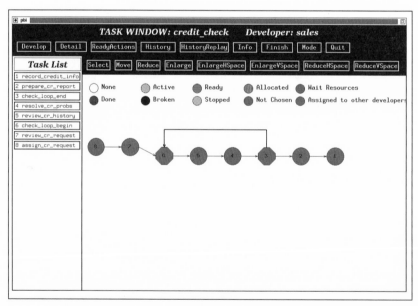

Figure 6. A third-level decomposition of the order-fulfillment process model.

partially decomposed OPMs, such OPMs can also be downloaded into the process driver to visually display and interactively walk through role-specific usage
scenarios. This is extremely useful in supporting an OPM construction effort
that is iterative, incremental, and improvement-oriented in an evolutionary

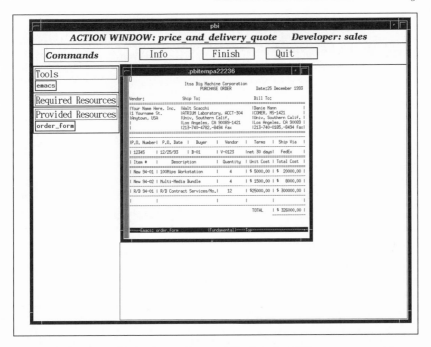

Figure 7. A lowest-level action workspace within the order fulfillment process model.

sense. Further, this prototyping capability can also be used to support training situations. This support is especially important when introducing new users to the concepts and mechanisms that support process-driven IT environments.

Integration and Enactment

The process driver and PBI provides IT tools, systems, and associated data resources (objects, files, databases, spreadsheets) that are served to users at the bottom level subtask actions so that they can perform their work. We refer to this capability as process enactment, meaning that users can perform or enact the modeled process tasks, subtasks, or actions assigned to them; and the IT tools, systems, and data resources are delivered to them at their displays and fingertips when needed. Figure 7 shows an example of a process enactment view, which provides the IT applications, tools, data objects, and workspace appropriate for the user assigned to this order-fulfillment process action.

Process enactment is a computational activity. It interprets an OPM or OPM instance as an input. Thus, the OPM or instance output from the Articulator represents a process enactment specification that is coded in something similar to an object-oriented operating system scripting language, or what others have called a process programming language (Osterweil 1987). In this sense, our process programs are automatically derived from the process model specification by way of a special-purpose application generator (Mi and Scacchi 1992, Karrer and Scacchi 1993). Accordingly, the process enactment specification can incorporate any operating system command, system invocation script, virtual mouse selections, or canned user input, as well as access protocols to heterogeneous information repositories (Noll and Scacchi 1991). This means it is possible for users to perform complex information processing tasks through a process-based interface that integrates access to local/networked data resources and IT tools/systems through a common GUI presentation (Mi and Scacchi 1992). As such, we are now working to prototype and demonstrate a number of process-driven environments in different business and government application domains that incorporate commercial off-the-shelf systems, internally developed systems, and prototype research software technologies that can operate over local-area and wide-area networks (Noll and Scacchi 1991).

Other Process Engineering Technologies

In addition to the computational mechanisms described so far, our approach utilizes mechanisms not described here. These include mechanisms for process scheduling and administration (Mi 1992), diagnosing, replanning, and rescheduling—articulation—of processes that unexpectedly break down or fail (Mi and Scacchi 1991; Mi 1992; Mi and Scacchi 1993); software re-engineering of processes and environments (Choi and Scacchi 1991); and knowledge-based process model repository (Mi, Lee, and Scacchi 1992).

Thus, we believe our approach can allow us to construct and demonstrate a computational framework for modeling, enacting, and integrating team-oriented process-driven work environments for redesigned business organizations.

Comparison with Other Ongoing Research

Much of the research in engineering process descriptions that influences our work at the USC ATRIUM Laboratory focuses on representations of the software engineering processes and architectures for process-centered software engineering environments. However, the Virtual Design Team effort at Stanford, described in the chapter by Levitt, is also investigating similar issues. Likewise, the ACTION system at USC described by Gasser, Hulthage, and Majchrzak can be viewed as a complementary effort that could serve as an organizational design "front-end" for configuring the architecture of organizational processes that can be modeled, simulated, and enacted through the Articulator environment.

Elsewhere, software process modeling, analysis, and simulation has been a research topic in a number of efforts (Curtis, Kellner, and Over 1992). Research at the Software Engineering Institute at Carnegie-Mellon University (Kellner 1991) has employed an explicitly enumerated state-space approach to process modeling, using the commercially available Statemate system. Kellner's approach to modeling and simulation has been successfully demonstrated on moderate sized project management processes. The PRISM project in Canada (Madhavji and Gruhn 1990) is focused on developing a process modeling and evolution methodology that is to be supported by future process-centered environments. However, at this time, neither of these two efforts addresses the support of process environment generation, enactment, replay or articulation.

A number of enactable representations of software engineering processes have been prototyped in recent years. For example, APPL/A (Sutton, Heimbigner, and Osterweil 1990) is a process programming language developed in the Arcadia project (Taylor et al. 1989). It expands the programming language Ada to include process constructors, relations, and other constructs to describe procedural aspects of a software process. Since APPL/A is targeted at process integration and enactment in an Ada-based environment, it is not at present well-suited for upstream process life cycle activities, such as incremental process modeling or simulation. In contrast, the PSS project in England (Bruynooghe et al. 1991) has developed a process modeling and enactment language based on an object-oriented knowledge representation notation. Grapple (Huff and Lesser 1988), on the other hand, relies on a set of goal operators and a planning mechanism to represent software processes. These are used to demonstrate goal-directed reasoning about software processes during modeling and enactment. AP5 (Balzer and Narayanaswamy 1993), developed at USC-ISI, and Marvel (Kaiser and Feiler 1987) developed at Columbia, use pattern-directed inference rules to model and trigger software process actions during process enactment. While Marvel has been extended to support the creation of process models (Kaiser, Barghouti, and Sokolsky 1990), its strength lies primarily in its ability to support rule-based process integration and enactment.

In the commercial arena, one recent process-centered environment is the process software life cycle support environment, ProSLCSE, from ISSI. We have found that the ProSLCSE representation of software processes lacks machine-readable data about the purpose and types of tasks and other activities. Next, Process WEAVER (Fernstrom 1993), a commercial product from Cap Gemini Innovation based in France, supports process modeling using a notational scheme derived from Petri-nets. In contrast, the computer-aided concurrent engineering product, CACE/PM from Perceptronics (Madni 1990), also employs a notational scheme derived from Petri-nets. However, CACE/PM offers a more substantial representational capability (such as rules, frames, attributes, and timing information), as well as supporting process model analysis and simulation. CACE/PM has, to date, been targeted to modeling development processes in the area of electronic design automation and manufacturing. However, it has not been applied to modeling and analyzing other technical or business processes.

In sum, no other process engineering environment today supports the full process life cycle. However, we have been able to demonstrate supporting mechanisms for the process life cycle activities described previously. Similarly, it should be noted that though our focus is targeted at engineering organizational processes, our approach can be applied to both complex technical domains (large-scale software engineering, electronic design automation, agile manufacturing) and to conventional business processes (new product development, corporate finance, and business planning), albeit in a radically innovative way (Davenport 1993).

Conclusion

This chapter provides a brief introduction to our approach and computational mechanisms to modeling, simulating, and integrating organizational processes that involve IT tools, systems, and data resources. These include a knowledge-based environment for re-engineering complex organization processes and other facilities for realizing and executing these processes. My colleagues and I are using our results to help redesign existing organizational processes that employ large teams and to provide a coherent, scalable IT infrastructure for enacting and integrating IT-based organizational processes.

Finally, in addition to the computational mechanisms described here, our approach utilizes mechanisms not described here. We are now investigating demonstrating mechanisms for acquiring and re-engineering action invocation histories into reusable process model fragments and coordinating remote user processes via email-based process deployment and retrieval. Thus, we believe our approach can allow us to construct and demonstrate an advanced IT for modeling, enacting, and integrating team-oriented process-driven IT-based work environments for redesigned business and government organizations.

In closing, I recommend readers interested in an up-to-date view of on-going research described in this chapter to examine an interactive presentation found on the World Wide Web, at www.usc.edu/dept/ATRIUM/Process_Life_Cycle. html for further details and examples.

Acknowledgments

This work is supported as part of the ATRIUM Laboratory at USC. Recent sponsors include Andersen Consulting's Center for Strategic Technology and Research (CSTaR), AT&T, EDS, Hewlett-Packard, IBM Canada Ltd., Intelligent

Systems Technology Inc., McKesson Water Products Company, Northrop-Grumman Corporation, Office of Naval Research (contract number N00014-94-1-0889), the Center for Service Excellence in the USC Marshall School of Business, and the USC Center for Software Engineering. However, no endorsements are implied. In addition, a number of people contributed to the ideas or system development work on which this report is based including Song C. Choi, Pankaj Garg, Anthony Karrer, Ming-Jun Lee, Jinhui Luo, Pei-Wei Mi, Mark Nissen, and John Noll. All of these contributions are greatly appreciated.

9

An Approach to Modeling
Communication and Information
Technology in Organizations

David J. Kaplan and Kathleen M. Carley

I magine a manager trying to make technology purchasing or scheduling decisions where a wide variety of technology and work arrangements are
possible. Should the manager select a collaborative setting? Perhaps an individual with many years of experience would be best. Maybe the presence of
video in a collaborative setting would be helpful; or, perhaps electronic manuals
should be the single most important item. Is the manager considering quality or
time as the decision criteria, or is the manager interested in minimizing the
physical handling of delicate machinery? Should the company invest in wearable technology or desktop technology?

To answer such questions, managers can consult many practical and academic articles that discuss the relative impacts or costs and benefits of various
telecommunication devices, software, computers, and so forth. Indeed many ex-
cellent scientific articles using either experimental or field approaches discuss
the relative social and information processing impacts of various information
technologies[1] (Fish, et al. 1993; McLeod 1992; Sproull and Kiesler 1991; Kraut,
Galegher and Egido 1990; Carley and Wendt 1991; Eveland and Bikson 1988).
While such research is valuable, it may not meet a specific manager's needs. Experimental research is limited by the number of technologies that can be simultaneously compared and the complexity of the organizational setting and
task that can be reasonably examined. Field research is limited in that researchers have little control over the relative impact of a wide variety of exogenous factors on their study's results. These problems are perhaps even more
acute—and certainly added complications arise—when one is dealing with "futuristic" technology that is still under development. One example of futuristic
technology is wearable technology.

Wearable technology is a general term for a collection of devices that incorpo-

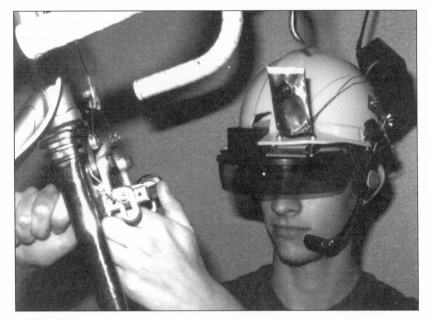

Figure 1. Example wearable system.

rate into wearable units one or more information technologies, such as a computer, telephone headset, radio transmitter, or video camera. Wearable technology should increase worker mobility and admit more rapid access to a remote expert or on-line manuals. For example, a wearable telephone headset with radio transmitter allows hands-free operation as well as increased user mobility. Heavy, difficult-to-manage paper documents can be replaced with wearable computer-based manuals whose output is displayed on a small, yet high resolution, head-mounted display, where manipulations are conducted with voice commands or simple control devices. An example of a wearable device is shown in figure 1. With such wearable technology, maintenance personnel, for example, do not have to carry manuals, have hands free for repair, and can contact a remote expert with questions when discrepancies occur between their observations and the on-line manual.

The use of computational techniques comprise an alternate approach to experiments and field studies for examining the potential impact of information technologies on organizations—particularly futuristic technologies. Questions about the relative impact of different and futuristic information technologies on organizational performance could be addressed if we had a computational framework where the organization, the individuals, the task, and the information technologies were simultaneously modeled. Such a model would be advantageous because it would allow us to examine the results of complex interactions among adaptive individuals, the organizational environment, and the information technology being employed. By using such a computational model, we could advance theories of how changes in any one of these complex factors might affect the others and overall organizational performance. In this chapter, we propose such a model, describe its necessary features, and illustrate its possible results. We are not arguing against the use of experiments and field studies for examining the impact of information technologies in organizations. On the contrary, we are arguing that a computational approach can, through theory development and initial exploration, help researchers determine which empirical investigations are most important.

The communicating and information technology model (COMIT) is such a computational model. COMIT is a prototype. It comprises a first step toward integrating, into a single framework, a model of the organization as an information processing agency, a model of individual action, a model of task, and a model of information technology. In describing this model, we point to critical issues in the interrelationship among organization, agents, tasks, and technology that are not well understood. We illustrate the type of results that are possible from such models by contrasting organizational performance under four different information technology environments — the individual acting alone with only a hard copy manual, the individual acting alone with an electronic manual, the individual interacting with a remote helper with an audio and hard copy manual, and the individual interacting with a remote helper with an audio, video, and electronic manual (the wearable technology condition). These conditions are interesting, in and of themselves, as they represent extremes in information technology possible with current technology. The value of this work includes a characterization of the complexity of such models, an extended checklist of features that these models should have, and an illustration of initial results.

COMIT seeks to simulate both macro and microlevel views of the organization with an emphasis on cooperative work. Cooperative and collaborative work bring together issues of agency, technology, task, and the impact of the organizational environment (Malone 1987; Kraut and Streeter 1995). Cooperative work can be supported by a variety of information technologies, such as telephone, video conferencing, or shared electronic manuals (Clark and Brennen 1991). These technologies allow groups of organizational actors freedom from copresence, admit access to remote experts, and alter the rate at which information can be accessed. COMIT must be flexible enough to represent a variety of organizational designs and tasks (such as those discussed by Levitt et al. [1994]; Decker and Lesser [1993]; Carley [1992]; Carley, et al. [1992]; and Cohen [1992]).

Our ultimate goal is to create a computational framework that integrates our understanding of individual decision making, organizations, and information technology and that can be used to predict some of the information processing effects of new information technologies and/or alternate organizational designs. Models that include aspects of organizational performance, individual decision making, and information technology exist (Masuch and LaPotin 1989; Carley 1992; Kaufer and Carley 1993; Decker and Lesser 1993). However, little work has been done to integrate these three aspects into a single composite model (Carley and Prietula 1994). An important exception here is the virtual design team (VDT) (Cohen 1992; Levit et al. 1994), where organizations are modeled as networks and information technologies affecting the rate and type of information that is transmitted. In the VDT model, individuals cannot learn; however, their experiences may vary. Further, within VDT order of information processing is the primary task. Essentially, VDT combines PERT chart information with information on the organizational hierarchy. COMIT is similar to VDT in its representation of task and experience and in its assignment of needed actions to steps. However, COMIT differs from VDT in a number of ways: there are only one or two individuals; the task is composed of a set of sequenced steps; each step has a set of subtasks; steps or substeps can be skipped; and information technologies alter the rate at which individuals can acquire information, whether individuals can access other individuals, and the communicative features of that interaction.

The COMIT Model

In this section we will describe the model. We begin with a brief discussion of the simulation's purpose, and then describe its process, paying special attention to the way actions are selected and performed. Next, parameters of the model are defined, followed by a discussion of each type of parameter. This section concludes with a brief example of a fairly skilled worker performing a diagnosis and repair task, aided by a reference manual.

Purpose

COMIT allows researchers to examine the performance of a small organization (one or two actors) doing a hierarchically decomposable task using various information technologies. The top-level process and parameter categories for COMIT are shown in figure 2. Illustrative information on each category is provided in the figure. To use COMIT, users adjust a set of parameters. These parameters describe the task representation, the agent or agents working on the task, the actions capable of being performed by the agents, the information technology used by the agents, and the type of descriptive output measures desired for analysis. After the parameters are adjusted, COMIT performs a virtual experiment with statistics about performance reported upon completion.[2]

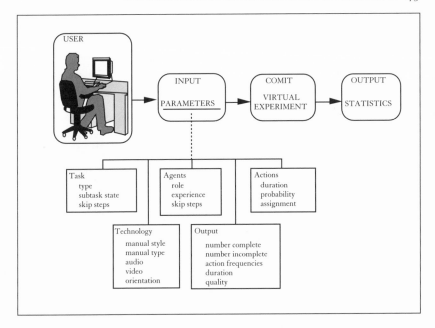

Figure 2. Overview of COMIT.

The COMIT Process

The process performed by COMIT is illustrated in figure 3. First, COMIT reads the set-up files provided by the user. These files specify task, agent, action, information technology (including manual), and output parameters. After set-up is complete, COMIT selects subtasks to perform based on the specified task-sequencing of subtasks, along with the worker agent's desire to continue or give up. Each subtask selected is performed until the worker agent gives up or completes the subtask (done status).

Each iteration of the action selection and performance section includes the selection of an action, performance of that action, performance of parallel actions or interrupts, and occasionally continuance of the performance of the selected action. The actions, parallel actions, and interrupts selected are those currently available. Their likelihood of selection is based on their probability of occurrence. Because some actions can be interrupted by a parallel action, such actions may continue after the interrupt.

After all subtasks have been performed or the worker agent has given up, statistics are reported to the user. These statistics include the duration and frequency of all actions reported by subtask or aggregated across the entire task. In typical Monte-Carlo fashion statistics aggregated across the simulations can be

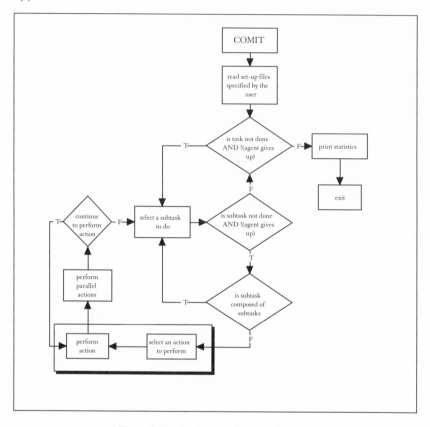

Figure 3. Top-level system diagram of COMIT.

reported for numerous simulations of the same organization. When many simulations are run, reporting is broken out by those simulations that have a "done" status for all subtasks and those simulations containing one or more subtasks with a status of "partially done" or "not done." A subtask—not composed of other subtasks—is "done" if the worker reaches a certain step, such as the eighth of ten steps (note that steps can be skipped along the way). A subtask is "partially done" if the worker reaches an earlier predefined step, such as the forth of ten steps. Otherwise a subtask is "not done." Subtasks composed of other subtasks have their status set to the maximum status of their subtasks.

Parameters

To discuss parameters concisely, we must first describe the topology developed that allows us differing degrees of abstraction from modeled items. Many mod-

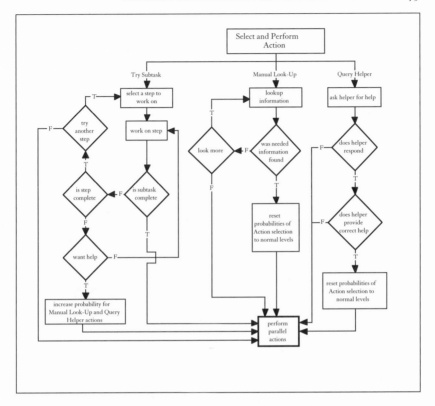

Figure 4. Detailed system diagram of action selection and performance.

eled items, such as a manual, require numerous variables to be adequately modeled. Other items, such as the probability of an action selection by an agent, require simply the specification of a value chosen from a range (for example, the selection of .5 from a range of 0 through 1). This topology was developed to enable users to interact with COMIT without a thorough knowledge of all its intricacies.

Much of what has been modeled requires a group of parameters rather than simply a limited set or range of values. For example, manuals are characterized by two metaparameters—manual type and manual style. For most users, simply noting that the manual has type "electronic" and that style is "reference" is sufficient. However, electronic manuals can also be characterized by setting the underlying parameters, such as speed of access or time required to read a page. These more detailed parameters allow researchers to model items at a more complex level, while the metaparameters provide simple access for users. Table 1 presents a subset of the parameters that can be manipulated by the user. Those in bold type are manipulated for the results presented in the Illustrative Results section.

Parameter	Topological Type	Values	Default
TASK			
Task representation	MP	Hartzell Task	Hartzell Task
Subtask state	LS	Done, Partially Done, Not Done	Not Done, each subtask
Skip steps	LS	Yes, No	Yes
AGENTS			
Role	**LS**	**worker, helper**	**worker, helper**
Worker experience	**M**	**0-100%**	**50%, each cell**
Worker probability skip steps	BCR	0..1	0.5
Presence of helper	**LS**	**Yes, No**	**No**
Helper experience	M	0-100%	100%, each cell
ACTIONS			
Duration of worker action	BCR	upper and lower bounds	action dependent
Duration of helper action	BCR	upper and lower bounds	action dependent
Probability selected by worker	BCR	0..1	action dependent
Probability selected by helper	BCR	0..1	action dependent
Assign actions to subtasks	M	True, False	All cells True
TECHNOLOGY			
Manual style	MP	reference, step-by-step	reference
Manual type	MP	physical, electronic	physical
Audio	LS	not present, present	not present
Video	LS	not present, present	not present
Orientation	LS	remote, face-to-face	remote
OUTPUT			
Number complete runs	BCR	0..1000	200
Number incomplete runs	BCR	0..1000	200
Report action frequencies	MP	Yes, No	Yes
Report task duration	MP	Yes, No	Yes
Report task quality	MP	Yes, No	Yes

Table 1. Illustrative parameters.

The topology consists of four types of parameters: bounded continuous range, limited set, matrix, and aggregate representation. Bounded continuous range (BCR) consist of a range of values bounded by an upper and a lower bound. For example, the probability of an action's selection by the helper may range from 0 to 1. Limited set (LS) consists of a set of values. For example, the status of a subtask is represented as one of three values: "done," "partially done," or "not done." Matrix (M) is a set of values in a two or more dimensional matrix. For example, the assignment of allowable actions for each subtask is represented as a two-dimensional matrix with true and false values in each cell. Each action specified by the user must be assigned to subtasks. While the default allows for all actions to be performed during any subtask, it is not always required. For example, it may be necessary for the worker to report only during a particular subtask. To represent this, a matrix of subtasks by actions is necessary. Finally, metaparameter (MP) is a parameter composed of multiple other parameters, each of which may vary in type.

Task

Users can manipulate three basic parameters in COMIT. The first, task representation, allows them to select a prespecified task. The second, subtask state, allows users to specify the beginning state of each subtask (i.e., whether it is "done," "partially done," or "not done"). For example, work in progress can be represented by specifying the beginning state of a subtask. Thus, a user could explore potential bottlenecks in the task. Finally, skip steps allows users to specify if the artificial agent can skip steps.

Only one task is currently prespecified within COMIT—the Hartzell task (figure 5). The Hartzell task is typical of a relatively simple sequential task that requires specialized knowledge to perform it well. This task involves the maintenance of a Hartzell constant speed propeller assembly. It consists of thirteen sequential subtasks. The measurement subtask (which is currently experimental work) is composed of a set of nonsequential subtasks (four measurements to be taken). In the future, we intend to calibrate COMIT by comparing its output with that from these experiments. A preliminary report on our experimental results appears in Siegel et al. (1995).

If the default task is not desired, users can specify an alternate task by listing all subtasks, their substructures, and the sequentiality among subtasks. COMIT allows any hierarchically decomposable task to be modeled as a set of subtasks.[3] Each subtask may have any number of subtasks. Each subtask, in turn, may also have subtasks. A subtask that does not contain subtasks will have, instead, a series of steps that the agent must take to complete the task.[4] Some subtasks are conditional on others. The sequencing of subtasks is specified by setting a matrix of linkages among subtasks.

Regardless of the task, each subtask and step can have, from the agent's perspective, one of three completion states: "done," "partially done," and "not done." By default, all subtasks and steps are initially in the "not done" state. As the worker agent performs the steps and subtasks, the completion state changes. To advance from one step or subtask to the next, the worker agent must achieve at least the prespecified required level of completion for this step or subtask. This level of required completion is specified by the researcher and may be "done," "partially done," or "not done." For example, in the Hartzell task, the worker agent cannot advance from Disassembly I to Disassembly II without first completing Disassembly I (status "done").

The worker agent can skip steps within a subtask, although quality will be diminished. Nevertheless, the subtask can still achieve a status of "done." Any number of steps within a subtask can also be skipped. Such steps will be left with a status of "not done." Similarly, subtasks can be skipped, but only according to the prespecified subtask ordering. If subtasks are skipped, the effect on

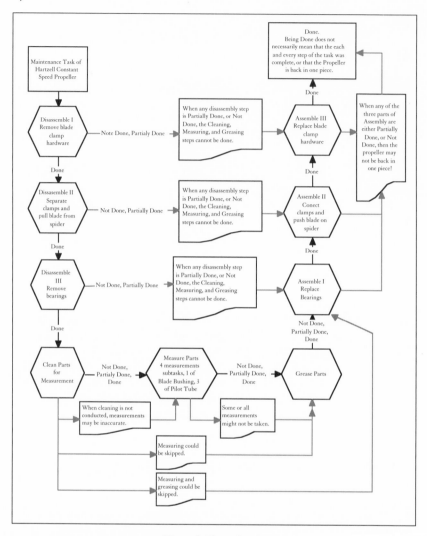

Figure 5. Hartzell task.

task completion will differ depending on the subtask that has been skipped. For example, in the Hartzell task, if the worker agent has "not done" or "partially done" Disassembly I, and decides not to try the subtask any longer, the only subtask that can be performed next is Assembly III. However, the critical measurement step cannot be performed because earlier subtasks were not completed. On the other hand, if the worker had decided to stop working on the clean subtask, leaving that subtask with a "not done" or "partially done," status the measurement subtask could still be performed.

Agents

Agents are characterized by their role (worker, helper), experience (task knowledge), and (if it is a worker) the likelihood that they will skip steps. COMIT can simulate organizations with a maximum of two agents, a worker and a helper. When both a worker and a helper are present, they work cooperatively to complete the specified task using various information technologies. Every simulated organization must contain a worker because only the worker agent performs tasks. The helper is optional. If a helper is present, the information technology chosen determines whether the helper is physically copresent (face-to-face condition) with the worker, or remote (communicating by means of a technology). Both workers and helpers vary in how much experience they have. Experience parameters apply to all subtasks and steps of the task, and have an initial experience level. The worker can learn from experience (by performing the task), by looking up information, or from helper communications. Learning raises the worker's experience level. The helper may initiate a communication with the worker, which may cause the worker to learn. Both workers and helpers can learn, although there is a cap at 100 percent experience. In addition, workers may vary in their likelihood to skip steps or subtasks. The worker probability skip steps parameter allows the user to specify the extent to which the worker is allowed to skip steps. The parameter of presence or absence of helper simply allows the user to specify whether or not the helper is present.

Learning is accomplished by either reading a manual or performing the work. If the agent looks up information and finds it, then it learns that information; otherwise it does not learn (i.e., it does not learn information it finds that is not relevant to the information it seeks). Agents learn about steps, but not subtasks. There is one piece of information for each step. Both workers and helpers are capable of learning by looking up information.

When a worker agent physically tries a subtask, it may learn, despite giving up. Thus, if the agent completes a subtask (status of "done"), then it gains complete experience. If the agent only partially completes a subtask, then it gains only partial experience. If the agent does not complete the subtask, then it learns nothing. However, if a worker has learned more (through lookups or helper agent provided information) than what it might get through experiential learning, then it retains its old experience (i.e., it never forgets, and knowledge is not additive; it is absolute each time). This learning mechanism only applies to the worker.

When a helper is present, the worker can learn by being told, as when the helper provides either solicited or unsolicited help. When help is provided, the worker learns an amount equal to the helper's knowledge on the step in question. Thus, a worker will learn under three different conditions. First, it will learn if at least one step was physically tried and a "partially done" status was achieved. In this case, only the worker learns. Second, it will learn when at least one lookup was made successfully. In this case, both worker and helper gain complete experience. Finally, the worker learns when the helper provides help to the worker at least once. In this case, only the worker learns.

If none of these conditions are met, no learning occurs. Thus, learning (or the lack thereof) does not necessarily rely on whether or not the worker gives up on the task.

Actions

Agents have a discrete set of actions they may perform, as described in table 2. Each action is listed along with the type of actor that can take the action. Each action has an associated probability of selection by the agent selecting the action. Many of these probabilities can change with the task state and/or the information technology. For example, if a worker realizes it needs information in order to complete a step, the probability of selecting actions such as look up or query helper will increase. This feature makes it possible for the researcher to implement assumptions such as individuals prefer to learn by being told rather than through trial and error. Increasing the probability of looking up information does not guarantee that the worker will look up information, nor that the agent will find the requisite information if it does look it up. Additionally, each action has some duration which is uniformly distributed over a range as specified by the user and which depends on the type of agent that can take that action. Finally, the user can specify during which subtasks/steps an action can be selected.

The worker can choose from an array of actions, provide unrequested updates to the helper, learn about the current subtask or step, give up on a subtask or step, or retry it upon failure. In addition, the worker knows the exact ordering of the subtasks and can recognize whether or not information is relevant to the current subtask or step, whereas the helper can respond to requests, view video, request situation updates, provide unsolicited help, ignore the worker, provide incorrect help if the worker and helper are not synchronized to the same step, and so forth. Both workers and helpers know the correct ordering of the subtasks to be performed, but each may have different experience for each step of a subtask.

There are both physical and cognitive actions. Cognitive actions occur in parallel with other actions and take no additional time. Physical parallel actions do take time. The minimum and maximum amount of time taken by each action is defined by the user and may be affected by the choice of information technology and agent experience.

Actions may not have the desired consequences. For example, the worker might ask for help but might not receive it or might receive inaccurate information. Further, the likelihood of some actions can change as a function of other actions. For example, although the worker can provide a situation description to the helper, the worker's desire to do so can change over time with respect to the last time a situation description was provided or as the helper reminds the worker to provide situation descriptions.

Action	Definition	Actor
Try Subtask	agent physically attempting a step	worker
Query Helper	agent requests step-specific information	worker
Manual Lookup	agent looks up information in a manual for a particular step	worker and helper
Report	agent makes a report	worker
Nontask Communication	communication between worker and helper not related to the task being performed	worker and helper
Waste Time	time spent not performing the task and not communicating	worker and helper
Parallel Cognitive Actions		
Update Desire to Provide Situation Description	adjusts agent's desire to provide a description of the step the agent is doing	worker
Update Desire to Provide Unsolicited Help	adjusts agent's desire to provide unsolicited help	helper
Update Experience	adjusts agent's desire to provide a description of which step the agent is doing	worker and helper
Parallel Physical Actions		
View Camera	agent can view the monitor and learn which step other agent is currently on	helper
Provide Situation Description	agent provides a description of which step the agent is working on	worker
Unsolicited Help	provide unsolicited help to the other agent	helper

Table 2. Available actions.

Technology

Information technology is characterized in terms of the way in which stored information is presented (manual style and manual type) and the way in which information is transmitted (audio, video, or orientation). With the parameters manual style and manual technology, a range of interesting mechanisms for retrieving information can be simulated. For example, a standard paper manual is physical in type and reference in style, whereas the same information presented in an on-line system would be electronic in type and possibly step-by-step in style. If an electronic manual is chosen, the user may allow the worker to use a check-list that automatically advances the manual's page to the appropriate next step. With the parameters (constraints) audio, video, and orientation, it is possible to characterize many different communication technologies. For example, discussions with a remote expert over the telephone has an audio constraint, no video, and a remote orientation.

Under a face-to-face orientation, the worker and helper agents are collocated. When worker and helper are not collocated, an audio channel exists between them. The audio channel in both the remote condition and the face-to-face condition is similarly modeled. The audio channel allows either agent to initiate a communication with the other agent and to respond to a communication if desired. No interrupts are possible, unlike a real telephone; however there is no coordination time required between communication turns, unlike a walkie-talkie. Video allows the helper to view the worker's workspace from the perspective of the worker. This can be accomplished, for example, by using a lipstick camera mounted on a visor or helmet of a worker. The quality is akin to that of NTSC video (30 frames per second), although the helper might not always choose to view the video signal.

Workers can look up information in both physical and electronic manuals, which differ in the time it takes to access information (search time).[5] Furthermore, information in the manual can be arranged either step-by-step or in a more standard reference format. This choice also affects the search time. A paper reference manual can be described as a random-access manual where access is accomplished through the use of an index. Thus, search time for such a manual should be fairly constant and the probability of finding the information with the use of an index should be uniform across the task. In contrast, a step-by-step manual is sequential. Thus, search time will vary depending on which section of the manual was last used relative to which section is needed. Thus, when using a step-by-step manual, an agent will have a high probability of finding information on the next step and a lower probability of finding information on preceding steps or subsequent steps.

Output

COMIT will generate a series of results for the specified organization. Since the program is not deterministic, a Monte Carlo approach should be taken. To specify the number of runs, the user can specify either the maximum number of simulations or the maximum number of simulations in which the worker completes the task with a "done" status. Depending on the task and the agents, there may be a large difference between these two. For example, in the Hartzell task it might take 1,100 to 1,700 runs (depending on the experience of the worker) to generate 200 runs where the worker actually completes the task.[6] This condition reflects the agent's relatively high likelihood of giving up on the task rather than finishing it. In reality, there may be many incomplete simulations performed before 200 complete simulations are found. COMIT continues virtual experiments until the requested number of simulations are found, or until the computer runs out of memory.

To a certain extent users can tailor the output. That is, users can specify whether they would like to have reported the frequencies of the various actions, the length of time it took to do the task or the various subtasks, or the quality with which the task is done.

Example

Imagine that you are trying to use COMIT to design a virtual experiment. You are interested in how long it will take an agent to perform the Hartzell task. The scenario you have in mind involves a fairly skilled worker performing the

NOT COMPLETED SIMULATIONS										
Simulations			Agents	Output Measures						
Requested Not Complete	Actual Not Complete	Total Run	Experience Worker	Time Taken	Status	Quality	Manual Look ups	Physical Task Tries	Reports	Skipped Steps
200	1065	1265	30%	4260.88	2.02	0.29	53.39	133.58	5.75	56.93
200	1174	1374	40%	4585.45	2.01	0.29	55.88	131.68	5.76	56.40
COMPLETED SIMULATIONS										
Simulations			Agents	Output Measures						
Requested Complete	Actual Complete	Total Run	Experience Worker	Time Taken	Status	Quality	Manual Look ups	Physical Task Tries	Reports	Skipped Steps
200	200	1265	30%	5771.91	1.00	0.55	89.64	252.34	13.03	21.05
200	200	1374	40%	5665.55	1.00	0.55	89.29	245.27	12.71	20.99

Table 3. Sample output.

diagnosis and repair task with only the aid of a reference-style manual and his or her own experience.

First you select a task—the Hartzell task. This selection sets the task representation parameter. Then you decide that the defaults for the next two task parameters, subtask state and skip steps, are appropriate for this experiment.

Next, you specify the information about agents. You decide not to have a helper; this decision requires no parameter changes, since helper present is "no" by default. The only agent parameter requiring change is worker experience. You set the worker's experience to 30 percent to reflect an "unskilled worker."

Next you adjust the action parameters. You choose not to change the assignment of actions to subtasks, but you do want to change two of the action selection probabilities (probability of selection by worker). For example, you might want to model the worker as someone who dislikes looking up information in a manual, but enjoys filing reports frequently. Thus, you reduce the probability of looking up information and increase the probability of filing reports from the respective default values.

The technology parameter defaults are all satisfactory to you. The worker has access to a physical reference manual. Without an electronic manual, the agent cannot have a checklist because that is electronic based. The remaining technology parameters do not apply to the solo condition.

Finally, you set the output parameters. As in any experiment, you must specify a sample size. In COMIT, you specify the number of complete and incomplete simulations to run. Because you are working in an exploratory mode, you request timing, quality, and frequencies of all actions. You decide on a sample size of 200 complete simulations. You are not interested in frequencies or quality; therefore, you set the frequencies of actions and report task quality to "no." The Duration's default is "yes," so you do not change this parameter.

Having set these parameters, you are now ready to run the virtual experiment. COMIT runs in batch mode and upon completion of the experiment reports both

	Low Technology			High Technology		
	Parameter Type	*Parameter*	*Value(s)*	*Parameter Type*	*Parameter*	*Value(s)*
Solo	AGENT	Helper Present	No	AGENT	Helper Present	No
	AGENT	Worker Experience	30-70%	AGENT	Worker Experience	30-70%
	AGENT	Helper Experience	N/A	AGENT	Helper Experience	N/A
	TECHNOLOGY	Manual Style	Reference	TECHNOLOGY	Manual Style	Step-By-Step
	TECHNOLOGY	Manual Type	Physical	TECHNOLOGY	Manual Type	Electronic
	TECHNOLOGY	Check-List	N/A	TECHNOLOGY	Check-List	Yes
	TECHNOLOGY	Audio	N/A	TECHNOLOGY	Audio	N/A
	TECHNOLOGY	Video	N/A	TECHNOLOGY	Video	N/A
Collaborative	AGENT	Worker Experience	30-70%	AGENT	Worker Experience	30-70%
	AGENT	Helper Present	Yes	AGENT	Helper Present	Yes
	AGENT	Helper Experience	100%	AGENT	Helper Experience	100%
	TECHNOLOGY	Manual Style	Reference	TECHNOLOGY	Manual Style	Step-By-Step
	TECHNOLOGY	Manual Type	Physical	TECHNOLOGY	Manual Type	Electronic
	TECHNOLOGY	Check-List	N/A	TECHNOLOGY	Check-List	Yes
	TECHNOLOGY	Audio	Present	TECHNOLOGY	Audio	Present
	TECHNOLOGY	Video	Not Present	TECHNOLOGY	Video	Present

Table 4. Experimental design.

the number of complete simulations and the average duration of all complete simulations. The output from this experiment is shown in table 3, along with the results of an identical experiment with worker experience of 40 percent.

Illustrative Results

Let us return to our hypothetical manager who is trying to make technology purchasing or scheduling decisions where a wide variety of technology and work arrangements are possible. By modeling and simulating the situation, the manager can make educated decisions about this rather complex scenario. To examine this scenario, we used COMIT to run virtual experiments with four conditions (see table 4). We examine extreme cases, from an environment that exists now—individuals working alone with hard copy manuals—to a futuristic view employing wearable technology—a worker and helper with lots of technology (audio, video, and an electronic manual). The experimental design is illustrated in table 4.

	Technology	
	Low	High
Solo	5608.6	5513.5
Collaborative	13266.5	11693.8

Table 5. Task completion time.

	Technology	
	Low	High
Solo	241.1	238.9
Collaborative	251.1	239.6

Table 6. Number of physical manipulations.

Let's imagine that the manager argues that some training has been provided and that all workers have some experience (say 50 percent) and all helpers are experts with complete experience (100 percent). If the manager was interested in making a decision based solely on reducing time, then he or she would select an individual worker with little technology (table 5). However, if the manager was more concerned with minimizing the physical manipulations of the machinery, then he or she would elect a collaborative condition loaded with technology (see table 6). Note that it appears that collaborative groups are more affected by technology than individual workers. Further analysis in which the degree of technology is varied in the collaborative setting might provide us with the optimal amount of technology for this particular task.

Now imagine that the manager has decided not to train the workers, a priori. Instead, the manager has a variety of employees to assign as workers to the task, but they vary in their experience. The manager still has highly skilled employees (100 percent experience) available to act as helpers. Now the decision space becomes a bit more complicated. Previously, we considered the case where the workers were all equally and partially skilled (50 percent experience). Now let us consider five levels of worker experience—30 percent, 40 percent, 50 percent, 60 percent, and 70 percent. As can be seen in tables 7 and 8, the relation between technology and the individual versus the collaborative condition depends on the experience of the worker.

Basing a scheduling decision on completion time had the manager schedule an individual worker with 50 percent experience in a low technology arrangement. The manager would make the same judgment for all workers with less

		Technology	
	Worker Experience	Low	High
Solo	30%	5771.9	5785.4
	40%	5665.5	5611.6
	50%	5608.6	5513.5
	60%	5393.2	5346.3
	70%	5233.2	5178.8
Collaborative	30%	13903.2	12040.4
	40%	13502.1	11847.1
	50%	13266.5	11693.8
	60%	12539.0	11296.2
	70%	11980.5	10867.3

Table 7. Task completion time as worker experience varies.

		Technology	
	Worker Experience	Low	High
Solo	30%	252.3	253.0
	40%	245.3	245.5
	50%	241.1	238.9
	60%	230.3	230.7
	70%	222.7	221.5
Collaborative	30%	267.2	249.0
	40%	256.9	244.1
	50%	251.1	239.6
	60%	237.7	228.9
	70%	227.9	220.6

Table 8. Number of physical manipulations as worker experience varies.

than 70 percent experience. Highly experienced workers complete the task more quickly with higher technology.

In the case of physical manipulations of the machinery, the manager is faced with an even more complex decision. If workers are working individually, technology has little impact on performance. However, under collaborative conditions, technology actually decreases the number of manipulations, even below what it would be if there were no helper.

This virtual experiment suggests some of the complexities in making decisions. Simple rules of thumb may not capture the dependencies between technologies, work conditions, and experience. By using COMIT, the manager can adjust parameters, do a series of what-if analyses, and locate more desirable conditions.

Discussion

With today's telecommuting technology and tomorrow's wearable technology, managers must begin to learn to evaluate the worth of these technologies in a variety of situations. COMIT is a prototype of the type of computational framework that is needed to examine the impact of technology, training, task, and organizational design on performance, given adaptive agents. The ultimate goal is to develop a tool like COMIT that could be used by researchers and managers as a decision aid to understand the effects such technologies and their application environments have on both cooperative and individual work in organizations.

COMIT allows users to model problems, such as diagnosis and repair, as a series of interlocked stages. In principle, it is therefore possible to use COMIT to examine either a user's specific needs or more generic tasks. Similarly, it is also possible to model a variety of technologies. These technologies include those that are widely available today (such as the telephone) as well as those that may be widely available in the near future (such as wearable computing). Further, COMIT has the flexibility to allow a user to describe both general classes of technologies (such as manuals) and specific subclasses (such as physical reference manuals or electronic step-by-step manuals). Finally, COMIT is flexible enough to allow users to model agents with varying capabilities. By varying an agent's task experience or willingness to provide feedback, users may be able to better understand the relationship between agents and differing technologies.

COMIT provides users with the ability to model task, technology, and agent with ease while remaining applicable to the user's domain. What COMIT lacks (aside from a user-friendly interface), are facilities for easily modeling new technologies, tasks involving more than two people, and complex organizational designs. The task of modeling new technologies is complex. Although some technologies have models associated with them (Clark and Brennen 1991; McCarthy and Monk 1994), new classes of technologies often emerge before a theoretical model is accepted. Researchers interested in building or maintaining systems such as COMIT should either select models that appear applicable or design new models. In addition, each technology may require the implementation of new source code.

COMIT's organizational component is composed of, at most, two people working in a predefined fashion. Consequently, COMIT is a microlevel simulation not currently capable of simulating the complexities of large organizational projects. While other simulations exist to model the macroworld (see Levitt, et al. 1994), they do not model the microlevel interactions COMIT models between individuals and technology. For COMIT to evolve into a system useful for examining larger projects and more complex organizational designs, care must be taken to ensure that the spirit of COMIT continues; namely that the computational model is flexible enough to apply to a wide variety of situations. In particular, COMIT needs to be expanded to include general features of information flow and the constraints of organizational design on performance.

We applied COMIT to a simple issue—should management invest in more technology for solo or collaborative repair work. Our findings suggest that a more experienced agent performs the task faster with more advanced technology, but hinders the less experienced. This simple experiment demonstrates that technology, training, and organizational design interact in complex ways to influence performance. Virtual experiments such as these are important for developing a theory of embedded information technology. The value of these experiments, however, will increase once models like COMIT are calibrated.

Specifically, the need to model environment, agent, task, and technology required us to make a number of assumptions not explicitly discussed in this chapter. Many of these assumptions, usually simplifying assumptions about human behavior, have their basis in experimental results, while others are based on experience and intuition. Those not yet based on experimental results should be verified to validate COMIT. Validation is a two-step process involving calibration and prediction.

The calibration of a computational model is an important step in making its results useful. Calibration of COMIT will require matching COMIT's predictions with the experimental results from human experiments. For example, we must create an experiment varying the technology and agent parameters. To test the quality or time issue as it relates to computer-based manuals, we can design a human experiment varying the type of manual used. To test telecommunication devices, we can vary the presence or absence of a helper with such devices. We intend to calibrate COMIT using data from a human experiment using the Hartzell task. Calibration of the simulation will be conducted by "training" COMIT using the results of 20 percent of the human subjects. This training will take place through a process of setting parameters in COMIT based on this 20 percent sample, and then predicting performance results for this sample.

Once the performance of the COMIT agents and the humans is matched in this small sample within some tolerance, COMIT should be able to predict the performance of the remaining 80 percent of the subjects. If the prediction matches the experimental results, the model has been validated.

Conclusion

As information technologies come to play an increasingly important role in organizations, the need for tools that allow users to preview the potential impacts of these technologies prior to their being established in the organization will grow. COMIT is a prototype system that illustrates some of the features of such a system. It is useful for building theory about the interaction between technology, task, and organization when agents are adaptive.

Acknowledgments

This work was supported in part by the ARPA SSTO HCI program under grant DACA88-94-C-0014 and the Human Computer Interaction Institute at Carnegie Mellon University.

Notes

1. We use the term information technology in its broadest sense to include tele and traditional communication technologies, as well as electronic and physical information systems.

2. Additionally, a trace can be printed as the simulation proceeds.

3. The number of subtasks is bounded only by the amount of memory on the researcher's computer.

4. All subtasks have ten steps.

5. Additional parameters can also be specified that determine whether the manual is random access or sequential access, the time to find information dependent on the current open manual page, and the probability of finding the information needed. This enables the creation of forms other than those described here.

6. This is based on an inexperienced worker working alone, and using only a hard copy manual.

IO

Organizational Mnemonics

Exploring the Role of Information Technology in Collective Remembering and Forgetting

Kent Sandoe

Why do certain features persist in organizations despite drastic changes in their personnel or their operating environments? Why do other features slip quietly into oblivion during periods of relative stability? How does the increasing use of highly automated forms of information technology influence these patterns of organizational remembering and forgetting? These are the central issues that are addressed in a simulation study aimed at furthering the understanding of the impact of information technology on the memory of organizations.

This chapter begins with a discussion of previous work that spans both organizational learning and organizational memory. It provides the necessary background for proposing a conceptual model of organizational remembering and forgetting. In the model, it is suggested that organizational remembering and forgetting occurs in three ways. First, an organization can remember structurally, through the establishment of rules, roles, and policies. Second, it can remember mutually, through the advisory relationships among its members. Finally, it can remember technologically, through the creation of physical or symbolic artifacts. These mnemonic forms are termed hierarchy, network, and hub, respectively.

The chapter next describes a simulation model that is derived from the conceptual model. The three mnemonic forms are simulated through different combinations of intelligent agents. Hierarchies consist of three tiers, with a CEO at the top, three managers at the second level, and nine analysts at the third level. Networks are modeled as all-channel networks, where each of nine agents is connected to all other agents. Hubs are modeled as wheel or star networks with nine agents connected to a centralized information source. To assess how changes in the workforce and instabilities in the organizational environment influence organizational remembering and forgetting, the three mnemonic forms are modeled under different levels of turbulence, turnover, and cost. The chapter discusses how the simulated forms are implemented using C++.

Next, the chapter highlights the major findings of the study. These findings indicate that hierarchies are most vulnerable to turbulence, networks to turnover, and hubs to cost. While hierarchies learn faster and are better than networks at resolving problems using their prior experience, networks outperform hierarchies at recognizing opportunities in the environment. Hubs outperform both hierarchies and networks in their ability to recognize opportunities and to successfully resolve them. However, they remain vulnerable to the costs of information technology.

Presentation of the findings leads to an important discussion of their limitations. These limitations are described for each of the components of the simulation model and relationships between them in terms of alternative ways that they could be represented. This is followed by an examination of some possible directions for further research, including additional simulation studies. Finally, the chapter concludes with a discussion of the implications of this work for the design of information systems and, more generally, for organizations, institutions, and society.

The symptoms of collective amnesia are not unfamiliar to executives and managers in today's organizations: fragmentation of social networks, training drain of employee turnover, undocumented and untraceable decision histories, and the endless reinvention of the same solutions for the same problems. Indeed, these symptoms are increasingly commonplace as sweeping changes in organizations, institutions, and technology undermine the two of the most important bases of organizational memory: social structures and individual minds. In our headlong rush from the iron cage of Weber's bureaucracy to the stream-lined efficiency of Drucker's flat organization, we have unwittingly reduced the mnemonic potential of the former's complex hierarchies and organizational structures. At the same time, the increased transience of workers at all levels of organizations has lessened their ability to serve as stable repositories of organizational memory.

If people and social structures are no longer sufficient to preserve an organization's memory, what is left but the slow and inevitable obliteration of the organizational past? There is a bright spot, however, in this gloomy portrayal of everyday life in postmodern times. Advanced information technologies (ITs) show great promise as tools to support remembering in organizations. IT has the potential to act as a mnemonic safety net for organizations: capturing, preserving, and providing access to many of the details of organizational life that might otherwise be lost through restructuring or turnover. However, as with any extension of individual or social capabilities through technology, the application of IT to organizational remembering brings both burdens and benefits to its users. Rigidity, stultification, a fixed worldview, the inability to respond innovatively in nonroutine situations—these are all possible drawbacks of an overly prescribed organizational memory. It is clear that there is a need to determine an appropriate role for IT in supporting organizational memory. To do so, we must first understand the practices of organizational remembering and forgetting and learn how information technology impacts these practices.

For a social scientist, attempting to understand the many subtle and complex ways that social entities remember and forget is a daunting task for several reasons. First, there is little in the way of theory or formal models of collective memory (Huber 1991; Walsh and Ungson 1991). Such theory or models would normally guide such an inquiry, providing the basis for extension, comparison, or refutation. Furthermore, the investigation of organizational remembering is made even more difficult by virtue of the fact that much of it is deeply embedded in organizational routines and practices that are seldom verbalized, seldom even thought about. Phenomena that lie beyond talk and thought are rarely tractable through conventional social science methods ranging from survey to intensive field-based observation.

One way to study these phenomena that avoids some of the limitations of traditional approaches is simulation. Simulation has proven to be a powerful technique for researchers investigating constructs closely related to organizational memory. For example, simulation has been used to model the influence of socialization processes on organizational adaptation and to study the relationship between stability and change within populations of organizations. In particular, the simulation described in this chapter is an outgrowth of the work of Kathleen Carley at Carnegie-Mellon University. In her simulation, Carley (1992) investigated the impact of personnel turnover on organizational learning.

This chapter demonstrates how simulation can be used to explore some assumptions about how organizations remember and forget and how IT may influence these processes. The first step is to gather these assumptions and organize them into a conceptual model. Thus, the chapter begins by describing the model in terms of processes and forms of memory. The next step requires careful reasoning about how these processes and forms might be instantiated in organizations and, more importantly, what are the critical factors that constrain and enable their reproduction within the environments in which they operate. This leads to the development of an overall plan for a computational model known as the simulation schema. The schema provides an outline for discussing each of the key components of the computational model in turn. Since the focus of the chapter is on building a computational model, the results of the simulation are described only briefly, and the chapter concludes by discussing the implications and future directions of this research.

Memory as Form and Process

In our daily lives, we all interact with other people in groups or organizations. Often, these interactions have a recurrent or periodic nature: we go to work every day, belong to social clubs, worship regularly, participate in civic activities, etc.... Many of these groups or organizations existed before we joined them and will continue to exist long after we depart. In fact, their composition may change entirely, many times over in the course of years. In spite of this change, significant features of these organizations persist: behaviors, routines, ways of operating, practices, etc. This phenomenon could be called the temporalizing of culture, the historicity of collective experience, or the structuration of social knowledge (Giddens 1979, 1984). We choose to term the persistence of social forms and the characteristics and consequences this persistence holds for social entities as "organizational memory."

Organizational memory can be defined as a framework of mutual understanding through which knowledgeable human agents maintain temporal and spatial continuity. As such, it guides and orients people in their everyday activity when working together and interacting in groups. But it is also a process whereby current activities are reconciled within a structure of prior interactions.

On the one hand, we can look at the framework or structure of organizational memory as memory itself, while the reconciliation process is remembering. For analytic purposes, this is often a useful distinction. But it must also be understood that the two, memory and remembering, are really aspects of the same thing. Memory, as framework, constrains and enables remembering and is both medium and outcome of this process. In a similar way, remembering, as process, is recursively implicated in the reproduction of memory (Giddens 1979).

To better understand the processes of remembering, I parse them into three temporal "stages": recognition, resolution, and evaluation. As with the distinction between form and process, it must be understood that these are not genuinely distinct or necessarily sequential processes or activities within organizations.

We can conceive of *recognition* as the process of remembering that reproduces memory through the interpretation of goals. Scanning the environment and matching external opportunities and risks with internal goals are examples of recognition. Organizational memory that results from and participates in recognition is often formally and informally articulated as goals, strategy, plans and forecasts.

Resolution is the process of remembering that reproduces memory through the interpretation of techniques. Performing tasks and making decisions based on memory are examples of resolution. The memory that resolution reproduces constitutes workflow descriptions, specification of how tasks are decomposed, forms of participation, and patterns of authority.

Remembering as *evaluation* reproduces organizational memory through the interpretation of criteria. Process review and performance comparison are activities of evaluation. Evaluation reproduces memory in the form of policies and norming patterns.

Three Forms of Memory

Individuals interact in ways that are at least partially determined by their history of past interactions. This structure of past interactions provides some stability for social encounters by eliminating the necessity for people continually and spontaneously to re-invent their actions when in the presence of others. Just as our ability to remember language and customs gives us a basis to interact in society, memory stored in social structures, in our mutuality with others, and in technology provides the basis of interaction for groups and organizations.

Structural memory is retained in social constructs such as norms, roles, and conventions of behavior. Such memory is typically embedded deep within an organization's established routines. Norms and conventions, for example, efficiently guide an organization with a minimum of thought or talk. It is not necessary, for example, for an organization to conduct an exhaustive search of its structural memory for the appropriate norm to apply in a given context; memory of this kind operates as a kind of habit or reflex. Of course, structural memories are occasionally formalized and recorded as, for example, policy and procedure manuals.

Mutual memory is the social memory that is retained in relationships between people. At one level, we can characterize it as the trust or mutual esteem that smoothes the way for interpersonal interactions. We can also think of this as the informal network that operates in most organizations: the tacit knowledge of who to go to under what circumstances.

Technological memory comprises an important organizational resource. Although commonly thought of as a means of production, technology is increasingly a means for coordinating activity. For example, coordination of projects is facilitated through the use of project management systems that permit the scheduling of activities as well as the tracking of project histories. Remembering through an organization's technology is primarily a discursive phenomenon. It is an effortful process whereby disembedded and decontextualized experience is translated to symbolic, artifactual form. A manual or automated inventory system, for example, represents the physical reality of stored goods, on the one hand, and individual agents' practical knowledge of orders placed and shipments pending, on the other, as symbolically articulated, highly formalized memory.

In the following section, the structural, mutual, and technological forms of memory described above are generalized into three mnemonic forms: hierarchy, network, and hub. While these are structures that are commonly studied in organizational research, they are used in somewhat nonconventional ways in the model. To highlight these differences, I will discuss each form, first in terms of its conventional usage (i.e., the location of strategy formulation, planning, and goal-setting; the nature of managerial decision-making and control; the role of information; and the capacity for innovation) and then in terms of its specific application as a mnemonic form.

Hierarchy

Since the days of Max Weber's ideal organizational forms, organizational researchers have extensively studied hierarchies. In hierarchically-structured organizations, strategy formulation, planning, and goal setting occur typically in the upper levels of management, at the "strategic apex." Hierarchies are noted for their efficiencies in task assignment and performance evaluation resulting largely from the specialization of work and differentiation of roles. In their use of information, hierarchies are criticized because of their tendency toward uncertainty absorption and toward information filtering. As environmental uncertainty increases, these tendencies result in poor performance. Individual decision makers are subject to the consequences of information diversity and overload because of the inherently limited cognitive abilities of human beings. Executives, in particular, focus more intently on recent successes than prior failures. With their restricted communication flows and sequential work processes, hierarchies tend to limit innovation.

In the model, hierarchies as mnemonic forms are characterized by anticipatory structures (goals, plans, strategy) that are highly stable, resulting in processes of recognition that are passive, automatic, and localized (usually at the top of the hierarchy). Structures of participation provide for decomposition of tasks, allowing resolution to occur through work specialization and aggregated decision making. The process of evaluation is highly prescribed by the form of memory itself and serves primarily to reinforce the status quo.

Network

As an alternative to the traditional hierarchical form, networks have been the focus of great interest on the part of organizational researchers in recent years. Networks are portrayed as organizational forms in their own right, as well as interorganizational systems or markets. Goal setting may be decentralized in networked or matrix forms, occur through the mutual adjustment of "adhocracies," or be driven by problems in a "garbage-can" process. In terms of managerial decision making and control, market or network structures can, under certain conditions, outperform hierarchies using techniques of bargaining and mutual influence. Because of their emphasis on lateral communication and integrative work processes, some researchers suggest that networks foster greater creativity. On the other hand, innovation may require such complex coordination that networks quickly become overwhelmed and performance declines.

In the networked mnemonic form, recognition is dispersed, resulting in anticipatory structures that are cooperative and/or competitive. Processes of reso-

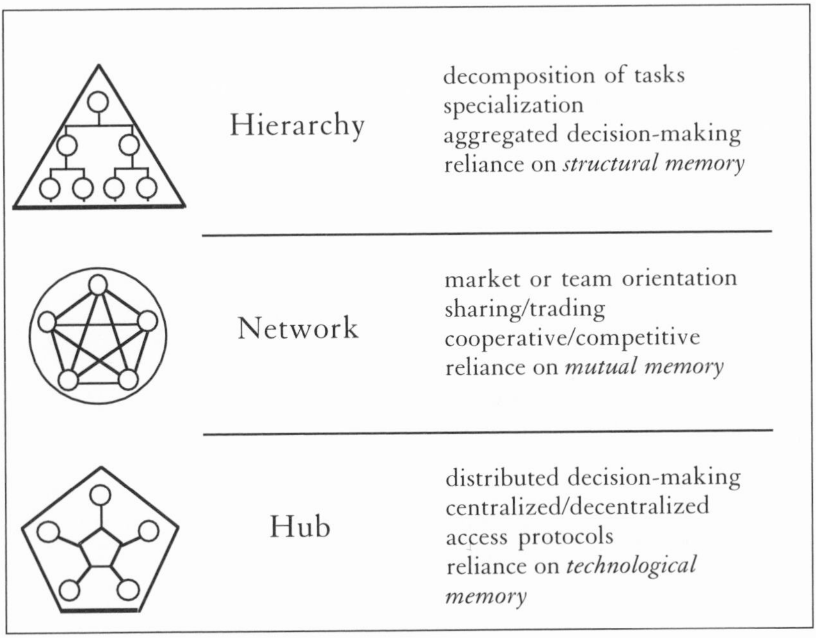

Figure 1. General mnemonic forms.

lution involve sharing and trading, resulting in market or team-oriented structures of participation. Evaluation is patterned on the nature of interpersonal relationships, causing structures of remembrance to take the form of socialization.

Hub

Compared with the attention paid to hierarchies and networks, hubs are relatively neglected in organizational research. One reason for this is that hubs are often viewed as either simple hierarchies or special cases of an idealized network. Both viewpoints are valid if an organizational form is described purely in terms of topology. However, it seems that hubs merit study as forms that are distinct from hierarchies and networks. First, hubs are unlike hierarchies in their decentralized managerial decision making and control. This provides a measure of flexibility not found in traditional hierarchies. For example, teams supported with information technology and decentralized, IT-dependent service organizations have advantages in coordination and task execution. At the same time, hubs are unlike networks in their centralization of information. In fact, hub-type alliances or constellations have been shown to overcome the complex coordination required for innovation in networks. However, such hub forms have significant costs that must be managed properly for their innovation advantages to be realized.

In its mnemonic form, the hub uses the articulation of goals to mediate the exhaustive-search-based activities of recognition. Techniques or generalized procedures provide the basis for the distribution of tasks and decision-making processes of resolution through participatory structures that focus on protocols, standards, and conditions of access. Criteria drive the activities of evaluation by continuously updating the form's memory.

The Role of the Environment

An organization's environment can be described as the set of exogenous forces and conditions that both surround and permeate it. As such, an organization's environment plays an important role in determining its success or failure. This importance has long been recognized in contingency theories (Thompson 1967, Lawrence and Lorsch 1967), bureaucratic models (Perrow 1979), and ecological theories (Hannan and Freeman 1977, Aldrich 1979) of organization.

Of most immediate concern to organizations is their task environment. The task environment presents organizations with opportunities and risks (Porter 1985). The kinds of tasks an organization faces vary considerably in the time and integrative effort required to resolve them (Kriger and Barnes 1992). Furthermore, assumptions about the nature of the environment clearly influence performance on decision-making tasks (Milliken and Vollrath 1991)

One type of task of particular interest in this study has been described by Carley as a "quasi-repetitive decision-making task" (Carley 1992). It is quasi-repetitive in that the same or similar tasks recur with some regularity, but with slightly different information and potentially requiring slightly different decisions. Carley points to many areas where this type of task is common in organizations, including policy-making, budgeting, and product development (Carley 1992).

One factor that is used to characterize the conditions under which decision-making tasks are performed is the degree of certainty. When the task environment changes rapidly, uncertainty increases and it becomes more difficult for organizations to make successful decisions (Daft and Weick 1984).

Environmental or market turbulence is often described as increasing levels of uncertainty or complexity in the task environment (Perrow 1979). Research has shown that turbulence increases vulnerability in vertically-integrated firms (D'Aveni and Ilinitch 1992), requires greater adaptability and flexible strategic response (Ulrich and Wiersema 1989), requires greater access to external information (Trippi and Salameh, 1989), and requires both learning and unlearning (Binsted 1989) and learning by doing (Marsick and

Cederholm 1988) on the part of managers and executives in organizations.

Because an important repository of organizational memory is the minds of individual agents, the arrival and departure of members have significant consequences for an organization's ability to remember. Indeed, researchers have noted a strong relationship between organizational learning and employee turnover (Huber 1991, Carley 1992, Neustadt and May 1986). In particular, success in knowledge-intensive firms has been attributed to their ability to manage turnover (Starbuck 1992). A contrary finding showed that the transmission of organizational culture among employees is unaffected by turnover (Harrison and Carroll 1991), indicating that factors other than individuals dominate this process. Finally, there is a clear relationship between performance, tenure, and turnover such that turnover is lower among high-performing, high-tenure individuals (Zenger 1992; Schwab 1991).

Organizational costs can be defined as those costs added to the costs of transactions by the existence of the organization. Generalizing about organizational costs is difficult because there are so many variations in cost across industries, classes of organizations, and locations. Malone (1987) developed a framework for examining organizational costs that is well suited to a comparative analysis of organizational forms with a focus on information technology and organizational remembering. He proposes three types of costs: production costs, coordination costs, and vulnerability costs (Malone 1987). In modeling organizational coordination, he represents these as waiting costs, messaging costs, and costs of component failure, respectively.

Prior research on the organizational impact of IT focused primarily on direct effects, for example, IT's impact on income and costs (Harris and Katz 1989), performance (Rice and Contractor 1990), and productivity (Davis 1991). These studies demonstrate that the impact of IT on organizations is subtle and complex. An adequate measure of performance must be able to address the multilevel impact of IT. For example, IT may impact organizational memory practices that may, in turn, impact overall organizational performance and productivity. The measures selected must capture these primary and secondary effects.

Simulation Schema

Simulations simplify reality. Of necessity, this simulation models only those factors crucial to an understanding of organizational memory. Endogenous factors included in the simulation are the forms and processes of memory described above; excluded are individual cognition and motivation, incentive and reward structures, and organizational leadership. Exogenous factors included in the simulation are instabilities in markets and workforce leading first to variations in the opportunities and risks presented by these markets and second, the skills and availability of labor; excluded are the effects of market competition and government regulation as well as the influence of labor unions and interorganizational systems.

The overall schema of the simulation is quite simple: a mnemonic form interprets a stream of events that differ in their potential benefit and cost, resulting in a measurable level of performance. By varying the composition and intensity of the event stream and the form of organization, different levels of performance are achieved. In addition to mnemonic forms and processes, the simulation models different levels of market stability, workforce stability, and cost to determine their effects on the model.

A fixed time-interval, stochastic simulation is employed in which each decision period requires four steps: (1) the environment presents the organization with three events; (2) using its past experience stored in memory, the organization selects one of these three events to resolve; (3) the organization splits up the event into tasks and makes an organizational decision; and (4) the organization evaluates its performance and updates its various memories.

In the following sections, each of the components shown in the simulation schema (figure 2) is described in detail. This description proceeds from the outside in: beginning with the task environment, internal and external constraints, and performance measures and then proceeding to the organizational actors and how they recognize, resolve, and evaluate their interactions with the task environment.

Events Stream

In the simulation, the external environment is modeled as a stream of events. Events are pattern-matching/decision-making problems and are represented as a string of twenty-seven bits. Initially, these events are external to the organization. Until events are selected by the organization for resolution, they are termed opportunities. At the beginning of each decision period, the organization is presented with three opportunities, drawn from a normal distribution of one thousand events. The organization must choose one of these opportunities to be its selected event for the decision period.

Every event has two attributes associated with it: first, a potential income and second, a "correct" decision. The potential income is computed relative to the magnitude of the event. The correct decision is based upon the number of ones versus zeros in the twenty-seven-bit event string, such that for a majority of ones, "yes" is the correct decision for the event and, for a majority of zeros, "no" is the correct decision for the event. The fact that there is an odd number of bits (27) in the event string ensures that there cannot be a tie—thus, there is always a correct decision. Although the ordering of the bits in an event makes no difference in terms of its correctness, it is important for the calculation of the potential income for the event. The leftmost bits represent greater magnitudes than

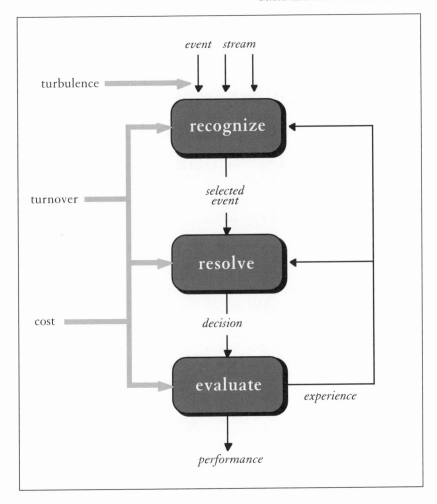

Figure 2. Simulation schema.

those to their right and thus are more significant in computing the event's overall magnitude.

At the outset, neither the organizations nor the agents that constitute them are provided with any knowledge or procedures that explicitly represent how correctness or income are calculated. Instead, they must develop this knowledge implicitly over the course of their simulated life by interacting with their environment and drawing on their experience in stored in memory.

The organizations in the simulation act as profit maximizers. Three goals drive the organizations in their effort to maximize profit: first, to recognize high-income opportunities in the environment, second, to process them success-

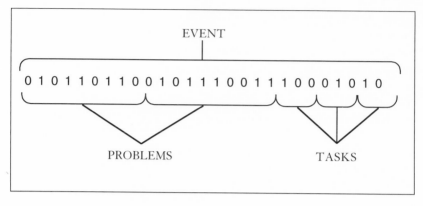

Figure 3. Event, problems, and tasks.

fully into decisions, and third, to minimize costs. Recognition occurs as the organization attempts to match its prior experience (stored as goals in memory) against the opportunities presented by the environment. If an organization recognizes more than one opportunity, it chooses the one that has produced the greatest profit in the past. If no opportunity is recognized, the organization chooses one opportunity at random.

Once an opportunity is recognized and selected, each of the three mnemonic forms uses different strategies to resolve the event into a decision of either "yes" or "no." In the case of hierarchies, the 27-bit event is decomposed into three 9-bit problems, and each 9-bit problem is further decomposed to three 3-bit tasks. (figure 3.) In the case of networks and hubs, the 27-bit event is decomposed into nine 3-bit tasks. In all forms, an agent can work on only one task during a decision period.

An organization is successful at resolving an event if its decision is the same as the correct decision for the selected event (i.e., "yes" for more ones than zeros, "no" for more zeros than ones). At the end of each decision period, the organization is either successful or unsuccessful. (The simulation does not model partial success at event resolution as is often the case in real life.) If an organization is successful at resolving its selected event, its profit for the decision period is equal to the income from the event less the costs of resolution. If an organization is unsuccessful, the income is zero and thus the organization has a loss for the decision period which is equal to the costs of resolution.

Turbulence

In the simulation, turbulence is modeled as cycles of upward and downward shifts in the mean of the distribution that is used to generate the event stream. A cycle of turbulence begins with an expansion of the range of possible events ac-

companied by a shift toward a new range of events. The expansion is represented by increasing the standard deviation of the distribution, and the shift is represented by either an increase or decrease in the mean of the distribution. The
period of market expansion (T_e) ends when the standard deviation has doubled
and the mean has shifted up or down by one standard deviation of the original
distribution.

Expansion is followed by a contraction of possible events represented by a reduction of the standard deviation back to its original size. Once the period of
contraction (T_c) is complete, the distribution for the new market looks exactly
like that of the original market except that it has shifted up or down by one
standard deviation.

After the market expands and then resettles at its new mean, there is a period
of relative stability (T_s), followed by another cycle of expansion and contraction,
reversing the direction of the previous shift. The degree of turbulence is determined by the frequency and magnitude of these cycles.

Turnover

In the simulation, turbulence in the workforce is modeled as turnover and is determined by the rate and type of departure. The departure rate is modeled as a
Poisson process that determines the likelihood of one or more employees departing in any given decision period. The type of departure (i.e., which employee is most likely to depart) is based upon a combination of tenure and performance. Each employee's performance score (R_e) is calculated from his or her
number of successes $(S_e$=absolute number of correct decisions in resolving tasks)
and the mean tenure of all employees (μ_T), such that:

$$R_e = \frac{S_e}{\mu_r}$$

The mean tenure of all employees (μ_T) is calculated from individual tenure
$(T_i$ = number of decision periods that employee has been a member of the organization), such that:

$$\mu_t = \frac{\sum_{i=1}^{n} T_i}{n}$$

Externally, turnover is determined by rate and type of replacement. For simplicity, the rate of replacement is equal to the rate of departure such that for every departure at the end of a given decision period, replacement occurs prior to
the beginning of the next period. In addition, while the experience of replacement workers can vary considerably, the simulation assumes that all replacement employees are novices (i.e., no prior experience and hence no memory).

Cost

For purposes of the simulation, two kinds of costs are modeled: production and coordination costs. Production costs are modeled as waiting costs caused by uncertainty in the system. Specifically, waiting occurs when agents in the various forms have insufficient information to complete tasks or make decisions; eventually, they are forced to guess. Coordination costs are (1) the costs associated with messages sent between the various components of each mnemonic form and (2) the search costs associated with examining each record of a centralized database. While messaging costs occur in all forms, search costs are associated with the hub form only. Vulnerability costs are modeled as the same for all organizational forms in this simulation.

Performance

Success. Successfully coping with events consists of applying prior experience to similar or dissimilar tasks to resolve them into correct decisions. If the decision of an organization for a given event is the same as the correct decision for that event, then the organization is said to have achieved success. In terms of the conceptual model, success can be thought of as a measure of the effectiveness of activities of resolution.

For any given decision period, an organization is either successful or not successful at resolving the selected event for that period. Over multiple decision periods, success is reported as the percentage of correct decisions made by a particular organization. An organization that does not learn through its interaction with its environment and from storing this experience as memory could be described as lacking intelligence. On average, such "zero-intelligence" organizations should achieve success about fifty percent of the time. Thus, success above a base-line rate of fifty percent is an indication of intelligence on the part of a simulated organization.

Income. As described above, events vary not only in their "correctness" but in their associated income. When matching past performance with opportunities presented by the environment, all organizations strive to recognize and select events with the greatest potential income. As they gain experience, organizations will improve their abilities to distinguish between opportunities that produce greater or lesser income.

At the end of each decision period, the income from the selected event is measured and captured irrespective of success or costs. Since income may be eliminated in the case of failure and is reduced by costs in the calculation of profit, the income measure represents potential versus actual income. As such, it is isolated from the direct effects of task resolution and therefore can be thought of as a measure of the effectiveness of the activities involved in recognition.

Profit. An organization may excel at recognizing high income events, but if it fails to resolve them successfully into correct decisions, overall performance will be low. Conversely, a mnemonic form may be very successful at resolving events but may not perform as well recognizing high-income events, resulting again in a low level of overall performance. Because profit takes into account both decision correctness and potential income, it measures the combined effects of recognition and resolution. In addition, profit measures the mnemonic form's ability to control costs as it gains experience with its task environment.

Organizational Actors

To cope successfully with events, organizations rely on their memory of past events to classify and assign portions of the event to appropriate agents for resolution. Agents draw on their experience with similar past tasks to resolve their currently assigned tasks. An important goal of this research is to determine the effects of structural, mutual, and technological features of organizations on remembering. To distinguish these effects from those of individual memory, the agents in all forms operate identically at the individual task resolution level.

Hierarchy

The hierarchies modeled in the simulation consist of three levels, each constituting a separate role classification with a distinct set of mnemonic practices. Thirteen agents are arrayed in the hierarchy as follows: nine *analysts*, three *managers*, and a *CEO*.

At the top of the hierarchy is a CEO. The CEO maintains a memory of those events with which the organization has had prior successful and profitable experience. This memory is used by the CEO to select events from among the opportunities presented by the environment at the beginning of each decision period. Because the memory does not contain failures or unprofitable successes, the events stored in it are defined as *goals*. In addition to the twenty-seven-bit event string, each goal includes the profit that it generated and the distribution order that indicates what part of the event was assigned to each of the three managers.

The memory is chronologically ordered with the most recently resolved event at the top. To model the cognitive limitations of individual decision-makers, the memory is limited in size to eighty-one goals and is subject to saliency effects such that more recent events are more fully remembered. Saliency effects are modeled by masking a portion of the twenty-seven-bit event string as follows. First, for the first twenty-seven goals, there is no masking; second, for goals twenty-eight through fifty-four, the least-significant (left-most) nine bits are masked; third, for goals fifty-five through eighty-one, the least-significant eighteen bits are masked.

Faced with three opportunities at the beginning of each decision period, the CEOs use their memory to select the opportunity with the highest potential profit. In the case of a tie or at least one of the opportunities not matching a goal in memory, the CEO selects the opportunity to be worked on at random, divides it into three problems, and randomly assigns each problem to one of the three managers.

The second level of the hierarchy consists of three managers. Each manager maintains a memory that consists of rankings of the performance for each of their three subordinate analysts. The memory consists of a list of each analyst's performance for each of the eight possible task types.

Upon receiving their assigned problems from the CEO, the managers divide the problems into three three-bit tasks and assign them to their subordinate analysts based upon the performance rankings. Beginning with the most significant task, each manager compares the task against its memory and selects the analyst with the highest performance for that task. In the case of a tie, the manager selects the analyst at random among the others and incurs waiting costs. The process is repeated for the remaining two tasks.

The third level of the hierarchy consists of three groups of three analysts, each subordinate to one manager. Analysts use their prior experience stored in their skills memories to resolve tasks assigned to them by their managers. When assigned tasks, they compare these tasks against their skills memory and respond with the decision that has led to the greatest success in the past. When their skills show more success with "yes," the analysts resolve tasks with a "yes" decision (equal to one). When the record shows more success with "no," the analysts resolve tasks with a "no" decision (equal to zero). When success is equal, the analysts guess (choose one or zero at random).

Once they have decided, the analysts pass their decisions back up the hierarchy to their superior managers. The managers collect the decisions of their subordinate analysts. The managers then decide either "yes" or "no" based on whichever decision agrees with the majority of their analysts' decisions. Since there are exactly three analysts for each manager, and because each analyst must respond with either a "yes" or "no" decision, there can be no ambiguity in the aggregation of the analysts' decisions.

Upon deciding, the managers pass their decisions up the hierarchy to the CEO. The CEO collects each of the managers' decisions. As in the case of the managers, the CEO aggregates them by deciding either "yes" or "no" based on whichever decision agrees with the majority of their managers' decisions. Also similar to the managers, since there are exactly three managers subordinate to the CEO, and because each manager must respond with either a "yes" or "no" decision, there can be no ambiguity in the aggregation of the managers' decisions. The CEO's decision is the final decision of the hierarchy for the decision period.

Performance is evaluated by first calculating the profit for the decision period. Profit is determined by subtracting the total costs for recognizing and resolving the event from the income generated by the event. The income (I_h) is based upon the magnitude of the event (E) adjusted by a constant profit factor (k_b), such that:

$$I_h = \frac{E}{k_b}$$

Costs for the hierarchy (C_h) are calculated as coordination costs incurred through messages sent by the CEO, managers, and analysts (M_c, M_m, M_a) and waiting time caused on the occasions when they were required to guess (W_c, W_m, W_a):

$$C_h = M_c + \sum_{m=1}^{3} M_m + \sum_{a=1}^{3} M_a + W_c + \sum_{m=1}^{3} W_m + \sum_{a=1}^{3} W_a$$

Thus, profit for the decision period for the hierarchy (P_h) is calculated as

$$P_h = I_h - C_h$$

Once the profit for the decision period has been calculated, if the decision was made successfully and profitably, the CEO adds a goal to the top of his or her goals memory. If the hierarchy fails by making the incorrect decision for an event, or if the costs of recognizing and resolving the event are greater than the income generated from it, no goal is added to the CEO's memory.

Next, the CEO informs the managers of the success or failure of the hierarchy's decision. The managers update each subordinate analyst's performance rating according to the following rule: (1) if the hierarchy was successful and the analyst's decision agreed with the manager's decision, or (2) the hierarchy was unsuccessful and the analyst's decision did not agree with the manager's decision, then (3) the analyst's performance score for the assigned task is incremented; otherwise, (4) the analyst's performance score for the assigned task is decremented.

The managers then inform each of their subordinate analysts of the success or failure of the hierarchy's decision. Analysts update their skills memories according to the following rule: (1) if the hierarchy was successful, increment the skills memory for the assigned task and decision; otherwise (2) decrement the skills memory for the assigned task and decision.

The evaluation rules for the managers and analysts in the hierarchy assume that, in addition to the information loss that occurs when the decisions are aggregated up the hierarchy, there is information filtering that occurs during the activities of evaluation. The managers and analysts receive no information about the hierarchy's final decision other than its success or failure. Thus, they have no basis with which to compare their decision and must assume that the successful or unsuccessful decision of the hierarchy was the same as theirs. This means that, in some cases, the decision of as many as five analysts and one manager may have been the opposite of the hierarchy's aggregate decision and still their incorrect decisions are treated as successful if the aggregate decision is correct (or vice versa).

Network

Networks are modeled as all-channel networks where each agent is connected to all other agents. Here, the agents are described as members, and all nine members are equal in roles and status with the exception of the leader, a position that is subject to change for each decision period. In addition to the members, there are thirty-six dyadic relationships between members that retain memory and influence the distribution of tasks.

The decision period begins as each member evaluates the same set of three opportunities presented by the environment against their individual goals memory (subject to the same size and saliency effects as CEOs in hierarchies). Each member submits a bid to become leader for the decision period for a specific event. The members calculate their bids based on their confidence that the recognized events can be successfully resolved. The more completely the event matches their goals, the higher the level of confidence. The member submitting the highest bid becomes the leader for that decision period only, and his or her selected event becomes the event chosen by the network.

The leader for the decision period initiates the division of the selected event into nine tasks. First, the leader removes the most significant task (leftmost three bits) from the event to be resolved later. Next, the leader passes the remainder of the event (*event fragment*) to his or her most valued relationship. Depending upon the strength of the relationship, a portion of the event fragment may be returned to the leader unresolved. In this case, the leader repeats the process by passing the event fragment to the next most valued relationship. This process repeats until the event is fully decomposed into tasks and distributed to members such that each member has one task. At this point, the leader resolves the task removed earlier in exactly the same fashion as in the case of the analysts in hierarchies described above.

Each relationship in the network maintains a memory of how successful it has been in resolving event fragments of various sizes. Successful two-way interactions result in an increase in the strength of the relationship, which is tracked on the basis of fragment size. The strength of the relationship determines how much of the event fragment is passed on to the corresponding member and how much is returned to the sender unresolved. At a minimum, all relationships are sufficiently strong to handle a fragment of one task. As a relationship grows stronger, it gradually increases its capacity for handling fragments of larger sizes.

When a member receives an event fragment from a relationship, he or she proceeds in the same manner as the leader. The only difference is that the size of the event fragment is smaller, by at least one task, than the original event. Also, the member cannot return anything to the relationship from which it receives an event fragment. Instead, after removing its task, it must choose from among its seven other relationships for the distribution of any remaining portion of the event fragment.

Once the event is fully distributed such that every member has one and only one task, each member then votes either "yes" or "no" based upon the resolution of their individual tasks. The decision of the network is the decision of the majority of its members. Since there is an odd number of members and each member must decide either "yes" or "no," the vote cannot result in an ambiguous decision.

Performance for the network is evaluated by first calculating the profit for the decision period. Like the hierarchy, profit is determined by subtracting the total costs for recognizing and resolving the event from the income generated by the event. The income (I_n) is based upon the magnitude of the event (E) adjusted by a constant profit factor (k_b), such that

$$I_n = \frac{E}{k_b}$$

Cost is calculated as coordination costs incurred through messages sent by the members (M), waiting time caused on the occasions that they were required to guess when tasks are ambiguous (W), and the costs of the voting sessions (V) necessary to establish the team leader and make the final decision:

$$C_n = \sum_{m=1}^{9} M_m + \sum_{m=1}^{9} W_m + V$$

Thus, profit for the decision period for the network (P_n) is calculated as:

$$P_n = I_n - C_n$$

Once the profit has been calculated and if the decision was made successfully and profitably, only those members whose decision concurs with the majority update their goals. If the network fails by making the incorrect decision for the selected event, or if the costs of recognizing and resolving the event are greater than the income generated from it, no goal is added to the memory of any of the members.

If the event is successfully resolved, the leader's capital is adjusted upward by the amount of the bid. This is done even if the event is not profitable. If the network fails to resolve the event into a correct decision, the leader's capital is adjusted downward by the amount of the bid or one-third of his or her remaining capital, whichever is greater. In effect, this results in the leader's being penalized for failure to a greater degree than he or she is rewarded for success. This failure penalty is designed to ensure a greater rotation in the leadership role since it is difficult for any single member to dominate this role over time.

Relationships are strengthened or weakened according to the event fragment size and performance of the network. If the network successfully resolves its selected event, the strength of each of the relationships that participated in its resolution is incremented for the corresponding fragment size. If the network fails to resolves its selected event into a correct decision, the strength of each of the relationships that participated in its resolution is decremented for the corresponding fragment size.

As in the case of the analysts in hierarchies described above, members update their skills memories according to the following rule: (1) if the network was successful, increment the skills memory for the assigned task and decision; otherwise (2) decrement the skills memory for the assigned task and decision.

Hub

Hubs are modeled as wheel or star networks. Here agents are described as *clients*. Each of nine clients is connected to a single, centralized information source *(server)*. All nine clients are equal in role and status.

The server's goals database is similar to the goals memory for the CEO in the hierarchy and the members in the network but each record contains more detailed information about each event. Specifically, the record lists the frequency for each type of task within the event and the distribution order for those clients who have successfully resolved their assigned tasks for the event.

The goals database is rank ordered by profit and is neither limited in size nor subject to saliency effects. However, because search is costly, the depth of the search is limited to a threshold that is recomputed each decision period.

Clients begin by requesting statistical information from the server on each of the three opportunities facing them at the start of each decision period. After comparing this information to their own abilities, the clients vote to choose an event for the decision period. Once an event is selected, each client creates a preference ranking that indicates the degree to which the tasks in the selected event match the client's skills. This ranking is used to create the distribution order for the tasks that make up the selected event.

Clients resolve their tasks in exactly the same manner as the analysts in hierarchies or members in networks. As in networks, the decision of the hub is the decision of the majority of its clients.

The performance for the hub is evaluated by calculating the net profit for the decision period. Like the hierarchies and networks, profit is determined by subtracting the total costs for recognizing and resolving the event from the income generated by the event. The income (I_b) is based upon the magnitude of the event (E) adjusted by a constant profit factor (k_b), such that:

$$I_b = \frac{E}{k_b}$$

Cost for the hub (C_b) is calculated as search costs incurred by the server in attempting to locate each of the three opportunities in its goals database $(S_i;$ n=number of seeks), coordination costs incurred through messages sent to and from the clients (M_c), and waiting time caused on the occasions when clients are required to guess when tasks are ambiguous (W_c):

$$C_b = \sum_{i=1}^{n} S_i + \sum_{c=1}^{9} M_c + \sum_{c=1}^{9} W_c$$

Profit for the decision period for the hub (P_b) is calculated as

$$P_b = I_b - C_b$$

Once the profit for the decision period is calculated and if the decision was made successfully and profitably, the server's goals database is updated. If the hub fails by making the incorrect decision for the selected event, or if the costs of recognizing and resolving the event are greater than the income generated from it, no goal is added to the server's memory.

If the event already exists in the server's goals database and performance has improved, the old record is updated with the new profit amount and any changes to the distribution order. In addition, because the goals database is maintained in descending order by profit, an improvement in performance means that the position of the record needs to be moved up in the database.

If the event does not exist in the database (i.e., the first time the hub has encountered this event), a new record is inserted in the database in profit order and the *threshold of innovation* is recomputed. The threshold of innovation represents a minimum level of performance that determines how deep the hub will search its goals database for a historical precedent before deciding to innovate.

The threshold of innovation (T) is calculated by taking the average performance for events where the hub has innovated successfully and profitably in the past $(P_{bi}; n = $ number of innovations):

$$T = \frac{\sum_{i=1}^{n} P_{b_i}}{n}$$

At the start of the first decision period, the threshold of innovation is zero. Each time the hub innovates successfully and profitably, the threshold is recomputed. If the hub does not innovate (i.e., when it has prior experience with the selected event), or when its innovation is unsuccessful or unprofitable, the threshold is not recomputed.

Outcomes and Conclusion

This section provides a brief overview of findings that resulted from running the simulation described above. These summary findings are discussed in terms of how turbulence and turnover impact the three organizational forms. The chapter concludes with a discussion of some future directions for this work.

Hierarchies

Of the three forms, the performance of hierarchies showed the greatest sensitivity to turbulence and were the least affected by turnover. These findings are consistent with the views of many organizational theorists on the effects of turbulence on hierarchical forms of organization. For example, despite his staunch defense of Weber's bureaucratic model of organizations, Perrow (1979) admits that. "...when such changes [in the environment] are frequent and rapid, the form of organization becomes so temporary that the efficiencies of bureaucracy cannot be realized" (p. 5). As a mnemonic form, the simulated hierarchies incorporate many of the features used by theorists to explain the difficulties hierarchies have in coping with turbulence, including weak feedback linkages (Burns and Flam 1987), rigidity (Aldrich 1979), and specialization leading to inefficiency and increased costs (Zeleny, Cornet, and Stoner 1990). The fact that hierarchies showed the least impact from turnover of all forms is consistent with Carley's (1992) finding that the effects of turnover are mitigated somewhat by organizational structure.

Networks

While turbulence showed the least impact on networks, turnover impacted them more than either of the other forms. Because this form retains its memory through its members and their relationships, it makes sense that turnover was most strongly felt in this form. Although the lack of work specialization in networks results in overall lower level of performance versus hierarchies and hubs, their ability to resolve tasks successfully is only mildly affected by a turbulent environment. In many ways networks are analogous to the task forces, teams, and matrix forms often discussed by organizational theorists. As such, they show much greater adaptability (Thompson 1967), receptiveness to experimentation (Drucker 1985), and flexibility due to lack of functional specialization (Davis and Lawrence 1977) in coping with uncertainty, instability, and change.

Hubs

In comparison to the other forms, hubs were mildly affected by both turbulence and turnover, but not to the degree of hierarchies and networks, respectively. In terms of overall performance, it is clear that hubs offer advantages over hierarchies and networks. They are better at recognizing opportunities in the environment, resolving them into successful decisions, and controlling costs. One reason for hubs' superior performance is that they retain some of the best features of both hierarchies and networks while not incorporating all of their major drawbacks. By centralizing information but not authority, hubs gain the efficiencies of specialization without the rigidity that hierarchical authority imposes through role structures. By distributing the activities of recognition but not the information services, hubs are effective at managing a complex environment without being encumbered by communication and negotiation overhead or being overly vulnerable to turnover.

It seems reasonable to conclude from the findings that IT can effectively support organizational remembering. While the hub form is slightly more vulnerable to costs than hierarchies or networks, this IT-based form offers significant performance advantages for organizations operating in turbulent times.

Future simulation studies can be embarked upon to investigate first, different kinds of tasks, situations, or problems; second, a wider range of market turbulence phenomena including seasonality and crises; third, a richer conception of turnover as an internal as well as external process, incorporating promotion, transfers, and replacement with various levels of experience; fourth, different assumptions regarding cost such as vulnerability costs resulting from the potential for errors and breakdowns; fifth, organizations that are more dynamic in terms of their internal structure and size; and sixth, the numerous and complex interrelationships among factors such as turbulence, turnover, and cost.

It seems likely that organizations will rely increasingly on IT-based memory. Such systems also have the potential to displace or alter existing forms of organizational memory, triggering organizational forgetting in potentially harmful ways. I hope that this work will provide guidance for the design of IT-based memory systems in such a way that they complement and support organizational remembering and forgetting in a positive and beneficial direction.

Validating and Docking

An Overview, Summary, and Challenge

Richard Burton

Simulating organizations is a rapidly growing science with many interesting and exciting developments. This book contains intriguing contributions to the science at the frontier and demonstrates possibilities for a next round of research. Each chapter stands on its own. The collection is even greater and gives the reader a good notion of where we are.

An overview chapter can be fashioned in many ways. I want to provide a brief summary of each chapter within a common framework. Burton and Obel (1995) provide one way to look at organizational simulation models. The validity of computational models focuses on three aspects: the purpose or question that the model addresses, the model and its simulation, and then the experimental design and analysis. These three considerations should be kept in balance; nonetheless, the purpose of the simulation is the anchor concern. Each chapter is summarized following this format.

Carley (1995) developed a perspective on computational and mathematical organization theory (CMOT) which includes a categorization scheme. She suggests four categories: organizational design, organizational learning, organizations and information technology, and organizational evolution and change. She then summarizes and gives an extended literature summary and review of CMOT using her scheme. I will suggest where each chapter fits within this framework.

The contribution of the collection is more demanding. Here I refer to the concept described in Axtell et al. (1996) of "docking," or aligning simulation models, as a challenge for the larger contribution. Each chapter is an interesting contribution and helps establish the frontier. Yet it is much more difficult to synthesize the contributions; docking is one way to search for deeper insight and greater understanding.

This chapter continues with a review of the validity model and its three elements. Carley's CMOT perspective is then described. I next turn to a brief summary of each chapter, where the validity model and the CMOT perspective are used as a very general guide. Docking is defined and applied. Finally, I look to the next areas where we need to make progress.

Validity—A Computational Model Framework

The validity of an organizational simulation is fundamental. The simulation validity helps us understand what we can learn, and cannot learn, about the underlying issue, here a better understanding of institutions and groups. Burton and Obel (1995) argue that an organizational simulation model can be summarized along three dimensions: the purpose or question, the computational model (i.e., the model statement and the simulation process), and the experimental design and the analysis of results. These dimensions should be kept in balance for an organizational simulation. Imbalance can lead to inefficiency and more importantly to misinterpretation of the model, its results, and their implications for practice and theory. Simple models are preferred, so long as they meet the purpose and address the research question.

The validity model is represented as a triangle in figure 1.

The model purpose or the question to be addressed provides the anchor. Organizational computational models can be constructed to investigate a wide variety of questions; it is a very versatile tool or laboratory. The purpose can include description of behavior, advice to managers, normative statements about what should be done, training of managers and novices, hypothesis testing, exploration of system behavior, theory generation, or alternative explanations of phenomena. No model can do all of these. A good computational model can do one well.

For each purpose, there are a number of models and simulations which can meet the purpose well. There are even more that will address it poorly for a variety of reasons, such as poor specification of variables, parameters and relations which may be too complex and detailed, over simplicity, focus on the wrong question. Finally, the experimental design and the analysis of data must relate to the question and stay within the context of the model and simulation. One frequent advantage of simulation modeling is that relatively simple experimental designs can be devised for the purpose or question. Very complex simulation models with ill-defined purpose usually create results that are difficult to interpret. Within the purpose, simple models and experiments are preferred.

The model is a convenient lens through which to look at the comprehensiveness of the organizational simulation and to relate it to the purpose or question at hand. In the following summary of the chapters, I have used the model as a very general guide, where the purpose is reviewed first, then the simulation model is described, and finally the experimental design and analysis are discussed. In each chapter, the simulation model is described in detail. This overview is not a sub-

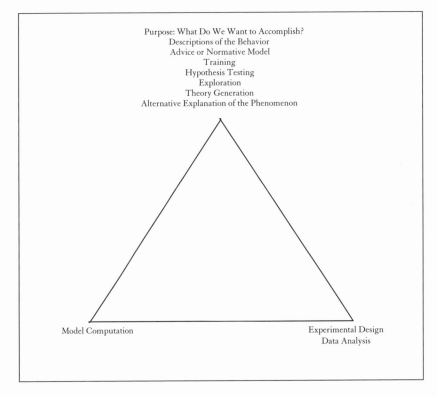

Purpose: What Do We Want to Accomplish?
Descriptions of the Behavior
Advice or Normative Model
Training
Hypothesis Testing
Exploration
Theory Generation
Alternative Explanation of the Phenomenon

Model Computation

Experimental Design
Data Analysis

Figure 1. Computation model design—balance and simplicity.
Reprinted from Burton and Obel 1995, p. 63.

stitute for the understanding you can obtain there—its purpose is the contribution of the research in terms of practice, and the relevant literature on organizational simulation. For some models, the purpose and the experimental design are more implicit; even so, the models are examples for which well-designed experiments can address interesting organizational questions.

CMOT Perspectives

Carley's (1995) framework provides an alternative way to view these contributions, that is, how each contributes to the four categories of her framework. The greatest effort has been given to organizational design, the first category. The general question is how to modify the design to meet task and environmental contingencies. Most experimental designs apply comparative static techniques to assess the effect of allocation, communication, and command structures; these are information models of organization. There is a cumulative body of research which she outlines and reviews.

The second category is organizational learning. There are two types of models: single agent and multiactor. Most of the models in this book are multiactor models. Organizational learning is tied to sharing and diffusion of information to improve organizational performance.

Organizations and information technology are in the third category. A key issue is how to consider and model alternative information technologies and then how to develop experiments which focus on improving performance.

Fnally, the fourth category is organizational evolution and change. Time-dependent models and their observation are obviously required to examine processes and the effect of their changes on performance. Carley notes that a focus on process, adaptation, task, and change can provide a more coherent understanding of organizations and how they work.

I now turn to a consideration of each organizational simulation model. Later on, I will examine some docking ideas.

The Studies

The three-element validity model serves as a general descriptive guide for the models on a chapter-by-chapter basis. I have tried to reflect and sometimes infer the purpose for the organizational simulation; the model itself; and the experimental design. To maintain the internal integrity of each chapter, I have used the language and definitions found therein; indeed, I have borrowed exact phrases and the occasional sentence without reference. My goal is to provide an organized overview within the validity model and to stay close to the chapter itself. I have also categorized each model using Carley's perspective to provide an alternative view of each contribution.

WebBots, Trust, and Organizational Science

Carley and Prietula create and examine the behavior of a new "critter"—the WebBot. A WebBot is a computer program that operates autonomously to accomplish a task as an intellectual advisor and assistant to a human counterpart (and other WebBots). Examples of what WebBots do include monitoring intranetwork events across a set of terminals, keeping an updated list of recent meetings, watching corporate knowledge bases, and scanning employee disks for viruses. WebBots are really not new; they exist today, and they can be viewed as generalized agents. What is new thinking about and examining their social and trust behaviors. WebBots are organizational members which act, communicate, remember, and require coordination. The specific question: to what extent does WebBot honesty affect individual and collective organizational behavior? More generally, Carley and Prietula are developing a new view of what we mean by organization in an information world.

The Soar architecture is the platform for the model. The WebBots communicate and remember, but they also have social memory (past interactions and what the experience was), rules of social engagement (would it tell the truth or not), and social judgment (a score card to judge others).

The experimental design varied the size of the organization and the honesty of the WebBots. Several outcome measures were used. They found some intriguing results. Untrustworthy agents first decline in terms of total time to complete a task, but then time begins to increase with a larger organizational size. Similarly for trustworthy WebBots. What is going on? As the size increases, the WebBots have increased waiting time and also communication time; both drive up the total time. But the average WebBot effort decreases, as one might expect. And over time, trustworthy WebBots ask more questions as they learn more, whereas untrustworthy agents ask fewer. Do WebBots behave like humans? What are the implications? These are intriguing questions.

Carley and Prietula conclude with some comments on the future form of organizational science. One observation is that the simulation of a WebBot organization is the organization itself. So, the WebBot is the real world. Have we come full circle?

This chapter examines WebBots as information technology. In the organization, they help human counterparts achieve goals; they are organizational players. It is an organizations and information technology model.

Team-Soar: A Model for Team Decision Making

Kang, Waisel, and Wallace want to understand better the nature of a "team"—a group with something in common, usually a goal or purpose. The study of high performance organizations, such as aircraft identification by the military, provide motivation. A team consists of highly differentiated and interdependent members with shared leadership, both individual and collective responsibility, and accountability. Individuals make decisions, as do teams, but teams proceed differently. They use multiple intelligences, often decomposing the problem into smaller subproblems which then require integration for a team solution. (This is characterized as distributed artificial intelligence, or DAI, when the intelligent agents are computational.) The literature suggests that teams make better decisions than individuals, especially for complex tasks. A team brings more information, knowledge, and reasoning capability to the problem situation.

The team is then modeled as Team-Soar, with a leader and several subunits. It captures the team description of iterated and distributed use of information among individuals to obtain a team decision.

Kang, Waisel and Wallace construct hypotheses about team behavior and then develop careful experimental designs and statistical analyses. Study I uses a 4 x 3 design in which the decision scheme (two kinds of majority win rules and two kinds of average win rules) and team informity, or information availability, were manipulated. The team performance was measured in two ways: decision deviation and disaster rate.

Study II is a 2 x 3 design that examines the impact of metaknowledge and information availability on the team wait time and the team decision cycles. The authors argue that computational models can provide insights that are difficult to sort out in the real world, can generate new and unanticipated insights, and can be useful precursors to human experiments. They confirm that more information does not always yield better decisions; the team performance was better than individual performances and yielded the unanticipated result that the metaknowledge affected team wait time and team decision cycles in opposite directions at medium and high informity levels. These are important insights about the "nature" of teams and suggest that human subject experiments should be developed to verify the insights.

Team-Soar is an organizational design model where the team is the organization. However, it also incorporates rather explicit specification of the information technology in terms of radar sources, but this is not the primary issue. Nonetheless, in Carley's terms the focus is the classical organizational design issues of task assignment, responsibility, and accountability.

An Organizational Ontology for Enterprise Modeling

Fox, Barbuceanu, and Gruninger explore an organizational ontology for the TOVE enterprise model, which links structure and behavior through the concept of empowerment. Empowerment is the right of an organizational agent to perform status-changing actions. This is an artificial intelligence (AI) perspective on organization as an information system. This second generation knowledge engineering model focuses on defining the competency for the ontology – its objects, attributes, and relations. The authors then specify the definitions and constraints which are represented in Prolog. The competency is tested with Prolog axioms. "Supply chain management" provides the real-world application and context for this research; they want to extend the MRP to include logistics and concurrent engineering.

The organization's competency is given in terms of structure and behavior. Structural competency includes who the members are, what the positions are, who fills the position, who communicates with whom, what kind of information is communicated, and who reports to whom. Behavior competency includes goals for the organization, the position, and the person. The assignment of activities and resources are also part of the behavior competency. Authority, empowerment, and commitment competency focus on who can do what. An organization is then a set of constraints on the activities performed by agents; it uses resources to achieve goals. These ideas are formalized in the first order logic and implemented in Prolog with the development of axioms. This is a preliminary exploration which develops the "rules of the game" and formalizes what we mean by empowerment in a formal and operational manner.

The model purpose and its specification are quite clear. The experimental design is yet to be developed for operational questions and designs.

In Carley's framework, it is an organizational design model with multiagents who must meet the competency requirements to obtain an organization.

An Approach to Modeling Communications and Information Technology in Organizations

Kaplan and Carley begin with an argument that computational modeling can be superior to field and experimental research, which is necessarily limited in its freedom to explore beyond normally accepted and observed parameter values and also known technologies—very limiting for new and "futuristic" technology in communications and information. Wearable technology integrates computation, voice, and sight technology simultaneously. Here computational methods provide alternative platforms for experimentation which can yield better answers at lower experimental cost, particularly for complex interactions among the several parts. It is somewhat analogous to flight simulation where an individual can learn to fly, test the limits, and crash without serious consequence.

Kaplan and Carley's purpose is to understand better the complexity of individual decision making, organizations, and information technology to predict the effects of new information technologies on organizational design. The COMIT model is a small organizational model that captures these complexities.

COMIT is a process model that specifies task, agent, action, information technology, and output parameters. The task can be specified in terms of subtasks and whether steps can be skipped or not. The agents are characterized by role, experience, and likelihood of skipping tasks. Actions include information choices such as "look up," as well as physical actions. Agents have choice and can learn. Information technology is characterized in terms of presentation, transmission, and retrieval alternatives.

The results are the organizational performance for the specified organization. Monte Carlo designs and large sample sizes are then used to test the effects of parameter variation in technology on solo or collaborative tasks. The results show interdependencies that rules of thumb miss. These insights are perhaps less likely discovered to be from independent analysis of parameters or from very complex models where it is difficult to sort out relations.

In Carley's framework, this chapter falls into the organizations and information technology category. COMIT is an explicit information technology model which links the choice of the information technology to the actual organizational use in solo and collaborative work.

For an organizational model of kindred spirit, although different in detail, see Levitt et al. (1994).

Modeling, Simulating, and Enacting Complex Organizational Processes—A Life Cycle Approach

Scacchi's purpose is to support the engineering of organizational processes throughout their life cycle; it is continuous organizational redesign. The focus is on the process engineering life cycle, which includes a large process list.

The Articulator uses a rule-based, object-oriented knowledge representation for modeling interrelated classes of organizational resources, which represents a resource-based theory of organizational processes. Agents perform tasks using tools and systems which consume or produce resources; for example, a manager can reduce staff effort in one area and assign staff to another or reduce the staff effort. The simulation or symbol execution reflects the process tasks and permits the dynamic modeling for different samples of parameter values.

What-if experiments for the design of processes are then possible. Construction and redesign are then generated for implementation in an ongoing fashion.

Scacchi's chapter, in Carley's terms, examines organization and information technology. Visualization in the Articulator is explicitly considered to ascertain the effect over the life cycle.

External Conditions and Organizational Decision Making Performance

Lin focuses on the understanding and design of high reliability organizations. A complex organization or the existence of high quality information is not sufficient. Simulation models are tools to examine other organizational possibilities. Lin examines the effect of external conditions on the decision- making performance in situations where we are concerned with the avoidance of severe mistakes. The particular motivation comes from the Cuban Missile Crisis and the Gulf War; a stylized radar task captures the main characteristics of the decision situation. This is a generalization of classic contingency theory—the effect of the environment on the performance and implications for the structure.

DYCORP is the computer simulation testbed. The radar task captures well the complex nature of the interrelationships and the difficulty in manipulating actual organizations. Time pressure is a central variable. The decision outcome calls the aircraft friendly, neutral, or hostile. An error can have severe consequences. And further, different kinds of errors have different consequences for different populations. The organizational design is varied in information terms: who knows what, when, and how decisions are made. Team voting, top-level decision making, hierarchical decision making, and two types of matrices are tested.

The experimental design systematically varies the time pressure and the organizational design and then observes the effect on the resulting decisions. The results go beyond the general contingency notion and add both precision and qualification—for an organization to achieve high performance, it should adopt an organizational design matched to the task environment. For little or extreme time pressure situations, the organizational design has little impact. However, for moderate time pressure and the performance either accuracy or type-1 errors, the design makes a difference. Perhaps many of our field studies were conducted for moderate time pressure situations; this variable is important and needs to added to our contingency notions. The question requires further exploration, both with computational methods and field studies. Yet, these kinds of controlled experiments are difficult to replicate in the field studies. Computational approaches can yield insights and add precision to theory which we would otherwise miss.

This chapter is again an organizations and information technology chapter. The focus is on reliability of the organization where the use of information follows a specification of the technology. DYCORP provides the platform for the simulation.

Fluctuating Efforts and Sustainable Cooperation

Huberman and Glance investigate the social dilemma of generating voluntary cooperation among individuals confronted with conflicting choices for time and effort. The dilemma is that the individual may help create a public good which is shared by many but where the individual costs do not merit the effort. The individual may choose to free ride on the efforts of others. This issue is fundamental and is at the heart of cooperative behavior in large organizations, political movements, and the adoption of new technologies. Indeed, it is fundamental to the maintenance of modern society and why it does not break down into anarchy. Political scientists and organizational theorists, at least, are interested in the question. It is driven by our interest in how to realize better organizations and better societies.

The model is dynamic, and the efforts of the individuals fluctuate over time, which could occur for a variety of reasons, both purposeful and random. The individual may participate in the cooperative activity or defect. This is the individual's choice and dilemma. That choice is influenced by the individual's expectation and by a mimicking; cooperation encourages cooperation, and defection encourages defection. The fluctuation can cause an individual to misperceive the actual level of cooperation and thus behave to cause a change in the equilibrium level.

The experimental design is relatively straightforward, namely, to observe the behavior and results of the dynamic simulation over time. The fluctuation has a paradoxical result that the average utility accrued by any individual decreases over time despite the fact that the average effort remains the same. Fluctuations are to be expected, rather than unusual. The dynamics of expectations and effort yield an interaction that decreases the amount of public good over time. This insight adds to our understanding of cooperative phenomena as it is likely to be experienced in the real world.

Huberman and Glance make an argument for simplicity and balance of the model. The question drives the model and yields insights that may be difficult to sort out from more complex models and the real world.

For the purposes of verifying these predictions, computer simulations have the advantage over social experiments in that the variables and parameters can be precisely specified. Although computer simulations are imperfect substitutes for real social dynamics, their relative simplicity and outcome clarity can be used as signs that this phenomenon can appear in real social settings, in particular, those situations where the average behavior of quantities reflecting collective actions seems at odds with what typical members of the group are doing.

As Burton and Obel argue, this is a basis for validity and indicates why we can and should utilize the power of computational organizational models.

In Carley's framework, this chapter is a contribution to organizational evolution and change. The organizational processes are well defined; the processes and organizational outcomes are observed over time to assess the relation between process and effect. We learn about change over time and more subtle observations than would be possible in comparative static models.

Task Environment Centered Simulation

The task environment gives the scope of the problems facing individuals, their complexity, and kinds and patterns of interrelationships between the tasks. A number of motivating illustrations shows how the approach models real-world situations and captures their essence: hospital scheduling, airline resource management, Internet information gathering, the pilot's associate, and the M-form organizational hypothesis. In all of these situations, the dependencies are the structure of the tasks and the uncertainty of the task structures. TÆMS is a framework to model and simulate complex, computationally intensive environments at multiple levels of abstraction and points of view. The purpose is to obtain better understanding of management issues and, in particular, the coordination issues.

Decker outlines and describes the TÆMS modeling approach and gives a number of illustrations. The model provides a framework and platform for a wide variety of investigations and studies.

Decker investigates organizational design with a focus on coordination mechanisms; it is a classical multiagent organizational design model.

In Carley's framework, this is organizational design—multiagent information processing models of organization.

Organizational Mnemonics—Exploring the Role of Information Technology in Collective Remembering and Forgetting

Sandoe demonstrates how simulation can be used to explore assumptions about how organizations remember and forget. In particular, we want to learn how information technology can influence these processes.

Organizational memory provides mutual understanding where knowledgeable human agents maintain temporal and spatial continuity; it guides and it orients. The process is to remember, which can be seen as three stages: recognition, resolution, and evaluation. Three forms of memory are structural memory, such as norms, roles, and conventions of behavior; mutual memory in relationships between people; and technological memory. Each form of memory has three mnemonic structures: hierarchy, network, and hub. The environment and its turbulence provide context for the model.

The computational schema is straightforward. The turbulent environment generates an event stream which results in turnover in the workforce. Costs are of two types: production and coordination, where coordination includes messages and search. Success is coping with the situation, and performance is measured in terms of income and profit. The mnemonic forms are carefully stated to reflect related real-world structures and processes.

Sandoe relates his results to organizational theory. Hierarchies were sensitive to turbulence but less affected by turnover; networks were less sensitive to turbulence but more to turnover; and finally, hubs were mildly affected by both turbulence and turnover. Information technology is utilized differentially by the three mnemonic forms and has varying effects. These results incorporate information technology issues in organizational theory and add precision to contingency notions.

In Carley's terms, this is an organizations and information technology issue. Sandoe addresses the effect of information technology on collective forgetting and remembering.

Designing Organizations for Computational Agents

So and Durfee are concerned with the design and self-design of organizations, which include humans or computer agents. The agents are communicating, autonomous, and computational. Reliability is a central concern, particularly where the agents tend to have a shorter life in the organization than the organization itself. More generally, they want to understand the design space for agents, differing tasks, and various performance goals.

Contingency theory is a theoretical organization perspective and is quite compatible with the DAI perspective. Their model includes specification of the task environment, the organization structure, and behavior and the performance requirements of reliability. Strategies for self-design are difficult to devise. The distributed network monitoring system provides a vehicle to develop the problem.

Future work requires refinement of the self-design function and the effort to expand on it. How much effort should agents spend on monitoring and redesign? How do we avoid spending too much time on monitoring and redesign and never actuality perform "work?" And should redesign be delegated to a special group? These are fundamental questions; it is a call for an ambitious agenda.

In Carley's framework, this chapter falls into the organizational design category. The multiagents are computational agents who are rather autonomous but with a focus on collective goals and their attainment. Efficiency and flexibility are central design issues.

Summary

Let's put it all together in a brief statement of important results. Here are a few insights:

- *Simulation and computational organizational models should reflect the real world but need not mimic the real world.* This is central to the validity argument and is found in a number of the chapters, most clearly in Huberman and Glance, Kaplan and Carley, and Kang et al., and is implied in the other chapters as well. Carley and Prietula take this view to the extreme where WebBots models become the real world, that is, the simulation *is* the organization.

- *Contingency notions of organizational design provide a framework for important questions.* The models add precision, clarification, and new insight to contingency notions. Huberman and Glance demonstrate that cooperation can deteriorate in a dynamic world; an insight that static equilibrium models overlook. Lin shows that time pressure has a differential effect on the organizational design. Kang and his colleagues confirm that more information is not always better for team performance. Sandoe shows us how turbulence and turnover affect the organizational structure of hierarchy, network, and hub. Carley and Prietula show that WebBot honesty and organizational size affect the development of organizational trust.

- *Information, its creation, modification, transmission, and use are what we mean by organization.* The information model of organization provides a fundamental view of organization, and simulation provides a means to examine organizational processes or work that yields insights not obtained using other approaches. The chapters herein move that frontier and establish a new point of departure. For a more historical view of the information processing view of organization, see Burton and Obel (1996).

There are many next steps; I would like to argue that docking is a next best step for our research agenda.

Docking—A Next (Best) Step

Axtell and his colleagues (1996) developed and tested "docking" or the alignment of simulation modeling. It is a compelling metaphor from space exploration and offers much promise to give simulation modeling greater validity. Docking is straightforward. We want to make two dissimilar models come together to address the same question or problem, to investigate their similarities and their differences, but most importantly, we want to gain new understanding of the question or issue. Insight is gained not only through parallel approaches to a problem, but also through meshing two approaches: do they give equivalent results, is one a special case of the other, are there new insights, do we have a parsimonious approach, is a third approach and model called for, to name a few.

Axtell and his colleagues docked the relatively simple Axelrod (1995) cultural model (ACM) with Epstein and Axtell's (1995) more complex model, Sugarscape. The purpose for ACM is to study the effects of a simple cultural mechanism and ecamine whether cultures will remain diverse or become eventually homogeneous under different circumstances. The transmission mechanism involves neighbors interacting on five attributes, where cultural change is more likely when the neighbors are the same and less likely when different. Sugarscape's purpose is to generate rich artificial histories. It takes a book to explain the model. These are significant model differences; were they able to dock the models? They tested whether the models were equivalent and would yield the same results. By simplifying Sugarscape to replicate more faithfully the Axelrod processes, they demonstrated equivalency. Similarly, they undertook an agent mobility experiment, which involved a sensitivity analysis. The models can yield equivalent results, and ACM can be viewed as a special case of Sugarscape, but within limits. Docking is not easy and involves the best of scientific judgment and technique. What do we mean operationally by "equivalent," how can we simplify a model without changing its essential elements, and how do we compare experiments? These difficulties may explain why docking is rare.

Our more usual approach is "orbiting without docking." We do a literature survey to show that what we are doing is important and germane. We may even do a thought exercise to compare our simulation models with other models and research—a kind of light touching. But true docking is rare. We rather use our time in creating and building new and more complex models. New and creative models are needed, but as a next best step we may learn more about the questions we are studying through docking as a way to accumulate our knowledge more rapidly than starting each time from the beginning. Axtell et al. argue that docking is essential to the progress of computational modeling. I agree.

In this book, there are no docking experiments. In terms of the validity model, docking must focus on the purpose or question, not on the model and simulation. There are a number of models that are built on the same platform. Lin; Kang, Waisel, and Wallace; Carley and Prietula; and Sandoe use Soar models investigating difficult issues. Soar is a versatile modeling approach. But we cannot accumulate understanding of the organizational issues or questions using this approach alone. In loose metaphor, they are in the same orbit but have not docked.

Can we devise any docking experiments, and what is there to learn? The purpose or the question is the beginning point, and I will not attempt to deal with the development of the actual docking experiments. Let me present some possibilities:

- *Trust and cooperation*. Huberman and Glance focus on cooperation, and Carley and Prietula on trust. Defection is a fundamental notion in both. These are very similar organizational concerns. Can these models be docked? I think we could learn more about mechanisms to realize nondefection, which could be quite insightful.

- *Reliability in organization*. Lin and Kang are Soar-based models which focus on reliability. Decker's modeling is different. What can we learn about reliability in organization by docking here?

These are only two possibilities of many. For n organizational simulations, there are $n(n - 1) / 2$ possibilities, or twenty-eight for the eight studies here. Clearly, not all would be interesting and worth the effort, but a few could be very important to our understanding of institutions and groups. We must first be concerned with the purpose for our models. This provides the foundation for docking of simulation models and greater understanding of organizations.

Bibliography

Abelson, R. P. 1968. Simulation of Social Behavior. In *Handbook of Social Psychology*, eds. C. Lindzey and E. Aronson, second edition, volume 2: 274-356. Reading, Mass.: Addison-Wesley.

Aldrich, H. E. 1979. *Organizations and Environment.* Englewood Cliffs, N. J.: Prentice Hall.

Auramaki, E.; Lehtinen, E.; and Lyytinen, K. 1988. A Speech-Act-Based Office Modeling Approach, *ACM Transactions on Office Information Systems* 6(2): 126-152. April.

Axelrod, R. The Convergence and Stability of Cultures: Local Convergence and Global Polarities. Santa Fe Institute Working Paper, 95-030028, Santa Fe, N. M.

Axtell, R.;Axelrod, R.; Epstein, J.; and Cohen, M. 1996. Aligning Simulation Models: A Case Study and Results. *Computational and Mathematical Organization Theory,* 1(2): 123-141.

Baligh, H. H.; Burton, R. M; and Obel, B. 1990. Devising Expert Systems in Organization Theory: The Organizational Consultant. In *Organization, Management, and Expert Systems,* ed. M. Masuch, 35-57. Berlin: Walter De Gruyter.

Balzer, R.; and Narayanaswamy, K. 1993. Mechanisms for Generic Process Support. In Proceedings of the First ACM SIGSOFT Symposium on the Foundations of Software Engineering, 9-20. *ACM Software Engineering Notes* 18(5). December.

Binsted, D. 1989. Learning to Cope with Change in the 1980s. *Management Decision* 27(4): 167-171.

Blackburn, J. 1991. *Time-Based Competition.* Concord, Ont.: Business One, Irwin.

Boddy, Mark; and Dean, Thomas. 1989. Solving Time-Dependent Planning Problems. In *Proceedings of the Eleventh International Joint Conference on Artificial Intelligence,* 979-984. Detroit, Michigan. August. San Francisco: Morgan Kaufmann Publishers.

Bond, A. H.; and Gasser, L. 1988. An Analysis of Problems and Research in DAI. In *Readings in Distributed Artificial Intelligence*, eds. A. H. Bond and L. Gasser, 3-35. San Francisco: Morgan Kaufmann Publishers.

Bruynooghe, R. F.; Parker, J. M.; et al. 1991. PSS: A System for Process Enactment. Paper presented at the First International Conference on the Software Process, 128-141. Redondo Beach, Calif.. October.

Burns, T. R., and Flam, H. 1987. *The Shaping of Social Organization: Social Rule System Theory With Applications.* London: Sage.

Burton, R. M.; and Obel, B. 1996. Organization. In *Encyclopedia of Operations Research and Management Science*, eds. S. Gass and C. Harris, 476-481, Boston: Kluwer Academic Publishers.

Burton, R. M.; and Obel, B. 1995. The Validity of Computational Models in Organization Science: From Model Realism to Purpose of the Model. *Computational and Mathematical Organization Theory* 1(1): 57-71.

Burton, R. M., and Obel, B. 1984. *Designing Efficient Organizations: Modeling and Experimentation*. Amsterdam: North Holland.

Carley, K. M. 1996. Communication Technologies and Their Effect on Cultural Homogeneity, Consensus, and the Diffusion of New Ideas. *Sociological Perspectives* 38(4):547-571.

Carley, K. M. 1995. Computational and Mathematical Organization Theory: Perspective and Directions. *Computational and Mathematical Organization Theory*, 1(1): 39-56.

Carley, K. M. 1992. Organizational Learning and Personnel Turnover. *Organization Science* 3(1): 20-46.

Carley, K. M. 1991. Designing Organizational Structures to Cope with Communication Breakdowns: A Simulation Model. *Industrial Crisis Quarterly* 5: 19-57.

Carley, K. M. 1990. Coordinating for Success: Trading Information Redundancy for Task Simplicity. In Proceedings of the Twenty-third Annual Hawaii International Conference on Systems Sciences. Kailua-Kona, Hawaii, 2-5 Jan. Los Alamitos, Calif.: IEEE Computer Society Press.

Carley, K. M. 1989. The Value of Cognitive Foundations for Dynamic Social Theory. *Journal of Mathematical Sociology* 14(2-3): 171-208.

Carley, K. M.; and Lin, Z. 1995. Organizational Designs Suited to High Performance Under Stress. *IEEE Transactions on Systems, Man, and Cybernetics* 25(2): 221-230.

Carley, K. M., and Prietula, M. J. 1994. ACTS Theory: Extending the Model of Bounded Rationality. In *Computational Organization Theory*, eds. K. M. Carley and M. J. Prietula, 4: 55-89. Hillsdale, N. J.: Lawrence Erlbaum Associates.

Carley, K. M., and Prietula, M. J., eds. 1994. *Computational Organization Theory*, 1-18. Hillsdale, N. J.: Lawrence Erlbaum Associates.

Carley, K. M.; and Newell, A. 1990. On the Nature of the Social Agent. Paper presented at the American Sociological Association Annual Meeting, Washington, D. C. August.

Carley, K. M.; and Wallace, W. A. 1995. Editorial. *Computational and Mathematical Organization Theory* 1(1): 5-7.

Carley, K. M.; and Wendt, K. 1991. Electronic Mail and Scientific Communication: A Study of the Soar Extended Research Group. *Knowledge: Creation, Diffusion, Utilization* 12: 406-440.

Carley, K. M.; Kjaer-Hansen, J.; Newell, A.; and Prietula, M. J. 1992. Plural-Soar: A Prolegomenon to Artificial Agents and Organizational Behavior. In *Artificial Intelligence in Organization and Management Theory*, eds. M. Masuch and M. Warglien, 87-118. Amsterdam: North-Holland.

Chaib-Draa, B.; Moulin, B.; Mandiau, R.; and Millot, P. 1992. Trends in Distributed Artificial Intelligence. *Artificial Intelligence Review* 6: 35-66.

Chandrasekaran, B. 1981. Natural and Social System Metaphors for Distributed Problem Solving: Introduction to the Issue. *IEEE Transactions on Systems, Man, and Cybernetics* SMC-11(1): 1-5.

Choe, S. C.; and Scacchi, W. 1989. Assuring the Correctness of Configured Software Descriptions. *ACM Software Engineering Notes,* 17(7): 67-76.

Choi, S. C.; and Scacchi, W. 1991. SOFTMAN: An Environment for Forward and Reverse CASE. *Information and Software Technology*, 33(9). November.

Clark, H. H.; and Brennen, S. E. 1991. Grounding in Communication. In *Perspectives on Socially Shared Cognition* , ed. L. B. Resnick, R. M. Levine, and S. D. Teasley, 127-149. Washington, D.C.: American Psychological Association Press.

Cohen, G. P. 1992. The Virtual Design Team: An Information Processing Model of Coordination in Project Design Teams. Ph.D. diss., Dept. of Civil Engineering, Stanford Univ., Stanford, Calif.

Cohen, M. D. 1986. Artificial Intelligence and the Dynamic Performance of Organization Designs. In *Ambiguity and Command: Organizational Perspectives on Military Decision Making,* ed. James G. March and Roger Weissinger-Baylon, 53-71. Marshfield, Mass.: Pitman Publishing.

Cohen, M. D.; March, J. G.; and Olsen, J. P. 1972. A Garbage Can Model of Organizational Choice. *Administrative Science Quarterly* 17(1): 1-25.

Cohen, Philip R.; and Levesque, Hector J. 1990. Intention is Choice with Commitment. *Artificial Intelligence*, 42(3): 213-261.

Cohen, P. R., and Feigenbaum, E. A. 1981. *The Handbook of Artificial Intelligence* vol 3, 3-21. Los Altos, Calif.: William Kaufmann, Inc.

Cohen, Paul; Greenberg, Michael; Hart, David; and Howe, Adele. 1989. Trial by Fire: Understanding the Design Requirements for Agents in Complex Environments. *AI Magazine*, 10(3): 33-48. Fall.

Collins, B. E., and Guetzkow, H. 1964. *A Social Psychology of Group Processes for Decision-Making*. New York: John Wiley and Sons.

Corkill, Daniel David. 1983. A Framework for Organizational Self-Design in Distributed Problem Solving Networks. Ph.D. diss., Univ. of Mass. February. (also published as Technical Report 82-33, Dept. of Computer and Information Science, Univ. of Massachusetts. December 1982).

Corkill, Daniel David; and Lesser, Victor R. 1983. The Use of Meta-level Control for Coordination in a Distributed Problem Solving Network. In *Proceedings of the Eighth International Joint Conference on Artificial Intelligence,* ed. Alan H. Bond and Les Gasser, 748-56. Karlsruhe, Federal Republic of Germany. August. San Francisco: Morgan Kaufmann Publishers.

Crowston, K. 1992. Modeling Cooperation in Organizations. In *Artificial Intelligence in Organization and Management Theory*, eds. M. Masuch and M. Warglien, 215-234. Amsterdam: North-Holland.

Curtis, B.; Kellner, M.; and Over, J. 1992. Process Modeling. *Communications ACM*, 35(9): 75-90.

D'Aveni, R. A.; and Ilinitch, A. Y. 1992. Complex Patterns Of Vertical Integration In The Forest Products Industry: Systematic And Bankruptcy Risks. *Academy of Management Journal* 35(3): 596-625. August.

Daft, R. L.; and Weick, K. 1984. Toward a Model of Organizations as Interpretation Systems. *Academy of Management Review* 9: 284-295.

Davenport, T. 1993. *Process Innovation: Reengineering Business Processes through Information Technology*. Cambridge, Mass.: Harvard Business School Press.

Davis, Randall, and Smith, Reid G. 1983. *Negotiation as a Metaphor for Distributed Problem Solving.* Cambridge, Mass.: The MIT Press.

Davis, S. M., and Lawrence, P. R. 1977. *Matrix.* Reading, Mass.: Addison-Wesley.

Davis, T. R. 1991. Information Technology and White-Collar Productivity. *Academy of Management Executive* 5(1).

Decker, Keith S. 1995. Environment Centered Analysis and Design of Coordination Mechanisms. Ph.D. diss., Dept. of Computer Science, Univ. of Mass.

Decker, Keith S.; and Lesser, Victor R. 1995. Designing a Family of Coordination Algorithms. In *Proceedings of the First International Conference on Multi-Agent Systems,* Menlo Park, Calif.: AAAI Press.

Decker, Keith S.; and Lesser, Victor R. 1993. A One-shot Dynamic Coordination Algorithm for Distributed Sensor Networks. In *Proceedings of the Eleventh National Conference on Artificial Intelligence,* 210-216. Washington. July. Menlo Park, Calif.: AAAI Press.

Decker, Keith S.; and Lesser, Victor R. 1993. An Approach to Analyzing the Need for Meta-level Communication. In *Proceedings of the Thirteenth International Joint Conference on Artificial Intelligence,* 360-366. Chambery, France. August. San Francisco: Morgan Kaufmann Publishers.

Decker, Keith S.; and Lesser, Victor R. 1993. Analyzing a Quantitative Coordination Relationship. *Group Decision and Negotiation* 2(3): 195-217.

Decker, Keith S.; and Lesser, Victor R. 1993. Quantitative Modeling of Complex Environments. *International Journal of Intelligent Systems in Accounting, Finance, and Management,* 2(4): 215-234. December.

Doran, J. 1989. Distributed Artificial Intelligence and the Modeling of Socio-Cultural Systems. In *Intelligence Systems in a Human Context: Development, Implications, and Applications,* eds. L. A. Murry and J. T. E. Richardson, 71-91. Oxford: Oxford Univ. Press.

Doran, J. 1985. The Computational Approach to Knowledge, Communication and Structure in Multi-Actor Systems. In *Social Action and Artificial Intelligence,* eds. G. N. Gilbert and C. Heath, 160-171. Aldershot: Gower.

Drazin, R.; and Van de Ven, A. H. 1985. Alternative Forms of Fit in Contingency Theory. *Administrative Science Quarterly* 30: 514-539.

Drucker, P. F. 1985. *Management: Tasks, Responsibilities, Practices.* New York: Harper & Row.

Duffy, L. 1993. Team Decision-Making Biases: An Information-Processing Perspective. In *Decision Making in Action: Models and Methods,* eds. G. A. Klein et al., 346-359. Norwood, N. J.: Ablex Publishing Co.

Durfee, Edmund H.; and Lesser, Victor R. 1991. Partial Global Planning: A Coordination Framework for Distributed Hypothesis Formation. *IEEE Transactions on Systems, Man, and Cybernetics,* 21(5): 1167-1183. September.

Durfee, Edmund H.; Lesser, Victor R.; and Corkill, Daniel David. 1987. Coherent Cooperation Among Communicating Problem Solvers. *IEEE Transactions on Computers,* C-36(11): 1275-1291. November.

Emery, Fred E. 1959. *Characteristics of Socio-Technical Systems.* Tavistock Document 527. London: Tavistock.

Epstein, J., and Axtell, R. 1995. *Growing Artificial Societies: Social Science from the Bottom Up.* Washington, DC: The Brookings Institute.

Eveland, J. D.; and Bikson, T. K. 1988. Work Group Structures and Computer Support: A Field Experiment. *Transactions on Office Information Systems* 6, 354-379.

Fadel, F.; Fox, M. S.; and Gruninger, M. 1994. A Resource Ontology for Enterprise Modeling. In *Proceedings of the Third Workshop on Enabling Technologies-Infrastructures for Collaborative Enterprises,* West Virginia Univ. , Morgantown, West Va., 17-19 April, 117-120. Los Alamitos, Calif.: IEEE Computer Society Press.

Fernstrom, C. 1993. Process WEAVER: Adding Process Support to UNIX. In Proceedings of the Second International Conference on the Software Process. Berlin, Germany. February.

Fish, R. S.; Kraut, R.; Root, R. W.; and Rice, R. E. 1993. Evaluating Video as a Technology for Informal Communication. *Communications of the ACM* 36(1), 48-61.

Flippo, E., and Munsinger, G. M. 1975. *Management.* New York: Allyn and Bacon, Inc.

Flores, F.; Graves, M.; Hartfield, B.; and Wionograd, T. 1988. Computer Systems and the Design of Organizational Interaction, *ACM Transactions on Office Information Systems* 6(2): 153-172. April.

Fox, M. S. 1981. An Organizational View of Distributed Systems. *IEEE Transactions on Systems, Man, and Cybernetics,* SMC-11(1): 70-80. January.

Fox, M. S.; Chionglo, J.; Fadel, F. 1993. A Common-Sense Model of the Enterprise. In Proceedings of the Industrial Engineering Research Conference., 425-429. Norcross, Ga.: Institute for Industrial Engineers.

Galbraith, J. 1977. *Organizational Design.* Reading, Mass.: Addison-Wesley.

Garg, P. K.; and Scacchi, W. 1989. ISHYS: Designing Intelligent Software Hypertext Systems. *IEEE Expert,* 4(3): 52-63.

Garvey, Alan; and Lesser, Victor. 1993. Design-To-Time Real-time Scheduling. *IEEE Transactions on Systems, Man, and Cybernetics,* 23(6): 1491-1502.

Garvey, Alan; Humphrey, Marty; and Lesser, Victor. 1993. Task Interdependencies in Design-to-time Real-time Scheduling. In *Proceedings of the Eleventh National Conference on Artificial Intelligence,* 580-585. Washington. July. Menlo Park, Calif.: AAAI Press.

Gasser, L. 1991. Social Conceptions of Knowledge and Action. *Artificial Intelligence,* 47(1): 107-138.

Gasser, L.; and Hill, R. W. 1990. Coordinated Problem Solvers. *Annual Review of Computer Science* 4: 203-253.

Gasser, L.; and Ishida, Toru 1991. A Dynamic Organizational Architecture for Adaptive Problem Solving. In *Proceedings of the National Conference on Artificial Intelligence,* 185-190. July. Menlo Park, Calif.: AAAI Press.

Giddens, A. 1984. *The Constitution of Society: An Introduction to the Theory of Structuration.* Berkeley, Calif.: University of California Press.

Giddens, A. 1979. *Central Problems in Social Theory.* Berkeley, Calif.: University of California Press.

Glazer, R.; Steckel, J. H.; and Winer, R. S. 1992. Locally Rational Decision Making: The Distracting Effect of Information on Managerial Performance. *Management Science* 38(2): 212-226.

Gmytrasiewicz, Piotr J.; Durfee, Edmund H.; and Wehe, David K. 1991. A Decision-theoretic Approach to Coordinating Multiagent Interactions. In *Proceedings of the Twelfth International Joint Conference on Artificial Intelligence,* 62-68, Sydney, Australia. August. San Francisco: Morgan Kaufmann Publishers.

Grant, R. M. 1991. The Resource-Based Theory of Competitive Advantage: Implications for Strategy Formulation. *California Management Review*, 33(3): 114-135.

Griffiths, D. G.; and Purohit, B. K. 1991. Fundamentals of Distributed Artificial Intelligence. *British Telecommunication Technology Journal* 9(3): 88-96.

Gruber, T. R. 1993. Toward Principles for the Design of Ontologies Used for Knowledge Sharing, Technical Report, KSL 93-04, August, Knowledge Systems Lab., Stanford Univ., Stanford, Calif.

Gruninger, M.; and Fox, M. S. 1994. The Role of Competency Questions in Enterprise Engineering. Paper presented at the IFIP Workshop on Benchmarking: Theory and Practice, Trondheim, Norway. June.

Hannan, M. T.; and Freeman, J. 1977. The Population Ecology of Organizations. *American Journal of Sociology* 82(5), 929-964.

Harris, S. E.; and Katz, J. L. 1989. Differentiating Organizational Performance Using Information Technology Managerial Control Ratios in the Insurance Industry. *Office: Technology and People* 5(4).

Harrison, J. R.; and Carroll, G. R. 1991. Keeping the Faith: A Model of Cultural Transmission in Formal Organizations. *Administrative Science Quarterly* 36(4): 552-582. December.

Hildum, David W. 1994. Flexibility in a Knowledge-Based System for Solving Dynamic Resource-Constrained Scheduling Problems. Ph.D diss., Dept. of Computer Science, Univ. of Massachusetts, Amherst. September.

Ho, Y. C. 1980. Team Decision Theory and Information Structures. In *Proceedings of the IEEE*, 68. June. New York: IEEE.

Hollenbeck, J. R.; Ilgen, D. R.; Sego, D. J.; Hedlund, J.; Major, D. A.; and Phillips, J. 1995. Multi-Level Theory of Team Decision-Making: Decision Performance in Teams Incorporating Distributed Expertise. *Journal of Applied Psychology* 80(2): 292-316.

Hollenbeck, J. R.; Sego, D. J.; et. al. Forthcoming. Team Decision Making Accuracy Under Difficult Conditions: Construct Validation of Potential Manipulations Using the TIDE[2] Simulation. In *Team Performance, Assessment and Measurement: Theory, Research and Applications*, eds. M. T. Brannick, E. Salas, and C. Prince, Hillsdale, N. J.: Lawrence Erlbaum Associates.

Hollenbeck, J. R.; Sego, D. J.; Ilgen, D. R.; and Major, D. A. 1991. Team Interactive Decision Exercise for Teams Incorporating Distributed Expertise (TIDE[2]): A Program and Paradigm for Team Research, Technical Report, N00179-91-1, Office of Naval Research, Michigan State Univ., Ann Arbor, Mich.

Horvitz, Eric J. 1988. Reasoning Under Varying and Uncertain Resource Constraints. In *Proceedings of the Seventh National Conference on Artificial Intelligence*. August. Menlo Park, Calif.: AAAI Press.

Huber, G. P. 1991. Organizational Learning: The Contributing Processes and Literatures. *Organization Science* 2(1): 88-115. February.

Huberman, B. A. 1992. The Value of Cooperation. In *Artificial Intelligence in Organization and Management Theory*, eds. M. Masuch and M. Warglien, 235-243. Amsterdam: North-Holland.

Huff, K. E.; and Lesser, V. R. 1988. A Plan-Based Intelligent Assistant That Supports the Process of Programming. *ACM Software Engineering Notes*, 13: 97-106. November.

Hunt, E. 1989. Cognitive Science: Definition, Status, and Questions. *Annual Review of Psychology* 40: 603-629.

Ilgen, D. R.; Major, D. A.; Hollenbeck, J. R.; and Sego, D. J. 1995. Raising an Individual Decision Making Model to the Team-Level: A New Research Model and Paradigm. In *Team Effectiveness and Decision Making in Organizations*, eds. R. Guzzo and E. Salas, San Francisco: Jossey-Bass.

Jennings, N. R. 1993. Commitments and Conventions: The Foundation of Coordination in Multi-agent Systems. *The Knowledge Engineering Review*, 8(3): 223-250.

Jin, Y.; and Levitt, R. E. 1993. *i*-AGENTS: Modeling Organizational Problem Solving in Multi-Agent Teams. *Intelligent Systems in Accounting, Finance and Management* 2: 247-270.

Kaiser, G. E.; and Feiler, P. 1987. An Architecture for Intelligent Assistance in Software Development. Paper presented at the Ninth International Conference on Software Engineering, 180-187. Monterey, Calif.. April.

Kaiser, G. E.; Barghouti, N. S.; and Sokolsky, M. H. 1990. Preliminary Experience with Process Modeling in the Marvel Software Development Environment Kernel. In Proceedings of the Twenty-third Annual Hawaii International Conference on System Science, 131-140. Kailua-Kona, Hawaii, 2-5 Jan. Los Alamitos, Calif.: IEEE Computer Society Press.

Karrer, A.; and Scacchi, W. 1993. Meta-Environments for Software Production. *International Journal of Software Engineering and Knowledge Engineering*, 3(1): 139-162.

Katz, Daniel, and Kahn, Robert L. 1966. *The Social Psychology of Organizations.* New York: John Wiley.

Katzenbach, J. R.; and Smith, D. K. 1993. The Discipline of Teams. *Harvard Business Review* 71(2): 111-121. March-April.

Kaufer, D. S., and Carley, K. M. 1993. *Communication at a Distance: The Effect of Print on Socio-Cultural Organization and Change.* Hillsdale, N. J.: Lawrence Erlbaum Associates.

Kellner, M. 1991. Software Process Modeling Support for Management Planning and Control. In *Proceedings of the First International Conference Software Process,* 8-28, October. Los Alamitos, Calif.: IEEE Computer Society Press.

Kim, H.; and Fox, M. S. 1993. Quality Systems Modeling: A Prospective for Enterprise Integration, In Proceedings of the Fourth Annual Meeting of the Production and Operations Management Society. Baltimore, MD: Production and Operations Management Society.

Kling, R., and Scacchi, W. 1982. The Web of Computing: Computer Technology as Social Organization. In *Advances in Computers*, ed. M. Yovits, 21: 3-90. New York: Academic Press.

Kraut, R., Galegher, J., and Egido, C., eds. 1990. *Intellectual Teamwork: Social and Technological Foundations of Cooperative Work.* Hillsdale, N. J.: Lawrence Erlbaum Associates.

Kraut, R.; and Streeter, L. A. 1995. Coordination in Software Development. *Communications of the ACM* 38(3): 69-81.

Kriger, M. P. and Barnes, L. B. 1992. Organizational Decision-Making as Hierarchical Levels of Drama. *Journal of Management Studies* 28(4): 439-457. July.

Laird, J.; Congdon, C. B.; Altmann, E.; and Doorenbos, R. 1993. Soar User's Manual: Version 6, Electrical Engineering and Computer Science Department, Univ. of Michigan, and School of Computer Science, Carnegie Mellon Univ.

Lant, T. K.; and Mezias, S. J. 1992. An Organizational Learning Model of Convergence and Reorientation. *Organization Science* 3(1): 47-71.

Lawrence, Paul R.; and Lorsch, Jay W. 1967. *Organization and Environment: Managing Differentiation and Integration*. Boston: Harvard Business School Press.

Lee, R. M. 1988. Bureaucracies as Deontic Systems, *ACM Transactions on Office Information Systems* 6(2): 87-108. April.

Levitt, R. E.; Cohen, P. G.; Kunz, J. C.; Nass, C.;Christiansen, T.; and Jin, Y. 1994. The Virtual Design Team: Simulating How Organizational Structure and Communication Tools Affect Team Performance. In *Computational Organization Theory*, eds. K. M. Carley and M. J. Prietula. Hillsdale, N. J.: Lawrence Erlbaum Associates.

Leymann, F.; and Altenhuber, W. 1994. Managing Business Processes as an Information Resource. *IBM Systems Journal*. 33(2): 326-348.

Lin, Z. 1994. A Theoretical Evaluation of Measures of Organizational Design: Interrelationship and Performance Predictability. In *Computational Organization Theory*, ed. K. M. Carley and M. J. Prietula, 6: 113-159. Hillsdale, N. J.: Lawrence Erlbaum Associates.

Lin, Z. 1993. Organizational Performance: Theory and Reality. Ph.D. diss., School of Public Policy and Management, Carnegie Mellon Univ., Pittsburgh, Penn.

Lin, Z.; and Carley, K. M. 1995. DYCORP: A Computational Framework for Examining Organizational Performance Under Dynamic Conditions, *The Journal of Mathematical Sociology* 20(2-3): 193-217.

Lin, Z.; and Carley, K. M. 1993. Proactive or Reactive: An Analysis of the Effect of Agent Style on Organizational Decision Making Performance. *International Journal of Intelligent Systems in Accounting, Finance, and Management* 2(4): 271-289. December.

Lucas, R. L.; and Jaffee, C. L. 1969. Effects of High-Rate Talkers on Group Voting Behavior in the Leaderless Group Problem-Solving Situation. *Psychological Reports* 25: 471-477.

Lupton, T. 1976. Best Fit in the Design of Organizations. In *Task and Organization*, ed. E. J. Miller, 121-149. New York: John Wiley and Sons.

Mackenzie, K. D. 1978. *Organizational Structures*. Arlington Heights, Illinois: AHM Publishing Co.

Madhavji, N.; and Gruhn, V. 1990. PRISM = Methodology + Process-Oriented Environment. In Proceedings of the Twelfth International Conference on Software Engineering, Mice France, 26-30 March. Los Alamitos, Calif.: IEEE Computer Society Press.

Madni, A. 1990. A Conceptual Framework and Enabling Technologies for Computer-Aided Concurrent Engineering (CACE). In *Proceedings of the Second International Conference on Human Aspects of Advanced Manufacturing and Hybrid Automation*. Honolulu, Hawaii, 12-16 August. Amsterdam: Elsevier Science Publishers.

Malone, T. W. 1987. Modeling Coordination in Organizations and Markets. *Management Science* 33(10): 1317-1332.

March, J. G., and Simon, H. A. 1958. *Organizations*. New York: Wiley.

Marsick, V. J.; and Cederholm, L. 1988. Developing Leadership in International Managers: An Urgent Challenge! *Columbia Journal of World Business* 23(4): 3-11. Winter.

Martial, Frank V. 1992. *Coordinating Plans of Autonomous Agents: Lecture Notes in Artificial Intelligence no. 610.* Berlin: Springer-Verlag.

Massey, A. P.; and Wallace, W. A. Forthcoming. Understanding and Facilitating Group Problem Structuring and Formulation: Mental Representation, Interaction and Representation Aids. *Decision Support Systems.*

Masuch, M. 1992. Artificial Intelligence in Organization and Management Theory. In *Artificial Intelligence in Organization and Management Theory,* eds. M. Masuch and M. Warglien, 1-19. Amsterdam: North-Holland.

Masuch, M.; and LaPotin, P. 1989. Beyond Garbage Cans: An AI Model of Organizational Choice. *Administrative Science Quarterly* 34: 38-67.

McCarthy, J. C.; and Monk, A. F. 1994. Channels, Conversation, Cooperation and Relevance: All You Wanted to Know About Communication But Were Afraid to Ask. *Collaborative Computing* 1(1): 35-60.

McFarland, D. 1974. *Management: Principles and Practices.* New York: Macmillan Publishing Co., Inc.

McGrath, J. E. 1984. *Groups: Interaction and Performance.* Englewood Cliffs, N. J.: Prentice-Hall.

McLeod, P. L. 1992. An Assessment of the Experimental Literature on Electronic Support of Group Work: Results of a Meta-Analysis. *Human-Computer Interaction* 7: 257-280.

Mi, P. 1992. Modeling and Analyzing the Software Process and Process Breakdowns. Ph.D. diss., Computer Science Dept., Univ. of Southern Calif., Los Angeles. September.

Mi, P.; and Scacchi, W. 1996. A Meta-Model for Formulating Knowledge-Based Models of Software Development. *Decision Support Systems,* 17(3): 313-330.

Mi, P.; and Scacchi, W. 1993. Articulation: An Integrated Approach to Diagnosis, Replanning, and Rescheduling. In *Proceedings of the Eighth Knowledge-Based Software Engineering Conference,* 77-84. Chicago, Ill., 20-23 Sept. Los Alamitos, Calif.: IEEE Computer Society Press.

Mi, P.; and Scacchi. W. 1992. Process Integration in CASE Environments. *IEEE Software,* 9(2): 45-53. March. Also appears in *Computer-Aided Software Engineering,* 2nd Edition, ed. E. Chikofski, IEEE Computer Society, 1993.

Mi, P.; and Scacchi, W. 1991. Modeling Articulation Work in Software Engineering Processes. In *Proceedings of the First International Conference on the Software Process,* 188-201. Redondo Beach, Calif., 21-26 October. Los Alamitos, Calif.: IEEE Computer Society Press.

Mi, P.; and Scacchi, W. 1990. A Knowledge-based Environment for Modeling and Simulating Software Engineering Processes. *IEEE Transactions on Knowledge and Data Engineering,* 2(3): 283-294. September.

Mi, P.; Lee, M.; and Scacchi, W. 1992. A Knowledge-based Software Process Library for Process-driven Software Development. Paper presented at the Seventh Knowledge-Based Software Engineering Conference, McLean, Virginia. September.

Miller, C. E. 1989. The Social Psychological Effects of Group Decision Rules. In *Psychology of Group Influence,* ed. P. B. Paulus, second edition, 327-355. Hillsdale, N. J.: Erlbaum.

Milliken, F. J.; and Vollrath, D. A. 1991. Strategic Decision-Making Tasks and Group Effectiveness: Insights from Theory and Research on Small Group Performance. *Human Relations* 44(12): 1229-1253. December.

Mintzberg, H. 1983. *Structure in Fives: Designing Effective Organizations*, Englewood Cliffs, N. J.: Prentice Hall, Inc.

Montgomery, Thomas A.; and Durfee, Edmund H. 1992. Search Reduction in Hierarchical Distributed Problem Solving. *Group Decision and Negotiation* 2(Special Issue): 301-317, 1993.

Neiman, D. E.;Hildum, D. W.; Lesser, V. R.; and Sandholm, T. W. 1994. Exploiting Meta-level Information in a Distributed Scheduling System. In *Proceedings of the Twelfth National Conference on Artificial Intelligence*. Seattle, Washington. August. Menlo Park, Calif.: AAAI Press.

Neustadt, R. E., and May, E. R. *Thinking in Time: The Uses of History for Decision-Makers*. New York: Free Press, 1986.

Newell, A. 1990. *Unified Theories of Cognition*. Cambridge, Mass.: Harvard Univ. Press.

Newell, A. 1980. Reasoning, Problem Solving and Decision Processes: The Problem Space as a Fundamental Category. In *Attention and Performance VIII*, ed. R. Nickerson, 693-718. Hillsdale, N. J.: Erlbaum.

Newell, A.; and Simon, H. A. 1976. Computer Science as Empirical Inquiry: Symbols and Search. *Communications of the ACM* 19(3): 113-126.

Newell, A., and Simon, H. A. 1972. *Human Problem Solving*. Englewood Cliffs, N. J.: Prentice-Hall.

Newell, A.; Yost, G. R.; Laird, J. E.; Rosenbloom, P. S.; and Altmann, E. 1993. Formulating the Problem Space Computational Model. In *The Soar Papers: Research on Integrated Intelligence*, eds. P. S. Rosenbloom, J. E. Laird, and A. Newell, 2(66): 1321-1359. Cambridge, Mass.: The MIT Press.

Noll, J.; and Scacchi, W. 1991. Integrating Diverse Information Repositories: A Distributed Hypertext Approach. *Computer*, 24(12): 38-45. December.

Novak, Vladimir J. A. 1982. *The Principle of Sociogenesis*. Praha: Academia Pub. House of the Czechoslovak Academy of Sciences.

Oates, Tim; Prasad, M. V. Nagendra; and Lesser, Victor R. 1994. Cooperative Information Gathering: A Distributed Problem Solving Approach, Technical Report, 94-66, Dept. of Computer Science, Univ. of Massachusetts, Amherst, Mass. September.

Orasanu, J.; and Salas, E. 1993. Team Decision Making in Complex Environments. In *Decision Making in Action: Models and Methods*, eds. G. A. Kle et al., 327-345. Norwood, N. J.: Ablex Publishing Co.

Osterweil, L. 1987. Software Processes are Software Too. Paper presented at the Ninth International Conference on Software Engineering, 2-13. Monterey, Calif., April.

Ow, P. S.; Prietula, M. J.; and Hsu, W. 1989. Configuring Knowledge-Based Systems to Organizational Structures: Issues and Examples in Multiple Agent Support. In *Expert Systems in Economics, Banking, and Management,* eds. L. F. Pau, J. Motiwalla, Y. H. Pao, and H. H. Teh, 309-318. Amsterdam: North-Holland.

Papageorgiou, C. P.; and Carley, K. 1993. A Cognitive Model of Decision Making: Chunking and the Radar Detection Task, Technical Report, CMU-CS-93-228, School of Computer Science, Carnegie Mellon Univ., Pittsburgh, Penn.

Pattison, H. Edward; Corkill, Daniel D.; and Lesser, Victor R. 1987. Instantiating Descriptions of Organizational Structures. In *Distributed Artificial Intelligence, Research Notes in Artificial Intelligence 3,* ed. Michael N. Huhns, 59-96. London: Pitman.

Perrow, C. 1979. *Complex Organizations: A Critical Essay.* Glenview, Illinois: Scott, Foresman.

Pinto, J. and Reiter, R. 1993. Temporal Reasoning in Logic Programming: A Case for the Situation Calculus. In *Proceedings of the Tenth International Conference on Logic Programming,* Budapest, 203-221. Cambridge, Mass.: The MIT Press.

Porter, M. E. *Competitive Advantage: Creating and Sustaining Superior Performance.* New York: Free Press, 1985.

Prietula, M. J.; and Carley, K. M. 1994. Computational Organization Theory: Autonomous Agents and Emergent Behavior. *Journal of Organizational Computing* 4(1): 41-83.

Pylyshyn, Z. W. 1989. Computing in Cognitive Science. In *Foundations of Cognitive Science,* ed. M. Posner, 52-91. Cambridge, Mass.: The MIT Press.

Reiter, R. 1991. The Frame Problem in the Situation Calculus: A Simple Solution (Sometimes) and a Completeness Result for Goal Regression. In *Artificial Intelligence and Mathematical Theory of Computation: Papers in Honor of John McCarthy,* ed. Vladimir Lifschitz. San Diego, Calif.: Academic Press.

Rice, R. E.; and Contractor, N. S. 1990. Conceptualizing Effects of Office Information Systems. *Decision Sciences* 21(2).

Robbins, S. P. 1990. *Organization Theory: Structure, Design, and Applications.* Englewood Cliffs, N. J.: Prentice Hall.

Roberts, K. 1990. Some Characteristics of One Type of High Reliability Organizations. *Organization Science* 1(2): 160-176.

Roberts, K. 1989. New Challenges to Organizational Research: High Reliability Organizations. *Industrial Crisis Quarterly* 33: 111-125.

Rosenschein, J. S.; and Genesereth, M. R. 1985. Deals Among Rational Agents. In *Proceedings of the Ninth International Joint Conference on Artificial Intelligence,* 91-99. Los Angeles, Calif., August. San Francisco: Morgan Kaufmann Publishers.

Russell, Stuart J.; and Zilberstein, Shlomo. 1991. Composing Real-Time Systems. In *Proceedings of the Twelfth International Joint Conference on Artificial Intelligence,* 212-217, Sydney, Australia. August. San Francisco: Morgan Kaufmann Publishers.

Sandhu, R. S.; Coyne, E. J.; Feinstein, H. L.; and Youman, C. E. Forthcoming. Role-based Access Control Models. *IEEE Computer.*

Sandhu, R. S.; Coyne, E. J.; Feinstein, H. L.; and Youman, C. E. 1994. Role-Based Access Control: A Multi-Dimensional View. Paper presented at the Tenth Annual Computer Security Applications Conference, 54-62. Orlando, Florida. 5-9 December.

Sathi, A.; Fox, M. S.; and Greenberg, M. 1985. Representation of Activity Knowledge for Project Management. *IEEE Transactions on Pattern Analysis and Machine Intelligence,* PAMI-7: 531-552. September.

Scacchi, W.; and Mi, P. 1993. Modeling, Integrating, and Enacting Software Engineering Processes. Paper presented at the Third Irvine Software Symposium. Irvine Research Unit in Software, Univ. of Calif. at Irvine. April.

Schoonhober, C. B. 1981. Problems with Contingency Theory: Testing Assumptions Hidden in the Language of Contingency Theory. *Administrative Science Quarterly* 26: 349-377.

Schwab, D. P. 1991. Contextual Variables in Employee Performance-Turnover Relationships. *Academy of Management Journal* 34(4): 966-975. December.

Scott, W. Richard. 1992. *Organizations: Rational, Natural and Open Systems*, third edition. Englewood Cliffs, N. J.: Prentice-Hall.

Searle, J. 1969. *Speech Acts*. Cambridge, UK: Cambridge Univ. Press.

Sen, S.; and Durfee, E. 1994. On the Design of an Adaptive Meeting Scheduler. In *Proceedings of the IEEE Conference on AI Applications*. Los Alamitos, Calif.: IEEE Computer Society Press.

Shoham, Yoav. 1991. AGENT: A Simple Agent Language and Its Interpreter. In *Proceedings of the Ninth National Conference on Artificial Intelligence*, 704-709. Anaheim, Calif.. July. Menlo Park, Calif.: AAAI Press.

Siegel, J.; Kraut, R.; John, B. E.; Carley, K. M. 1995. An Empirical Study of Collaborative Wearable Computer Systems. In *Human Factors in Computing Systems: CHI '95 Conference Companion*, ed. I. M. R. Katz and L. Marks, 312-313. New York: ACM Press.

Simon, H. A. 1982. *Models of Bounded Rationality, Volume 2*. Cambridge, Mass.: The MIT Press.

Simon, H. A. 1962. The Proverbs of Administration. *Public Administration Reviews* 6: 53-67.

Simon, H. A. 1957. *Models of Man*. New York: Wiley.

Simon, H. A.; and Kaplan, C. A. 1989. Foundations of Cognitive Science. In *Foundations of Cognitive Science*, ed. M. Posner, 1-47. Cambridge, Mass.: The MIT Press.

Smith, David; and Broadwell, Martin. 1987. Plan Coordination in Support of Expert Systems Integration. Paper presented at the the Eighth International Workshop on Expert Systems and their Applications. Avignon, France, 30-May-3 June 1998.

So, Young-pa; and Durfee, Edmund H. 1995. Local Sophistication and Organizational Performance. Paper presented at 1995 Workshop on Mathematical and Computational Organization Theory, Washington D.C., 3-4 May.

So, Young-pa; and Durfee, Edmund H. 1994. Modeling and Designing Computational Organizations. In Computational Organization Design: Papers from the 1994 Spring Symposium, 181-186. Tech. Rep. SS-94-07, American Association for Artificial Intelligence, Menlo Park, Calif.

So, Young-pa; and Durfee, Edmund H. 1993. An Organizational Self-design Model for Organizational Change. In AI and Theories of Groups & Organizations: Conceptual & Empirical Research: Papers from the 1993 Workshop, 8-15. Tech. Rep. WS-93-03, American Association for Artificial Intelligence, Menlo Park, Calif.

So, Young-pa; and Durfee, Edmund H. 1992. A Distributed Problem Solving Infrastructure for Computer Network Management,. In *International Journal of Intelligent and Cooperative Information Systems,* 1(2).

Sproull, L., and Kiesler, S. 1991. *Connections: New Ways of Working in the Networked Organization*. Cambridge, Mass.: The MIT Press.

Starbuck, W. H. 1992. Learning by Knowledge-Intensive Firms. *Journal of Management Studies* 29(6): 713-740. November.

Stasser, G. 1988. Computer Simulation as a Research Tool: The DISCUSS Model of Group Decision Making. *Journal of Experimental Social Psychology* 24: 393-422.

Stinchcombe, Arthur L. 1990. *Information and Organizations*. Berkeley, Calif.: University of California Press.

Sueyoshi, T.; and Tokoro, M. 1991. Dynamic Modeling of Agents for Coordination. In *Decentralized Artificial Intelligence 2*, eds. Y. Demazeau and J. Müller, 161-176. Amsterdam: North-Holland.

Sutton, S.; Heimbigner, D.; and Osterweil, L. J. 1990. Language Constructs for Managing Change in Process-Centered Environments. In *Proceedings of the Fourth ACM SIG-SOFT Symposium on Software Development Environments*, 206-217. Irvine, Calif.. 3-5 December. New York: ACM Press.

Sycara, K.; Roth, S.; Sadeh, N.; and Fox, M. 1991. Distributed Constrained Heuristic Search. *IEEE Transactions on Systems, Man, and Cybernetics*, 21(6): 1446-1461. November/December.

Taylor, F. W. 1911. *The Principles of Scientific Management*. New York: Harper.

Taylor, R. N.; Belz, F. C.; Clarke, L. A.; and Osterweil, L. 1989. Foundations for the Arcadia Environment Architecture. *ACM SIGPLAN Notices*, 1-13. February.

Tham, D.; Fox, M. S.; and Gruninger, M. 1994. A Cost Ontology for Enterprise Modeling. Paper presented at the Third Workshop on Enabling Technologies-Infrastructures for Collaborative Enterprises, West Virginia Univ.

Thompson, J. D. 1967. *Organizations in Action*. New York: McGraw-Hill.

Tindale, R. S.; and Davis, J. H. 1983. Group Decision Making and Jury Verdicts. In *Small Groups and Social Interactions*, eds. H. H. Blumberg, A. P. Hare, V. Kent, and M. Davis, 2: 9-37. New York: Wiley.

Trippi, R. R.; and Salameh, T. T. 1989. Strategic Information Systems: Current Research Issues. *Journal of Information Systems Management* 6(3): 30-35.

Trist, Eric L. 1981. The Evolution of Sociotechnical Systems as a Conceptual Framework and as an Action Research Program. In *Perspectives on Organization Design and Behavior,* ed. Andrew H. Van de Ven and William F. Joyce, 19-75. New York: John Wiley, Wiley-Interscience.

Ulrich, D.; and Wiersema, M. F. 1989. Gaining Strategic and Organizational Capability in a Turbulent Business Environment. *Academy of Management Executive* 3(2): 115-123. May.

Votta, L. 1993. Comparing One Formal To One Informal Process Description. Paper presented at the Eighth International Software Process Workshop. Dagstuhl, Germany: IEEE Computer Society. February.

Walsh, J. P. and Ungson, G. R. 1991. Organizational Memory. *Academy of Management Review* 16(1): 57-91.

Weber, M. 1987. *Economy and Society*. Berkeley, Calif.: University of California Press.

Westbrook, D. L.; Anderson, S. D.; Hart, D. M.; and Cohen, P. R. 1994. Common Lisp Instrumentation Package: User Manual, Technical Report, 94-26, Department of Computer Science, Univ. of Massachusetts, Amherst, Mass.

Winograd, T. 1987-1988. A Language/Action Perspective on the Design of Cooperative Work. *Human Computer Interaction* 3(1): 3-30.

Yost, G. R.; and Newell, A. 1993. A Problem Space Approach to Expert System Specification. In *The Soar Papers: Research on Integrated Intelligence*, eds. P. S. Rosenbloom, J. E. Laird, and A. Newell, 2(46): 982-988. Cambridge, Mass.: The MIT Press.

Yu, E. S. K.; and Mylopoulos, J. 1994. From E-R to "A-R" — Modeling Strategic Acto Relationships for Business Process Reengineering, Paper presented at the Thirteenth International Conference on the Entity-Relationship Approach. Manchester, UK. 13-16 December.

Zannetos, Z. S. 1987. Intelligent Management Systems: Design and Implementation. In *Economics and Artificial Intelligence*, ed. Jean-Louis Roos, IFAC Proceedings Series 12: 55-60. New York: Pergamon Press.

Zeleny, M.; Cornet, R. J.; and Stoner, J. A. F. 1990. Moving from the Age of Specialization to the Era of Integration. *Human Systems Management* 9(3): 153-171.

Zenger, T. R. 1992. Why Do Employers Only Reward Extreme Performance? Examining the Relationships Among Performance, Pay, and Turnover. *Administrative Science Quarterly* 37(2): 198-219. June.

Zlotkin, G.; and Rosenschein, J. S. 1991. Incomplete Information and Deception in Multi-agent Negotiation. In *Proceedings of the Twelfth International Joint Conference on Artificial Intelligence,* 225-231. Sydney, Australia. August. San Francisco: Morgan Kaufmann Publishers.

Index